REVOLUTION
RANGERS - 1986-92

REVOLUTION
RANGERS - 1986-92
MARTYN RAMSAY
FOREWORD BY PROFESSOR GRAHAM WALKER

First published 2023 by DB Publishing, an imprint of JMD Media Ltd, Nottingham, United Kingdom.

ISBN 9781780916446

Printed in the UK

CONTENTS

ACKNOWLEDGEMENT

Although the cover of this book bears my name, there are a number of people whose input has made it what it is.

Firstly, the four gentlemen with whom I have spent a couple of hours every week for over a year recording 55 episodes of the podcast *Dominant: The Souness and Smith Years*. With different generational perspectives, we have shared memories, insights and debated long into the night about an era that means so much to every one of us. To John Cowden, Alan Bradley, Andy McGowan and especially to David Edgar, I give thanks for your contributions that have enriched my project, and to the latter, for the opportunity to continue to make shows that interest me. Hopefully, the 72 hours of audio that we have created will continue to entertain and educate down the years.

Secondly, my thanks must go to a whole host of experts on whom I leaned so as to get the most accurate wider picture possible. In many ways this is a story of modern Britain, and who better to ask than Dominic Sandbrook for guidance and reassurance? His kindness and support was greatly appreciated. To Professor Graham Walker, for being an excellent soundboard on the chapter on sectarianism and for kindly agreeing to write the foreword. The king of long-form sports writing, Rob Smyth, and his equally erudite colleague at *The Guardian* Scott Murray, for their help with the wider footballing context. The doyen of football business analysis, Kieran Maguire, for expert guidance when writing about the Rangers chairmen. Mark Dingwall, for his insight into the nascent world of football fanzines. Alistair Bain, for some much-needed assistance with the tactical outlooks of the two managers. And finally, those two esteemed Rangers historians, David Mason and Robert McElroy, for their memories of the time.

Campbell Ogilvie was very generous with his time and his detailed reflections of the revolution were priceless. So too, the help of Ross Lawrence for allowing me access to some family reflections on a time of great change and upheaval.

Finally to the team at DB Publishing – Steve Caron, Michelle Grainger and Gareth Davis – for their patience and ability to pick up on all the mistakes that I miss!

FOREWORD

Rangers supporters who lived through the years covered in this book will be indebted to Martyn Ramsay for bringing back to life the excitement and non-stop drama of a pivotal era in the club's history. This is a book which takes as its theme not only the Rangers revolution conducted principally by Graeme Souness after he took over as player-manager in 1986, but also that of Scottish football more broadly. It is a book, moreover, which puts the on-field happenings illuminatingly in the context of changes in society and the popular cultural *zeitgeist* of the times.

The perpetual turbulence of the five-year Souness era culminating in the hand-over in 1991 to the steadier managerial figure of Walter Smith, cannot be over-stressed. There was little in the way of order: just constant change, ever-present controversy, thrills, spills, self-inflicted setbacks, and glorious triumphs. Just as his arrival dragged Rangers out of an under-achieving torpor and freed it from hidebound practices, so his departure probably delivered blessings of another kind, allowing the club to continue to win honours, at least domestically, in a more settled atmosphere.

The Souness Revolution was made possible by several factors, all assessed authoritatively in this book. There was the decision of the majority shareholder Lawrence Marlborough to install as chief executive David Holmes in order to reorganise the club from the top and take it in a new modernising direction. Holmes is in many ways an unjustly forgotten figure, and Martyn gives him the long-overdue credit he deserves for his quiet but firm steering of the club in the early phase of Souness's management. Then there was the ban on English teams playing in European competition following the tragedy of Heysel in 1985, and the opportunities this opened up for a new manager whose horizons were well beyond Scotland from the outset. Overnight, Souness reversed the customary flow of talent from north of the border to the south. Souness's outlook drew him to the world of business, and he was instrumental in persuading David Murray to buy a controlling stake in Rangers in 1988. The Souness–Murray partnership ensured that Rangers were at the forefront of speculation over a European super league and, although it did not come to fruition as envisaged, this all added to the intoxicating experience of supporting the club in these years. Moreover, it was no coincidence that Rangers made the most sensational signing of a player in Scottish football history, Maurice Johnston in 1989, when these two risk-takers and turbo-driven characters were at the helm. Martyn's book provides a scintillating appraisal of this landmark event and of the context of religio-sectarian controversy in which it occurred and to which it inevitably contributed.

The book is richly informative on topics as varied as the media of this pre-internet age; football supporters' culture and the phenomenon of the 'fanzines'; and the growing commercial character of football. At root, however, it is a lucidly written account of Rangers' playing fortunes: the players, tactics and formations, dressing room tensions and bust-ups, and the goals, the victories, and the trophies. Rangers fans who want to replay in their minds that spine-tingling Ibrox night when Rangers defeated Dynamo Kiev, the 5-1 rout of Celtic when Wilkins struck the goal 'made in England', the breathtaking last day title decider against Aberdeen in 1991, and so much more, need look no further for stimulation than the pages of this superb book.

INTRODUCTION

'These prizes reflect the wining of the imaginations of over one million people who came to Ibrox over the season. In winning this league championship trophy, Rangers transformed the entire landscape of Scottish football. It will never be the same again.'
Archie Macpherson, That Championship Season: Rangers 86-87

It really wouldn't. As symbolic and emotionally significant as it was, that title win in 1986/87 was much more than the footballing story of a great old club regaining its place at the top of the game or, as in 1974/75, an outpouring of joy and relief for some long-suffering supporters. It represented the future in a way that no other achievement ever did. The decade or so that followed produced a level of success at Ibrox that had never been enjoyed before and hasn't been since. Nor was it some kind of sporting inevitability; that oft-quoted – but deeply flawed and illusory – theory of the cyclical nature of football. As if Rangers were simply waiting their turn for a place in the sun as other clubs would now have to do, as if it was some natural part of the unwritten laws of the game. The old rules were over. They had been ripped up and thrown away. This was a revolution – one credited to a football club and its manager – but a revolution nonetheless. That title triumph was the most important in the modern history of both Rangers Football Club and Scottish football.

Modern was the operative word. On and off the pitch, the success of that season and the many that followed was brought about by fresh thinking, a broader vision and burning ambition. Future Scottish champions would have to match that sense of scale and thus the era of heterogeneity that characterised the wilderness years for Rangers which preceded 1986 – where Aberdeen and Dundee United joined Celtic in the winner's circle and Hearts really should have – was over for good. Ally McCoist was one of a few Rangers players who was being paid at the imposed club wage cap of £350 per week (£18,200 a year) before the arrival of Graeme Souness and Walter Smith in April 1986. At the time, the average weekly salary for a male in the United Kingdom was £203.60, less than the basic wage of Scotland's hottest centre-forward but not exactly in another world. Ten years later, that average had increased from £10,587 per annum to £20,150. In 1996 Rangers were paying Paul Gascoigne £15,000 per week.

To what extent Rangers shaped change in football outside of Scotland, or were instead shaped by it, is one of the major themes of this book. This was an internal revolution set during a time of great transformation, both in the sport and in Scotland itself, and a proper history of the era has to set events at Ibrox in the context of a game that was almost unrecognisable by the end of the 20th century and a country that was rapidly developing too. From Whitehall to the Waddell Suite, it really was a landscape that was being altered in a seemingly irreversible way.

In order to do that, I have tackled broader themes than simply goals, saves and transfers. I felt that trying to squeeze them into the more chronological season chapters would be too clunky so instead there are six shorter chapters – more like essays than anything else – interspersed throughout the book, so as to give those issues the appropriate time and space. None of these chapters are exhaustive – each subject could be a book in its own – but I have tried to bring through what I believe to be the most important themes in each. In doing so I have broken the golden rule of any dinner party by discussing both politics and religion; firstly because I had no other choice and secondly, because it is such a terrible rule to begin with. Those two subjects are often the source of the most interesting and revealing discussions and the story of Rangers throughout this era cannot possibly be told without the cognisance of the surrounding political turmoil and growing secularisation.

The experience of the supporters is also too often overlooked by histories of the era and the growth of fanzine culture – in the window of time before the arguments of the pub and supporters' buses were taken to internet message boards and social media – is examined, as well as the changes in how ordinary fans consumed the sport itself. Finally there are two comparison pieces on the men who shared the two biggest jobs at Ibrox: manager and chairman. The psychology, tactical awareness and market success of Souness and Smith are analysed in the context of the prevailing norms of the time and the stewardship of the two Davids – Holmes and Murray – is assessed as Rangers moved from a chairman who was put in place to do a particular job to an owner who couldn't help but adopt a more 'hands-on' philosophy. For better and for worse.

The six season chapters – the overwhelming thrust of the book – stop in the summer of 1992. This is the first book of two that will tell the whole overarching story of Rangers during the Souness and Smith years, between 1986 and 1998, and on the face of it this is a neat and convenient place to end being as it is, slap bang in the middle of that era. It also has a satisfying symmetry as the six years before and after that summer delivered ten trophies each, including five league titles and one solitary campaign of European respectability.

But that is not why I decided to finish where I did. I could have gone a season earlier and split it up between the Souness and Smith terms or I could have finished with a bang a season later, as Rangers enjoyed their greatest ever year. However, both of those would have been equally as arbitrary. The truth of the matter is that by the summer of 1992, the revolution was over. If the overriding theme of the whole Souness and Smith era, both inside and outside of Ibrox, is one of modernisation – and I would strongly argue that it is – then the first half of this period, 1986 to 1992, is broadly one of *successful* modernisation at Rangers. When the ambition was rooted in reality, when the club was often leading the way for change and, at worst, was closely in the slipstream of it and when words from the top of the club, more often than not, matched its deeds. There is an overwhelming forward drive in these six years that shaped the future and placed Rangers at the forefront. The story of what came after 1992 – a slowing-down of that momentum and ambition, when the vision became smaller rather than bigger and when the public utterances became detached from action – is one for another day.

There is another reason for tackling this era. In my first book, The 50 Greatest Rangers Games, fans included 21 matches from between 1986 and 1998 in that list and I felt that was a number that seemed fair and reasonable given the demographic of the voters and the overwhelming success of the period. However, what was interesting is that ten of those matches were bookends. Three of them took place in that first season and seven of them – a third of the total – were chosen in a period of just over 12 months between Paul Gascoigne's title-winning hat-trick against Aberdeen in April 1996 to Brian Laudrup's header that sealed nine in a row in May 1997. So much weight has been placed on those who finished the job and that memorable first season, about which so much has been written already. Understandable as that may be, it does a disservice to some far more interesting stories, none more so than how Souness lost his grip in 1987/88 and how he regained it with interest the following year. It forgets a very finely balanced football team and some unsung heroes of the age. I would dearly hope that some of those names and games are better understood and appreciated as a result of this book.

Finally, this is unashamedly my era. My footballing consciousness started with the Mexico World Cup in 1986, my first Rangers game was in the September of that year and I would be nearly into adulthood – 17 years, five months and a day if you wish to be precise – until I experienced how it felt to go through a season without seeing Rangers win a trophy. It's not a love letter, although there will be moments of genuine affection. Historians should be able to be aware of their biases and false memories, distorted as they are by nostalgia, and still be critical in their assessment decades later when blessed with a different perspective. Despite that, what I hope I have captured in these pages is the sense of excitement that seemed to be a permanent state of emotion during these years. The landscape was changing and for those older than me who had seen things I hadn't, their thrill could not be hidden. It was infectious. For us all, it was a period in history where it genuinely felt like Rangers could sign anyone and win anything. Ambition and hope was limitless.

It was our time and this is how it happened.

PROLOGUE

'British football is in crisis: a slum sport played in slum stadiums and increasingly watched by slum people, who deter decent folk from turning up.'
Sunday Times, 19 May 1985

'Nothing is inevitable until it happens.'
A.J.P. Taylor, historian

This time Graeme Souness was seated and subdued.

Twelve months earlier, he had been swaggering around Rome's modern colosseum with the European Champions' Cup in his hands and the world at his feet. The all-action midfield gladiator; powerful and stylish in equal measure. The captain of Liverpool, with whom he had just won his final prize in a long, glittering collection, and the captain of Scotland, from where, it could be argued, a better all-round footballer has never been produced. Souness was a force of nature. A dominant, adrenaline-fuelled presence, on that night as he had been throughout his career. His eyes bulging down the camera lens, dressed as he was in that iconic pin-stripe shirt.

This time he was dressed in sombre black, appropriately as it would turn out, as he, Terry Venables and Jimmy Hill struggled to make sense of the horror coming through from Brussels to their television studio in London. Crowd disturbances were, by then, depressingly familiar to British viewers but these scenes were different. The showpiece event of the footballing calendar was thrown into tragic chaos by hooliganism, poor planning and a crumbling stadium. The Heysel disaster, where 39 Italian fans were killed and over 600 were injured, was the sickening culmination of an English football fan culture spiralling out of control and an ineffective and, indeed, indifferent approach to governance by the game's authorities.

The three men tried valiantly to make sense of it all as well as filling the televisual vacuum that the lengthy delay to kick-off had created. Although now detached from the decaying national game, with Souness playing for Sampdoria in Italy and Venables in Spain managing Barcelona, their instant reactions were very much in sync with the reactionary politics that would follow at home. National service, tougher policing and a system of identification were all proposed in the studio as they would later be in Downing Street. 'You're talking about animals,' said Souness of elements of the support who once chanted his name. 'They act like animals so they should be treated like animals.' Hill was so shaken by the crisis that he mistakenly passed over to John Motson instead of his commentary colleague and rival, Barry Davies, who was actually the BBC's man in position in Belgium.

Souness could never have imagined that the tragedy unfolding before him that evening would be the first in a series of events throughout the next year, which would change the fortunes of his first true footballing love and, in turn, his life. Early on in the broadcast he was asked if the match should take place at all. 'No I don't think so,' he replied, still shocked and softly spoken. 'I think it's a very sad day for football. I feel for the parents who are maybe watching this programme wondering if it's any of their kids who are involved in it.'

He continued, somewhat prophetically, 'I think maybe we've seen the last English team play in a European competition for a long, long time Jim.'

* * *

'The world of football is in a state of shock,' said David Will, SFA president and a member of UEFA's Executive Committee, on Thursday, 30 May 1985, the day after the disaster. 'However, I must say that my fellow committee members at UEFA are heartily sick of this.' That sickness was felt just as acutely back in England. Liverpool immediately withdrew themselves from the next season's UEFA Cup and the following day, after some pressure from government, the FA banned all of its clubs from European competition for one year. The language used by FA secretary Ted Croker was very much in keeping with the infamous 'Slum Game' editorial in the Sunday Times ten days before Heysel, 'We have got to do something about the scum we are stuck with at football matches.' He would stay consistent to that line during the crisis talks in Downing Street. When Margaret Thatcher reportedly told him that she did not want his sport's hooligans in her country, he famously replied, 'These people are society's problems and we don't want your hooligans in our sport, prime minister.'

The reactionary response to Heysel was seen by some as an opportunistic attack on the city of Liverpool specifically and working-class culture in general. As Tony Evans, the football writer and Liverpool fan who was in the stadium that night and who wrote a brutally emotional mea culpa piece years later, put it, 'At a time when we [the city of Liverpool] were politically, economically and socially under pressure, the thing we had as flag-bearers were the football teams, who were the best in Europe.' Although the methods in the years to follow – ID cards, high fences and all – would support the argument of 1980s class warfare and a government who were out of touch with the game, the immediate response on all sides of the deep political divide in Britain at the time was supportive of withdrawal. The Guardian's editorial called for self-quarantine of 'our sad, sick game. We are the root of the contagion. We are the home of the virus, and we must act accordingly. It will of course do the game great harm. International stars will move abroad. Standards will waver. Gates will plummet. But the only way of treating a virulent and mysterious virus is the most rigid quarantine.'

Heysel, of course, was not an isolated incident and, although the language of the Sunday Times editorial – published in the wake of the Bradford fire tragedy – was elitist and provocative, there was some truth contained therein. Attendances at English football were plummeting, so much so that the following season would see levels not witnessed in the First Division since the First World War and, in the Second Division, since 1906/07. This latest shameful episode was just another act in over ten years of worsening violence. Tottenham Hotspur were handed a home ban when fans rioted in the UEFA Cup Final second leg in Rotterdam in 1974. Leeds United were banned for four years, cut to two, after rioting during the 1975 European Cup Final against Bayern Munich in Paris. Manchester United had to play home ties in the European Cup Winners' Cup in 1977 away from Old Trafford after trouble in Saint-Étienne in the first round and West Ham had to play behind closed doors three years later in the same competition after rioting in Madrid in their first leg against Castilla CF. Aston Villa fans rioted in Anderlecht during their victorious 1982 European Cup run while Manchester United fans did the same in Valencia in the following season's UEFA Cup and a Spurs fan was shot dead in a bar before the 1984 UEFA Cup Final first leg against Anderlecht, leading to 200 fans being arrested during the subsequent riots. And this does not include the England national team, which was left out of any proposed ban. There was trouble in Turin during a European Championship match against Belgium in 1980 and more damage was inflicted on the cities of Basel, Oslo and Copenhagen during 1981 and 1982.

Kenny Dalglish, writing years later, felt that it was the 'height of irresponsibility for Thatcher to come out so quickly with such rash statements when she didn't know the facts. She probably got all the English clubs banned. If she'd kept her mouth shut, the rest of them might not have suffered.' Given the endemic levels of violence by then running through the English game, and that it was relatively rare for Liverpool to be involved, it was not conceivable that UEFA would simply target one club. All were likely to be affected. The only question was for how long would they be exiled.

On Sunday, 2 June 1985 UEFA banned English clubs from all European competitions indefinitely and it was the nature of the punishment that would allow the following period in Rangers' history to take place in the manner and pace in which it did. UEFA could have accepted the self-imposed FA ban, in which case English clubs would have been able to compete again at the start of the 1986/87 season. They could have gone higher but kept it fixed – say a two-year ban for all clubs and an extra season for Liverpool – and still it would have been highly unlikely for Rangers to have been able to attract the quality of player that they did for as long. The ban was severe – understandable given its proximity to such horrible tragedy – and a touch cynical given that it would allow the English grip on UEFA's top contest to loosen significantly, but it was the vacuum of uncertainty that caused the greatest damage to English clubs and the greatest opportunity for those alert to it.

Reviews would continue intermittently. In March 1986 UEFA president Jacques Georges made it clear that the governing body would never be rushed into relaxing their position. 'We will decide what to do once the commission produces a report,' he said in the build-up to the international friendlies that month. 'It is premature to say whether at that stage we will decide on an immediate readmission or admission within a year, or to keep the ban. We are in no hurry, we cannot afford to come up with the wrong decisions.' The FA would often talk optimistically as the years went by but they were continually hamstrung by events such as a 150-man brawl between West Ham United and Manchester United fans on a ferry to their respective European pre-season tours in 1986, the stabbing of a West German supporter at a friendly with England in 1987 and widespread hooliganism at the European Championship in West Germany in the summer of 1988.

On the eve of the 1990 World Cup, the new UEFA president Lennart Johansson gave only a ten per cent chance of readmission the following season, but – despite familiar scenes on the island of Sardinia – on 9 July, two days after the World Cup Final, it was all over. The new UEFA position was that a continuation of the ban would be 'a victory for violence' and it would be reasonable to argue that the impact of England on the field that summer – the FIFA Fair Play Award, Paul Gascoigne's tears, Bobby Robson's avuncular humanity – had as much to do with the change of heart as the increasingly relaxed and festive atmosphere of the England support in the stadia. Liverpool, as First Division champions, were given an extra year ban but FA Cup winners Manchester United would go into the Cup Winners' Cup and Aston Villa would take the one UEFA Cup place for 1990/91, meaning that the standby club for that slot – Celtic – would have to put their passports away, only a month before the new season was due to start.

In the immediate aftermath of Heysel, the anxiety wasn't confined to Albion. For many on the continent, this was a British issue and the blanket should cover all four home nations. Scotland had suffered its own share of football violence in the 1970s but the alcohol ban, placed into legislation after the Hampden riot following the Old Firm Scottish Cup Final in 1980, was starting to have a positive impact albeit with some notable exceptions such as the 'Janefield Street Riot' four weeks previously when a wall and railings collapsed on fans and passersby after a police charge at the end of the final Old Firm game of the season. Belgium's interior minister Charles-Ferdinand Nothomb announced a ban on all British football clubs, including school teams, from playing in Belgium. It was eventually rescinded before Scotland's Euro '88 qualifier in April 1987 and the wider concerns were quickly assuaged for Scotland, Wales and Northern Ireland – by Thatcher among others – but there was a definite feeling during that summer that they were all effectively under an informal suspended sentence. Rangers quickly felt the pressure and pulled out of a pre-season trip to Germany in the summer of 1985 including games against 1860 Munich, Karlstad and Saarbrücken with manager Jock Wallace summing up the position, succinctly as ever by saying, 'If we don't go there can't be any trouble.'

The picture, however, would become much clearer as 1985 turned into 1986. This was a situation that England alone would be forced to deal with. Many football writers predicted an increased drain in talent, already under way, from the First Division southwards and eastwards to the continent's biggest leagues. None were suggesting that some of those biggest English names could head north to Scotland, thus bucking the traditional market trend that had been set in stone since the dawn of the professional game itself. That would take a significant change in ambition.

It would take a revolution.

* * *

'We cannot make anyone, whether they be a manager or player come to this club. The people we approached chose not to come,' said a floundering Rangers chairman, John Paton, in October 1985 as tensions inside Glasgow's Mitchell Theatre grew like never before at the club's AGM. It was the perfect crystallisation of the state of ineptitude that had existed inside the Ibrox boardroom for far too long. The biggest and wealthiest club in Scotland couldn't even attract the country's best managers. Within 40 days, however, that debilitating deadlock would be blown away.

No sooner had the Glasgow comedian Andy Cameron been surrounded by warm laughs inside the auditorium than they had turned to heckles. It was he who had attacked Paton on the shambolic process that the club had gone through to appoint a successor to John Greig in the autumn of 1983, when they were turned down by Scotland's two leading managerial lights, Alex Ferguson and Jim McLean. 'I want to know why there wasn't a queue outside the door,' he demanded. 'It's a disgrace.' It was his next point that led some shareholders to suggest that he should play in 'Hibernian halls' for the foreseeable future. Cameron alleged that McLean in particular had turned the job down because he wasn't allowed to sign a Roman Catholic. 'It's obvious to us that you'll never sign a Catholic – why don't you be honest about it?' he asked amid the increasing discontent around him. 'I don't care if you never sign a Catholic player or sign ten. What matters is that Rangers have the best team.'

The signing 'policy' was now dominating the newspaper editorials any time the Rangers managerial position was discussed. The Glasgow Herald stated shortly after Greig's departure, 'The club has, in short, been presented with a momentous opportunity; it must seize it. No explicit statement has yet been issued that Catholics can be signed by the new manager, whoever he is. That statement must be issued by the board, immediately and unequivocally.' However, there is no evidence at all that McLean had doubts about the assurances he was given to sign whomever he wished or if he had, that they were the significant factor in refusing. Walter Smith, his assistant at Tannadice, sensed that there were some misgivings when the two discussed the proposal but that McLean had in fact decided to accept, before that fateful Monday lunchtime meeting with the full Dundee United board where he was finally convinced to stay. United could never match the Rangers offer of £70,000 a year but the reported pitch of a £50,000 testimonial was not insignificant, especially on top of the fact that McLean had, by that point, deep emotional ties at the club as well as an outside chance of winning the European Cup that season.[1]

The same question has dominated the Alex Ferguson story over the years as he has shared many and varied narratives for his rejection in print. In his 1999 book Managing My Life, Ferguson stated it was the main reason for turning down

---

1   Dundee United had just qualified for the quarter-finals of the European Cup the week before McLean was offered the Rangers job. The tournament would resume in March and United were only knocked out in the semi-finals by AS Roma in very dubious circumstances.

the then vice-chairman John Paton's advances, 'The truth is that I was already reluctant to entertain exposing my family to the risk of a recurrence of the bigotry I had encountered at Ibrox in my playing days … Cathy's religion would probably have been enough in itself to convince me that returning to Rangers was not a good idea.' This is in contrast to the more contemporaneous account he gave in his 1985 book A Light In The North, where he wrote, 'Although I did discuss the religious subject with John Paton it was not an issue with me. As far as I am concerned managing footballers is all that matters.' This was a reaction to a Radio 2 news item what had made him 'absolutely livid', in which it proclaimed that he would be the Rangers manager the next day and that his first signing would be a Roman Catholic. His biographer Michael Crick offered up the credible explanation that Ferguson's rage would be specifically related to the thought that any director would dictate to him who he had to sign as well as some reluctance at being publicly associated with such a vigorous rejection of an employment policy that some of his friends and heroes – Scot Symon, Willie Waddell and John Greig – had perpetuated. The least credible explanation was given by Ferguson to the Rangers Monthly magazine in early 2001 where he said that he had questioned the ambition of the club in 1983 when he asked Paton 'why the club didn't have the best players from England. It wasn't difficult, it was just a matter of finding who you wanted and then buying them.' Such a transfer vision in Scotland, pre-Heysel, is a post-hoc fantasy. A case of looking back at how history unraveled and deciding that you would have done exactly the same, only sooner.

What is more certain is that both men felt a sense of unease about the functionality of the football club itself. In Ferguson's first book, he recalled a conversation with his previous manager Scot Symon who, instinctively, told him that he must accept but that his only reservation related to the boardroom. 'Who on the board of Glasgow Rangers held power at the particular time and were they the same group as was offering me the manager's place?' was the question posed by Symon to Ferguson. 'He was able to find out some of these answers himself but when we spoke on the telephone the next evening he remained unsure about the unity of the board. His information was that two separate directors were competing for the chairman's seat. Now, such an issue may be largely irrelevant to the ordinary football supporter … but to a manager it is all-important. At the end of the day, the most important relationship in the running of a club – and particularly of a big rich club like Rangers – is between the manager and the chairman.'

The reality was that, by the middle of the 1980s, too many men wanted to be a director of Rangers Football Club because of the status that it would bestow on them inside business and social circles rather than because they wanted to gain a position of influence from which to drive the club forward and, because of that superficial focus, it naturally led to an interminably long period of in-fighting. An Evening Times editorial likened the never-ending 'manoeuvrings behind the club's red brick facade' as something that would be beyond a Dallas scriptwriter and called it a state of flux in recent years which has 'seen directors come and go like players in a transfer free-for-all'. This was perhaps exemplified by Jack Gillespie, the Lenzie car garage owner, whose rise in the business world ran parallel with his desire to have a position of prominence at his boyhood heroes. His purchase of Matt Taylor's shareholding, among others, led to him becoming the second-largest shareholder in the club by 1977 and thus forcing his way on to the board. He was made vice-chairman in March 1983 but would not see out a full year in post before being deposed in yet another reshuffle, only to be back in that role 20 months later, in early November 1985, as the bitter game of musical chairs continued. Few knew that the most significant round of all was soon to come.

Gillespie's dream of becoming the chairman of Rangers was well-known but his self-confidence and the significance of his role in helping finance the stadium reconstruction didn't appear to be shared and respected by his fellow directors who felt, because of his stock, that he was a presence to be tolerated rather than coveted. Gillespie, however, did seem to know what Rangers required in order to regain success, and he was the only member of the board who would admit that John Greig wasn't the answer. As early as March 1983 he sounded alarm bells over the managerial position when he said, 'Mr Greig could still have a very long career here. He could maybe have a short career … Football is a very cut-throat business.' When the crisis did eventually loom over Ibrox in the following October, Gillespie voted to sack the manager but the then chairman Rae Simpson, John Paton and Willie Waddell didn't, which only helped to prolong an environment of dithering inaction which in turn, heaped more pressure on a struggling club legend. Greig resigned the following day.

It was as much the board's structure, rather than solely the personalities on it, that was a weight around the club. More and more clubs were moving towards an increasingly autonomous boardroom dynamic whereas both Rangers and Celtic could often be hamstrung by contesting blocks of power. The kind of ambition required to flourish, post-Heysel, would struggle to be realised if it meant that competing family interests had to always be appeased, as those at Parkhead would find out soon enough. Domination on the park would need a dominant presence off of it.

After a long series of calls from Lake Tahoe, Jack Gillespie agreed a deal that would realistically end his dreams of the top seat but would change the course of Rangers history forever. On Wednesday, 20 November 1985, it was announced that Lawrence Marlborough – grandson of the former Rangers chairman John Lawrence and now in control of the family construction business including their stake in Rangers – had agreed to pay £1m to Gillespie for his 80,000 shares over the course of the next five years. With the significant Rangers losses impacting on the accounts of the Lawrence Group, Marlborough knew that it was time to either get out completely or grab control and risk it all on a turnaround. As much as success on the Ibrox pitch would have been welcome to a lifelong supporter, it would also have been a very visible corporate and public relations success which, in turn, would be good for business. The casinos around Tahoe are perhaps smaller than its more famous Nevadan neighbour, but the gambler's instinct still runs through it. Marlborough chose to lay it out on the table and roll the dice.

The move still needed a willing party on the other end, however. For all that Gillespie's critics would point to their perception of a self-serving egotist, this was a pivotal moment where a man sacrificed his ultimate personal ambition for the greater good and it finally ended the era of small-minded, attritional protectionism. Gillespie was healthily rewarded of course but it was still a deal that ended a debilitating deadlock. Many shareholders complained at the time that they had been blind-sided and sold down the river but something had to give and Gillespie realised it. 'I have the interests of Rangers at heart,' he said that day. 'I feel the best way forward for the club is for the major shareholders to join forces.' He would keep his position on the board as part of the arrangement but would now vote with Marlborough. Or rather, vote with Marlborough's man.

Due to the pressures of his business interests on the other side of the Atlantic and a natural inclination to stay out of the Ibrox limelight, Marlborough had stepped down as vice-chair in February 1983 and for exactly the same reasons he decided to appoint his chairman and managing director from John Lawrence (Glasgow) Ltd. building group to take responsibility on Edmiston Drive in 1985. David Holmes, a Falkirk fan with a sharp business brain who had started as a training officer before rising to the top, was handed the controls of the biggest institution in Scotland and now it was control in the very real sense of the word. This deal meant that, for the first time in its history, Rangers Football Club had a single majority shareholder. The era of the gentlemanly badge of honour and boardroom stalemate was over.

'It's not the Rangers I know,' complained Tom Dawson, by then a former director of Rangers, on Wednesday, 12 February 1986, the day that Holmes ruthlessly cut the board down to size by asking Dawson, James Robinson and Rae Simpson to leave.[2] In his Evening Times column the late James Sanderson – who coined the infamous 'were you at the game today, caller?' catchphrase on Radio Clyde's Open Line – likened Holmes to a bungling hitman doing an untidy and unprofessional job and, because of his initial reluctance to work openly with the media, just another 'Scarlet Pimpernel' like his absentee boss. 'What do Holmes and Co. expect to do that Messrs Robinson, Dawson and Simpson could not?' That question would be answered before 1986 was out.

Dawson was correct, of course. It really wasn't the Rangers that he knew. It was now going to be a more streamlined executive with every director responsible for a specific job, demonstrated by the appointment of Freddie Fletcher, the marketing manager at the Lawrence group, later that month. He was made a director with a tight remit around sponsorship and was tasked with generating matchday income like never before. Talent was now a prerequisite for admission and it would have to be, as Holmes soon made clear, 'In the end the board, and individual directors, will be responsible for their performance to John Lawrence (Glasgow) Ltd. As with any business they will be judged on their performance and treated accordingly ... The club will generate its own cash. It will not be supported by the John Lawrence group or anyone else.' Rangers now had a board in place that was prepared to be more dynamic and more ambitious than any Scottish football fan could possibly realise. It had shedded some of the old and archaic fashions and traditions. It was following a trend that would become more and more in vogue within football and business alike throughout this era. Rangers were becoming modern.

---

2   This move left a four-man board: Holmes, Gillespie, the (nominal) chairman John Paton and
      Hugh Adams who had done impressive work with the Rangers Pools scheme.

But what of the main job at Ibrox? Anyone paying even a passing glance to the remarks by David Holmes in February 1986 would know that Jock Wallace, struggling to find results and with his contract due up in the summer, would not be the manager in August. 'The manager's contract runs until the end of the year. We have not even discussed it,' said Holmes. 'Like everyone else from the directors downwards he is answerable to someone for his performance. Some of the decisions that have to be taken will be hard but if the end result is that Rangers run out winners we are all winners in the end.'

It has often been a point of intrigue, not to mention a rich source for counter-factual historical fantasists, that Rangers – now with a united boardroom, financial ambition and the willingness to give a new manager total control in a post-Heysel world – didn't ask the question once again of Alex Ferguson. Perhaps pride was a factor after such an embarrassing rejection, detailed further in a book that was only published the year before. In the 2021 film Sir Alex Ferguson: Never Give In, he made that clear that his infamous post-match tirade after the 1983 Scottish Cup Final win over Rangers where he eviscerated his Aberdeen players (who had just won their second trophy in the space of a week following their European Cup Winners' Cup heroics against Real Madrid) for not beating Rangers badly enough. Trembling with fury, Ferguson didn't simply want to be victorious over Rangers in a cup final, he wanted to embarrass them, such was the simmering rage that he still felt following his treatment and subsequent sale after the 1969 Scottish Cup Final.[3]

Rangers hiring a manager who, less than three years before, had shown such visceral hatred for the club was perhaps never going to be a productive match.[4] However, given that Holmes didn't even entertain that type of football manager, it is clear that he sought something completely different with which to spearhead the revolution. Many would point to Ferguson's Manchester United success as evidence of what inevitably would have been at Ibrox, however it would not have been that simple. A development of an already promising youth system would unquestionably have happened – and the failure to capitalise on that would be a theme throughout the real history that was to follow – but that might still have been dependent on finding an Eric Harrison figure to run it.[5] Although talented youngsters were starting to come through, Rangers supporters in 1986, with no league title in eight years, would not have been sold on waiting on another generation for success. Nor is it credible to believe that Ferguson would have had the necessary charismatic pulling power when it came to raiding the English First Division.[6] It wouldn't be until 1989 that he started getting to grips with

---

3   Ferguson was at fault for the first goal in a 4-0 defeat by Celtic and was frozen out at Ibrox before being replaced by Colin Stein. Both playing careers would suggest that it was the correct footballing decision, although handled badly.

4   It is, however, an intriguing coincidence that Ferguson only told Aberdeen that he definitely wanted a new challenge in the week following their Scottish Cup semi-final win in April 1986, during the week that Rangers appointed their new manager.

5   Harrison was arguably the man who shaped Manchester United's youth development the most and has been given the credit, by Ferguson himself, for the 'Class of '92'.

6   In his first summer at Old Trafford, Ferguson failed to persuade Mark Hateley, Peter Beardsley and Kevin Drinkell to move to Manchester United and passed on the opportunity to sign John Barnes.

that market and even then, it was younger players he managed to persuade such as Gary Pallister, Paul Ince and Denis Irwin. Once more, we should beware the seduction of the inevitable in history.

It was Graeme Souness himself who first conjured up the notion of him being player-manager at Rangers. In the September of 1985, as Scotland prepared for that fateful World Cup qualifier against Wales in Cardiff, he contributed to the BBC Scotland documentary Only A Game?, which would be shown in May 1986 in the run up to the finals. 'I'm a professional footballer who plays for money,' said Souness when asked to open up on the topic of the professional game in this country. 'I can earn a great deal more by playing football outside of Scotland than I could in Scotland. So that's why I play football outside of Scotland.' Then there was a pause and grin before he added, 'But I'd still like to be player-manager of Rangers one day. I'd settle for manager. Jock Wallace watch out!'

David Holmes once said that he was lying in bed one night when the thought of Souness joining Rangers first came to him. Some fans have also claimed to have had the same notion as they trudged towards the warm refuge provided by the pub, after another grim Ibrox performance in the early part of 1986. Those accounts might all be true but it is highly doubtful that the image of a Scottish Liverpool legend in a player-manager role would have entered their minds in the first place, if the general idea hadn't been put into practice already.

* * *

Jimmy Hill had an important talking point all ready to use before the question of life and death made everything else suddenly seem trivial. The big news on the day of that 1985 European Cup Final was that it would be Joe Fagan's last game in charge of Liverpool and the speculation was that Kenny Dalglish was prepared to step up into a player-manager role. It was an unfashionable hybrid in football. Herbert Chapman had done it as a bridge between being a footballer and a manger at Northampton Town back in the Edwardian period before he revolutionised the status of the latter, but by this time it was seen as something of a stop-gap appointment for older professionals such as Johnny Giles at West Bromwich Albion in the 1970s.

Souness had expected Fagan to go on for another year and for Dalglish to retire and take up the manager's position in the normal way in the summer of 1986. 'It's maybe a wee bit early for Kenny now,' he said. Terry Venables thought that it would be too hard to do both jobs at that level and he should make his mistakes further down the footballing pyramid before returning to Anfield at a more suitable time. Hill then pressed Souness on whether he would do that kind of job at this stage of his career. 'I don't think so, no,' came the reply. There were far more important considerations for Souness to process at that specific time but even then, it just wasn't the kind of role that was used at a club as big as Liverpool. Or Rangers, for that matter.

'This is worst Liverpool side I've ever played in,' said Alan Hansen to his manager prior to Liverpool's visit to Tottenham at the start of March 1986. Eleven points behind Everton, with a game in hand and three points for a win, Dalglish felt that the team spirit was still good and that, if they could get on a run, they would still win the title. An instinctive Ian Rush winner in the final minute provided the spark for exactly that and, by 10 May, they had won the First Division and FA Cup double. In truth, they had just suffered a bad winter. At the turn of the year Liverpool were in third place, in the hunt for all three trophies, and the new project seemed to be working. At the turn of the year, David Holmes made a call to Genoa.

Holmes later wrote, 'I looked at how Graeme's friend Kenny Dalglish had stolen a march on him with his instant success as Liverpool's player-manager and decided that was the best way to sell the job to him.' It wasn't simply a case of Holmes being tempted by a novel, if exciting, fad. This was a Liverpool idea and, in 1986, that was as good a guarantee of success at it was possible to find in the capricious world of football. The accounts of the pursuit of Graeme Souness vary wildly, somewhat appropriate for a story that some people still struggled to believe when they were in the room watching it unfold. For example the man himself, in his 1999 autobiography Souness: The Management Years, wrote that he first had a discussion with Walter Smith about the job at a Scotland camp before a game with Yugoslavia in February 1986.[7] That fixture does not exist. Scotland didn't have a match at all that month and wouldn't play Yugoslavia again until 1988. Smith did write about that first discussion at Turnberry during an international week but that it was in late March for the friendly at home to Romania. That does indeed check out but Smith says that he was first approached at the Gleneagles hotel in the February, which was contradicted years later by Sir Alex Ferguson, who said that he approached Smith while on Scotland duty in Tel Aviv at the end of January, about potentially coming with him to Arsenal should he take up that offer. That is when Smith told him that he couldn't accept as he was heading to Ibrox after the World Cup and would fill him in on the detail much later. Souness wasn't in the squad for that match.

Ferguson's Israel account, given to the Rangers matchday programme for Smith's final match at Ibrox in 2011, seems too specific to be confused so it appears clear that both men received an initial approach in the January of 1986. The first broker was the former Sun and Glasgow Herald football writer Ken Gallacher, who was asked by John Paton to make contact with Souness in Italy in advance of a call from Holmes, before the three men met in the Mayfair Hotel in London. Holmes took a day trip to Milan for one final meeting but it was merely a formality as Souness had, by then, made up his mind to take the job which would start after the World Cup. It was Holmes who strongly advised that Souness take on an experienced assistant who knew Scottish football well and there was simply no better choice than Smith, already assumed to be the next big thing in Scottish football management. By 26 March the two were already discussing their plans in Smith's hotel room for how they would revitalise their faded old club, always wary of someone bursting in to find them discussing an agenda that had nothing to do with Mexico.

---

7   Walter Smith was, by then, an assistant to Alex Ferguson in his temporary role as Scotland manager for the forthcoming World Cup in Mexico that summer.

On the weekend prior to that Scotland friendly, Rangers drew 4-4 with Celtic at Ibrox in a ridiculous farce played out in torrential rain. Archie Macpherson has said that after the game, 'Jock Wallace came up to Holmes in the boardroom. Jock was singing "The Sash". Jock wasn't a bigot, he was what I would call a traditional bluenose, but Holmes said to himself, "We've just drawn at home when our great rivals have ten men and the manager's singing 'The Sash'. I've had enough of this." So he spoke to Marlborough, who said, "Change the place".' Macpherson was simultaneously right and wrong. The die had been cast for Wallace long before that match but the need for reform was obvious to anyone who was paying attention. The only question was whether could Holmes afford to wait until the end of the season as, with the team's current form as it was, there was no guarantee that Rangers would secure that final spot for European qualification.

In the end, as is so often the case, the decision was forced by other events. Scottish Television's Jim White had also been to Italy that spring to talk with Souness, this time for a pre-Mexico piece and on life in Serie A in general. On Sunday, 6 April, White had been tipped off by his Sampdoria press office contacts that his man was 'coming to your city, he's coming to Rangers'. Alan Ferguson, a Glasgow PR consultant who was working with Rangers at the time, had already advised Souness to start throwing journalists off the scent by suggesting that he might take up a player-manager role in England. On Friday, 4 April Chick Young had a back-page splash in the Evening Times with quotes from Souness saying that he has been offered a job which he was desperate to take but that it was now in the hands of Sampdoria president Paulo Mantovani. 'The club concerned is almost certainly Arsenal or Tottenham,' wrote Young before finishing with, 'Ironically, the news of his future could be broken in Glasgow, for he flies here on Monday for a dinner date in the city.' Whether Young was a stooge or an accomplice[8], it was rendered irrelevant by the Sunday night when White had his story. Ferguson's advice to Holmes was to act quickly which, by the standards of mid-1980s media[9], meant a 5pm press conference the next day to announce a sudden managerial sacking and an imminent arrival.

The Scottish Cup semi-finals had pride of place in the Scottish footballing calendar that weekend and, as Rangers were not involved, they had arranged a 'glamour' friendly against Tottenham Hotspur at Ibrox.[10] Only 12,655 people turned up to watch a sad home team limp to a 2-0 defeat. David Holmes wasn't even in attendance. As that game was being played, he was at the Pond Hotel in the west end of Glasgow finalising an agreement with Walter Smith. So hasty was it that Smith didn't even ask about what he'd be paid. Later that week, when Rangers needed Smith to come in immediately and see out the rest of the season, Jim McLean and Dundee United chose to be difficult and asked for £50,000 compensation. Smith was furious at this given that McLean had sold him to Dumbarton as a player for £7,000 and then bought him back for just over half that fee. However, according to Smith, 'David Holmes picked up the phone and

8   The fact that Young fully expected to be sitting next to Souness at a Variety Club dinner the night that it was announced would suggest that it was the former.

9   STV did not have a lunchtime bulletin so White could only use the 6pm slot.

10   A similar match had been arranged for the previous round, when Rangers hosted Chelsea.

called [Dundee United chairman] George Fox. He had a speaker switched on so that I could hear the entire conversation and he simply asked him where the £50,000 cheque had to be sent. When he was told to send the money to George Fox's house, he sat down and wrote out the cheque in front of me, summoned a courier and had it delivered to Carnoustie that evening. That cleared the decks for me to start the job immediately.'

Campbell Ogilvie's announcement on the Monday evening was short and to the point. Jock Wallace's time had regrettably come to an end by mutual consent and that Rangers had entered into talks with Sampdoria where they wished to invite Souness to be their player-manager. There were audible groans from journalists that this was all that they had been dragged out for. The following morning, after clandestine car rides and diverted flights and after bringing their new man into Ibrox through the back door, the groans had turned to gasps. It wasn't standard practice for Rangers to invite the nation's press into the famous Blue Room but there was nothing standard about that morning. There was even a dramatic pause after Holmes had uttered those words, 'So, gentlemen, can I just say to you, welcome to our new player-manager, Graeme Souness.' With typical nonchalance, the new boss was on the phone to a friend at the time and had to quickly hang up before walking through that door to a cacophony of flashes and excitement.

'I've got a lemon in my pocket,' Holmes told White on STV. 'I suck it every now and then to keep the smile off my face. If this club was going to be ambitious then you have to go for the very best and I think Graeme is the very best.' The front page of the newspapers naturally focussed on Souness's commitment to signing Catholics, especially as his wife was one, whereas the back pages struggled immediately to make sense of it all. Comparisons were made with the appointment of John Greig, who too lacked the relevant experience, and a catalogue of problems were listed for the new man to address. The Evening Times had an extremely interesting cartoon of Souness – the boy from Edinburgh who had never played a minute of domestic football in his home country – entitled 'Where Is Ibrox?'. It depicted him wearing a Gucci suit with an 'A to B of football management' and a map of Scottish football grounds in the pockets while carrying a suitcase bulging with cash and an I.O.U. He had a bottle of Brut aftershave – seemingly the height of cosmopolitan fashion according to mid-1980s Glasgow – and was wearing a badge that says 'I Love Me'. A man who was respected but never loved in Scotland, who was the living embodiment of a political philosophy that contrasted with so much of the city, was now in charge of its biggest club. This wasn't a local appointment.

His horizons weren't local either. It was Souness who first grasped the possibilities that Rangers now had in the transfer market. Although genuinely humbled to have been given this opportunity at such a big club, he didn't waste any time by being overawed. He wanted to reverse the traditional flow of talent south, of which he had of course been a part, and attempted to bring the best of England north. Such was the bitter competition in Scotland, he knew that there was little point in trying to raid rival clubs who simply wouldn't sell at a reasonable price. Foreign investments were risky as if they didn't work out, their value wouldn't recover whereas the English market would still pay a fair rate if a particular experiment went wrong. 'It seemed a logical step but some of the Rangers board expressed surprise at the idea and were worried that the fans would resist a Sassenach invasion,' Souness later wrote. 'I disagreed. I believed the public would welcome any new faces who would help to make Rangers the number one team again.'

For better or worse, Souness was a manager who acted on instinct. His first one was correct and it would change Scottish football at a stroke.

* * *

Essentially the story of the Rangers revolution and the era of dominance that followed is one of vision. It was forged by those who had it, those who lost it and those who never possessed it to begin with. Those who were able to grasp the zeitgeist of the era and those who were beholden to the practices of the past. It is a story of barriers and limitations being blown apart only for new boundaries to rise up with even tighter restrictions. Paeans for those ambitions that were realised, laments for what might have been.

And the preamble to this drama, the events between May 1985 and April 1986, is characterised by exactly the same theme. This Rangers story was, indirectly, shaped by those who lacked vision. The countless figures in English football and in government, either through procrastination or counter-productive reactionary approaches, who helped create and then extend their footballing isolation while causing further tragedy, before realising that the solution was staring back at them from the corner of their living rooms. Those club chairmen in Scotland who lacked the foresight and ambition to capitalise on the opportunity that they had been given to change the traditional direction of the footballing market. It was shaped even more, of course, by those who really did had vision. The Liverpool board for revitalising the tired concept of the player-manager by successfully infusing it with a living legend. Lawrence Marlborough and Jack Gillespie, who realised that the internecine bickering had to cease in order pull this giant back on to its feet and for trusting that job to a dynamic corporate operator who really did understand that sometimes less can deliver more. Graeme Souness himself, whose plans for revolutionising the footballing operation were a shock even for this fresh and invigorated board.

And finally the vision of Willie Waddell, who 15 years previously, while the rest of British football looked upon the Ibrox disaster with genuine sympathy but naive ignorance, sought to create a lasting monument to those who never came home by building a football stadium fit for the 21st century when those closest to it had barely left the 19th. His patience and providence meant that, as the rest of British football resisted modernity, Rangers could attract new players by allying a space-age ground to the financial ambition of their new board and the overpowering charisma of their new manager.

The common history of this era tells us that it was simply Rangers' time. 'The circle will turn again,' said John Greig in March 1986. Then in a punditry capacity with BBC Radio Scotland, he was trying to assure the long-suffering Rangers fans that their chance would come around soon. That is how the cyclical nature of football works after all. Except that it is never as simple as that. As seductive as that long view of history is, it is ultimately illusory. It fails to properly recognise the role of agency and fortune, both of which were hugely significant factors in this story. UEFA's tough response to a tragedy opened up a window of opportunity where one Rangers director had to forego ego at the same time as an exciting new brand of football management was being used to great success. If just one of those decisions wasn't taken then the tale that is about to be told, would not flow in the way in which it did.

The circumstances of 1985 and 1986 had created a possibility where an ambitious Scottish club could build the foundations of a golden era and Rangers, at exactly the right moment in history, had the figures in place to take advantage of that. None more so than the man who breezed through the Blue Room door on that April morning.

Finally, Rangers were ready.

1

IGNITION

SEASON 1986/87

'They say there is a bit of me in Graeme's play and for sure he has the ability to give the opposition players that feeling of inadequacy which I could give them.'
Jim Baxter

'Example is not the main thing in influencing others. It is the only thing.'
Albert Schweitzer, Philosopher

Even with the Ibrox pitch holding up under the falling sleet and snow, Graeme Souness looked a class apart. Alan McInally and Mo Johnston were physically close to him but looked so much in awe, they might as well have been watching from the main stand as he pivoted one way then the next before taking a moment, amid the mayhem, to just pause on the ball as if he had suspended time itself. The comparisons to Jim Baxter were almost immediate, with Archie Macpherson admitting in his post-match summary that he had never seen a Rangers player dominate the midfield like that in an Old Firm game since the great man's heyday. It was Souness's first appearance in the famous old fixture – the new year game no less – and few matches that season were laden with such significance and symbolism. A 2-0 victory would bring Rangers to within touching distance of the top spot and a platform from which to exert a level of pressure in the chase with which Celtic wouldn't cope. Souness's control of the that game became iconic because he was naturally seen as the father of the revolution that was starting to gain an unstoppable momentum.

It was called the 'Rangers Revival' at the time but, as the years have passed, the 'Souness Revolution' has become more en vogue. A one-man force of nature, turning Scottish football on its head. His band of merry Englishmen are usually credited shortly after and then, eventually, David Holmes and Walter Smith get some acknowledgement for their support. Our need for icons, heroes and saviours may be innately human but it never provides us with proper perspective.

The story of 1986/87 is really one of influence more than mercenary expediency. It is about the increased contribution from older faces as much as it was about the glittering performances from new ones. This famous success would not have been possible without the weight of goals from Ally McCoist and Robert Fleck and the odd crucial one from Dave McPherson. The consistent reliability of Stuart Munro and the maverick uncertainty of Ted McMinn. The dynamic energy of young talent like Ian Durrant and Derek Ferguson as well as the new life that was breathed into the fading light of Davie Cooper. Terry Butcher and Chris Woods were almost ever-present but Souness played in only half the games that season and Graham Roberts just a third. Rangers built new foundations in the summer of 1986 but it wasn't an oligarch-fuelled re-fit, with a shiny new player for every position. In an 11-a-side sport, there is only so much impact that three or four men can have in a single match. The potential impact that they can have on their team-mates, however, is almost limitless.

This is not a story about how a handful of professional footballers changed a handful of games. It is about how they changed an entire culture.

* * *

Walter Smith was appalled as he stood in the Rangers dressing room on his first day at work. The first team squad would pick up training gear from a pile dumped in the middle of the floor and, even worse, it would just be hung up in old-fashioned drying rooms afterwards to be used again the next day, filthy and stiff. Writing years later, Smith noted that this wouldn't have been acceptable at Dundee United, from where he had just arrived, and it certainly jarred with his idealistic impression of what life at Rangers would – and should – be like, 'I had had a vision of Ibrox all my life, in which everything at the stadium was as near-perfect as you can get at a football club. But back then, for whatever reasons, the infrastructure of the club was not right. That had to be overhauled dramatically.' Standards were not, as men of Smith's generation would say, 'Rangers-class'. A shibboleth for a job measured perfectly to the best possible grade. The mythology created by Bill Struth and cultivated by Scot Symon had been tarnished by decades of complacency and incompetence. An aura had vanished.

Smith was initially alone in trying to steer Rangers towards the end of season 1985/86 and keep control of that European qualification place, so vital as it would be to all that was to follow. A 2-1 defeat at Clydebank on 12 April had left Rangers in a perilous position with only a single point separating them from the chasing Dundee, with only three matches left to play. The uncertainty around Alex Totten – Jock Wallace's assistant who was unfairly left in a state of limbo – was not helping matters and David Holmes eventually had to bring the succession planning forward and get Souness's assistant in place while he played out the remainder of the Serie A season. Three days later a deal was done with Dundee United for Smith, now that their title challenge had ended, while Totten, John Hagart and Stan Anderson were thanked for their service and waved goodbye.

There was no sudden bounce in form as Rangers continued their losing streak with another 2-1 defeat away to St Mirren the following weekend, and more importantly they were now behind Dundee in the race for Europe. Smith turned to the former Coventry City and Dundee manager Don Mackay to come in and assist with the crucial final fortnight of the league season starting with the least-attractive fixture imaginable. One year on, a trip to Aberdeen would be a piece of heaven for Rangers but at this point in history it was the stuff of nightmares.

One win in the previous 25 visits, a run that included 17 defeats, did not augur well for a stumbling side that simply could not afford to lose. There was, however, a remarkable response and one small, early indication of what might be possible. Rangers didn't win but were fully deserving of the point in a 1-1 draw where they were the better side and were only pulled back late on when John Hewitt cancelled out a fantastic Ted McMinn strike. What is perhaps more revealing are the early signs of Smith's calm but firm assurance around the club during that week. Davie Cooper, for example, turned in a fine performance after some close work with Smith and encouraged by the promise of what was around the corner. 'His talent is not in question,' said Smith immediately after the game, 'but Davie needs to be confident. It was clear that his confidence had gone down in recent months along with the rest of the Rangers team.' Ally McCoist, who was enjoying a very healthy goal return that season, was told after the St Mirren game that just scoring wouldn't be enough and that there would have to be a lot more to his game that benefited the group as a whole. There was also evidence that Smith realised that buying an entire new team was neither realistic nor required, as he explained, 'Since we have come in, there has been a lot of talk about needing something like six new players – but I don't think that is necessary. It has been my opinion for some time that there are good football players at Rangers.'

What they needed was guidance and inspiration and if the first part was already in place then the latter was to finally arrive in time for the season's finale. Souness had met his new players already, of course. He had flown over a couple of times to check in and had some brief, but clear, words with them on that whirlwind day in April. He was used to success and he expected more of it so things would have to change and, as a result, those players would either have to be fully on board or would miss out completely. 'My first impression was of the immediate presence of the man,' wrote Ally McCoist in the early 1990s. 'He was dressed immaculately; he looked fit and tanned and he spoke with firm authority.' It was a common early impression on those players.

Dundee's defeat at Parkhead in their penultimate fixture meant that Rangers held all the cards going into the final day and, with Souness in the Ibrox dugout for the very first time, they didn't disappoint as they managed a 2-0 win over Motherwell with goals from McCoist and McPherson. The 21,500 may have been the biggest crowd of the day in Scotland but it still only represented a half-full Ibrox, where it was clear that more work was required to routinely tempt fans back into the stadium. European football may have been secured for the following season but the glum faces around the dressing room was an early sign of the culture change that the new management had to address. Dundee's sensational win on the final day against Hearts wasn't enough to pip Rangers for that crucial spot but it did open the door to an unlikely and dramatic Celtic title win which, with the help of a very accommodating St Mirren at Love Street, they managed to burst open. 'Surely the most important thing was that Rangers had qualified for Europe?' Souness remarked a few weeks later. His surprise suggested a naivety around the nature of this rivalry which, never having lived in Glasgow, he hadn't properly absorbed. In reality it is a truth inherent in all footballing rivalries, that any success is only ever relative to the other side's. Souness was correct in one respect, however, in that it demonstrated an obsessive insecurity which can easily corrode and distort the measure of one's own worth. Fortunately his new side would have a chance to make a mark on the new champions before the season had fully concluded.

The Glasgow Cup Final – by that time something of an anachronism purely for the reserves – would get the full treatment in 1986 as both sides of the Old Firm promised to field full-strength teams in a match moved to the Friday night so as not to overshadow the Scottish Cup Final the following day. Such was the promise of the new champions coming up against Souness's men that over 40,000 made their way to Ibrox that night, causing traffic chaos that held up Rangers' centre-forward, never known for his punctuality at the best of times. Ally McCoist made amends with a hat-trick in a 3-2 victory with the winner – in extra time – a fantastic 25-yard dipping shot that was worthy of clinching any final. The impact of those two wins, in the space of a week, should not be underplayed. Failure to qualify for Europe would have derailed every recruitment plan that Souness had in waiting and, even though it was effectively a friendly, the chance to deflate, if not completely burst, the Celtic title balloon did leave questions in the mind of the new champions. It was telling that, in the build-up to the game, manager Davie Hay chose not to talk about the prospects of a new 'Celtic Era' after their league win, but of an 'Old Firm' one where Glasgow as a whole was going to re-emerge in its footballing prominence, 'All the signs are that ourselves and Rangers can go on from here to bigger and better things and it is an exciting time for the Old Firm in general.' He wasn't wrong of course – no club outside the two has won the title since, at the time of writing – but it is indicative of the threat that was felt by rivals almost immediately from a club who hadn't been close to being champions for the best part of a decade.

Even Souness was taken aback by the atmosphere but the events of that evening further demonstrated what could be achieved if the correct building blocks were in place. Smith agreed some time later when he said, 'It told us the power that the fans could generate and demonstrated to the pair of us just what could be done if we turned things around.' Earlier that day the pair had cut Derek Johnstone, Dave MacKinnon, Billy Davies, Andy Bruce and Eric Ferguson from the Rangers books while also placing Dougie Bell and John MacDonald on the transfer list.[11] It was only after the game was over that Souness technically made his first signing with the extension of McCoist's contract. What was supposed to be a deal tied up before the game was given a touch more value with an Old Firm hat-trick but McCoist saw fit to protract matters even further by pretending not to be interested. His joke fell on exasperated ears as David Holmes replied, 'Ally, it's been a long day. Would you just sign this and let me get to my bed?' There was never any question of McCoist seriously stalling. He knew exactly which way the wind was changing, 'Rangers and Graeme Souness were going places. No way I was going to miss out. I signed.' The questions over who would be next to put pen to paper would only intensify from this point forward and it was even a hot topic of conversation during the greatest show on earth.

From Scotland's World Cup training camp in Santa Fe, New Mexico to the England base up in Colorado Springs, the transfer activity of Glasgow Rangers was not far from players' thoughts. It was understandable that it would dominate

---

11   MacDonald would move to Barnsley that summer but Bell would stay for the season.

the Scotland squad given how involved their captain and assistant manager were and that one of their players was a big target. Richard Gough wanted to move to Ibrox but, as he and Walter Smith knew all too well, it was never going to happen given Jim McLean's refusal to sell such an important player to a rival club. Souness called back to Glasgow every day while out in the USA but promised that, when the squad touched down in Mexico, his focus would be on the tournament itself. It's quite possible that even he believed it.

It was on the flight out of London that Souness gave an exclusive to Chick Young, then of the Evening Times, about his big summer plans and, of course, the religion question. 'Do they want a sectarian team or a successful one?' Souness challenged the Rangers support, via Young. 'I will sign a Catholic player. There will be no hedging of bets on this.' It could quite easily have been done before that flight took off, with serious interest in Ally Dick of Tottenham Hotspur, however the way that the player – and his family – leaked the story was not to Souness's liking and the deal was off. He was adamant though, that Rangers would go big on at least one target that summer. Some journalists, such as Alex 'Candid' Cameron, were initially carried away with the assumption that it would be the Brazilian Falcão of AS Roma but, even though Rangers were now willing to compete with any English club, Serie A terms were out of reach. It would, surely, then have to come from England.

'It was unheard of,' wrote Smith in his autobiography. 'Top English players simply didn't come to Scotland to ply their trade. They had their own big clubs and all the time they were being told that our Premier League was a second-rate affair. Graeme was going to change all of that. Dramatically!' England's number one, Peter Shilton, had been sounded out early on but wasn't interested while just before Bobby Robson's side were due to leave Heathrow, the media had started to report that Rangers had joined Spurs and Manchester United in their interest in the Ipswich Town central defender Terry Butcher, who was definitely leaving Portman Road after their relegation that season. Speculation over player movement in an international camp is nothing new but it was heightened in 1986 with the new reality for English clubs finally dawning. According to Butcher it was Souness and Rangers that dominated the conversation, especially as it 'ran totally against the grain'. It was known that a member of that England squad had already signed up and, when Butcher discovered that it was Chris Woods, he thought his team-mate was 'mad' for deciding so soon. 'What would happen to his England prospects if he was playing in Scotland?' he fretted.

Woods himself had no such reservations, especially since his conversation with the new Rangers manager at Wembley just a few weeks before, when England beat Scotland 2-1 with the current boss and future captain both on the score sheet. Souness was first impressed when he saw him in action against his Liverpool side in the 1978 League Cup Final, when he was then an understudy to Shilton at club level with Nottingham Forest, as he would later be in the international side. Both Souness and Shilton had to sit out the final as they watched Forest frustrate the English champions over two matches.[12] Souness knew then the value of a goalkeeper as that Liverpool side would consistently enjoy the lion's share of

---

12   Forest won the replay 1-0 after the initial 0-0 draw.

possession in those encounters but, because of Shilton and Woods, wouldn't score. 'That taught me how important it was to have a class performer in that position,' he wrote years later, 'and I was prepared to pay big money for the right man.' Once the World Cup was over he would break the world record for a goalkeeper when Rangers paid £600,000 for Woods.

In the meantime there was still a tournament to be played although, naturally, Scotland wouldn't overstay their welcome. Their group was devilish and the first two defeats – to the Danish side that had impressed at the 1984 European Championship and the West Germany team that would reach the final – were close and somewhat unfortunate. Critics suggested that Souness was a detriment to the side as every attacking endeavour had to go through him, thus making Scotland predictable and ponderous. His display against the West Germans did not lack urgency or class but it took its toll in terms of weight loss in the baking Mexican heat and Alex Ferguson decided to do without his skipper for the decisive final game against Uruguay. Playing against ten men for 89 minutes, Scotland toiled to create much at all and their World Cup was over, as was Souness's international career.

Just as Alan Davidson of the Evening Times penned a lament on the state of all three home international sides, England – and especially Gary Lineker – eventually found some form which would take them to the quarter-finals and that famous match in the Azteca with Diego Maradona, the backdrop of the Belgrano and all of that. Terry Butcher had managed to handle the transfer speculation from outside the camp and the persistent pleading of Woods and the journalist Bob Harris[13] to join Rangers on the inside. With the exception of a clumsy moment early on in the second-round match against Paraguay and, of course, him being the last England player to see the back of Maradona's blue and silver shirt for that second Argentina goal, Butcher had a fine tournament which he finished as England captain due to Bryan Robson's injury and the suspension of Ray Wilkins. For all the talk, by the end of July there was only one club ready to walk as Rangers offered Ipswich over £700,000 in cash to move into pole position to have a formal discussions with the player.

Butcher was drunk as he picked up the phone at 3am in his hotel room, high up in the Hollywood hills. He was in Los Angeles as part of a Rest of the World XI that had played the Americas earlier that Sunday in Pasadena's Rose Bowl in a charity match for UNICEF. Butcher had scored, along with Paolo Rossi before Diego intervened and took the match to penalties.[14] Now he was making arrangements to meet Souness when his flight arrived at Heathrow the next day. The agreement was to meet at the Sheraton Skyline but Butcher, somewhat hazy from the night before, had forgotten that important detail and headed for the Holiday Inn in hope. Once the mistake was rectified, Souness scrambled over to meet his man. If Butcher thought that it would be a polite discussion over strong coffee about a manager's plans before he could head back home to sleep off his hangover and think it over, he was in for a surprise as Souness got him on the next

---

13   Harris was in the England camp with the *Daily Mirror* at the time and was a close friend of Souness.

14   The Americas would win the shoot-out.

shuttle to Edinburgh and then drove him to the stadium immediately. Ibrox was always the ace he felt that he had up his sleeve, as long as he could get players there before they spoke to anyone else. According to Souness, there was no way he could let Butcher go back to England without signing. The deal was done in principle that day and Butcher would train with the squad over the next three days but it wasn't signed and sealed until the Friday.

Although Souness was persuasive, the deal was attractive, a countryman was already in place and his wife Rita firmly behind the idea of moving the family up north, Butcher held off for another offer. Although somewhat faded, like Rangers had been, he felt that Manchester United was still England's glamour club and has admitted since that if they had matched the Rangers figure then he would have reneged and signed with them instead. Rangers have Bobby Charlton to thank for that, vetoing Ron Atkinson's move for Butcher as he was of the opinion that the Old Trafford boss had more than enough quality in that position already, and Tottenham wanted to see him down there in training before doing a deal with Ipswich. Although he still had reservations about Scottish football being 'something of a backwater', Butcher had been impressed with the way that Rangers had treated him and, perhaps most importantly, was given assurances from Bobby Robson that the move wouldn't affect his England status. In addition to the early signing of striker Colin West from Watford, on August 1 Souness completed his big money summer by finally landing his captain.

There were reports that the proposed move for Gough would have been in addition to the Butcher deal but, given that Souness and Smith had to stop there as their initial summer budget had been reached, those weren't realistic. At the unveiling, Souness sent a parting shot to McLean by saying that it was 'sad for Scottish football that this money has gone outside the country when it could have stayed in the game up here. However, we met with obstacles to doing that and it wasn't our fault that we had to go and outbid the biggest teams in England.' Gough would get his move eventually and he would prove to be a longer-lasting success than Butcher but, in hindsight, Jim McLean's obstinacy was to Rangers' ultimate advantage as few signings would have the impact of this one.

Jock Wallace's planned transfer activity in the summer of 1986 would have comprised bids for Gordon Durie of Hibs, John Brown of Dundee and Craig Levein at Hearts. Two of them would eventually arrive at Ibrox – going on to be fine servants of the club – and Levein wouldn't have looked too far out of place had he joined, such was his potential. The signings would have been treated positively in some quarters, evidence that Rangers were building something around Scottish youth if somewhat lacking in ready made quality. Compared to Souness, Butcher and Woods, however, it was small-time both in terms of vision and outlay. It was considered aggressive when both Rangers and Celtic spent nearly half a million pounds each in 1984/85 but these three signings, plus West, took Rangers' spending to just over £1.8m.[15] Despite Davie Hay's assurances that the Celtic board would support him in the close-season to match Rangers' ambition, they barely spent a penny on a young Anton Rogan from Lisburn Distillery. The

---

15   Jimmy Nicholl would also arrive on the eve of the season in a deal that involved Bobby Willliamson heading down to West Bromwich Albion.

nation's footballing landscape had changed in the blink of a Scottish summer and the rest of the field were too shaken to adequately respond.

Although the transfer activity created headlines, Souness and Smith were quietly making other big changes to the Rangers culture as they got into the business of pre-season training, both in Glasgow and with a tour of West Germany. On the field it was clear that Liverpool was the new manager's main influence and in particular, using a more patient build-up in play from the back. As the preparations for the new season intensified, Souness knew that it was not a style of play that would be adopted by the support immediately but that would be very much their problem. 'I expect to be criticised for the way we play but it's my way and I'm not about to change it.,' he said after the final friendly, a 2-0 defeat at home to Bayern Munich. 'In some ways it is almost a re-education because it is my view that Scottish football in general has gone nowhere for years.' There were positive signs that the new approach was taking root, both in that defeat as well as throughout the tour and a 1-1 draw at White Hart Lane, a testimonial for Tottenham's Paul Miller. 'The players are thinking more about the game than they used to. Sometimes they have tended to play with the heart rather than the head, but we're changing that,' said Souness. It was early evidence of aggressive modernisation.

Off the field, it was Souness's Italian experience that was driving changes in professionalism that were badly needed at Ibrox. Despite both Souness being at the end of his playing career and the much mythologised standards of fitness brought to Rangers by Jock Wallace, he soon found himself to be on a different level from his much younger players. Pre-season training was very different than what had gone before with more emphasis on suppleness and stretching than punishing runs up sand dunes. Double sessions were now fuelled by pasta and filled with fresh, modern ideas from Europe's pre-eminent football league. The little things changed too. Players would spend the night before all games together in a hotel, even when playing at home. Flip-flops were compulsory in order to protect the players' main asset: their feet. Golf was banned because of the regular midweek commitments. 'I want their muscles to feel 100 per cent right. The whole commitment must be to Rangers.', said the new manager. Jacuzzis and saunas were installed, as well as proper washing machines, and the club suit – which was now mandatory attire in order to enter the front door – was made by Armani and not Slaters. The little things all add up and were appreciated by the players. 'He knew football players were creatures of routine who liked to be looked after well so they could give of their best on a Saturday and he transformed the place from the bottom up to make sure that it worked that way,' wrote Ian Durrant. 'Those added pieces of professionalism sound trivial but they mattered.'

James Sanderson wrote in his Evening Times column two weeks before the first match of the new season, a trip to Easter Road to face Hibs, 'It is obvious the Souness and Smith regime know the score, but they will now find the honeymoon is over.' In Scotland, nothing attracts attention and suspicion quite like spending money and the pressure and attention was inevitable. One newspaper had a cartoon of Souness's pre-season training differing from Wallace's only in that he had replaced Gullane Sands with a bundle of tenners for players to jump over.

Nevertheless, the squad felt ready for big kick-off. 'All around Ibrox there was a feeling of real optimism,' said Walter Smith, 'where in previous seasons there had only been pessimism.' For all Sanderson's tabloid hysteria there was one cool observation that Souness would have done well to pay heed, 'Our domestic game, for him, is a minefield that is booby-trapped with problems. He will have, with Smith's help, to adapt fast and accurately.'

'The man responsible for creating the greatest interest in the start of a new season for years,' said Jock Brown on commentary before kick-off as the camera caught the player-manager in close up, his first competitive game in Scotland. It was a beautiful August day, the kind you can't help but feel are almost obligatory on the opening day of a season, and – in a purely footballing sense – much of the first 45 minutes contained signs of how the first half of the campaign would play out as Rangers matched quality with unnecessary error. Butcher at times looked commanding, the play had much of the patience that Souness demanded – if a ball was long then it was more a case of it being sprayed, usually by him, than punted – and the passing and movement that led to McCoist being fouled for a penalty was genuinely graceful and intelligent. McCoist would convert but unfortunately it was sandwiched by two Hibs goals that left the high-profile signings looking momentarily overpriced. Butcher was caught comically under a long ball and allowed Steve Cowan to get away from him and square across the Rangers box for Stuart Beedie to fire Hibs in front, and then Woods should have done a lot more to stop another simple cross for Cowan to tap Hibs back into a lead that they would not give up. 'What a waste of money!' was the inevitable chant ringing around the ground, especially as West missed a glorious chance to score a Rangers second at 1-1. The goalmouth action, however, is not why the match is so vividly remembered.

'Some very inflammatory shouts from McCluskey right at the beginning of the match went a long way to creating the atmosphere on the park that day.,' recalled McCoist. 'One of the nastiest games I've ever played in … I've never – and I mean never – seen a team so fired up against us as Hibs were that afternoon.' The initial tempo of the match didn't reflect the simmering tension but it wouldn't be long before the lid blew off. It was Souness who was first to bite with an outrageous tackle on Billy Kirkwood, whom Smith had warned him about prior to the match. It was a clear booking that he took with a barely suppressed smile on his face and, as a marked man, it was a deliberate case of getting his retaliation in early but it started a chain reaction that led to mayhem. Woods was bundled to the ground by George McCluskey at a corner soon after, which resulted in referee Mick Delaney being surrounded by blue shirts demanding action. It wouldn't be long until they all met again. Souness was tackled, unfairly, by Stuart Beedie and he should have gone down to claim the free kick but instead he bundled headlong into McCluskey which sparked a melee in the centre circle where Souness lashed out with a kick on McCluskey that left a gash requiring nine stitches. It was bedlam as every single Rangers player, including Woods, got involved. Only the Hibs goalkeeper Alan Rough stayed in his penalty box as 21 players were later booked, Souness handed a three-game ban and Rangers and Hibs fined £5,000 and £1,000 respectively. It was a straight red for the new player-manager and, as he walked off the field – just as his opponent was carried off – he caught a glimpse of his father James in the stand looking down and shaking his head. It was, as Souness described, one of the all-time lows of his career.

'In 37 minutes I watched 12 months of work walk out the door,' recalled David Holmes at the end of the season. He went straight back home with his wife Betty, closed the curtains and didn't surface again until the Monday as the inevitable backlash began. 'The dressing room afterwards was silent, stunned. We'd been billed as invincible and we believed it.,' said Ian Durrant. Butcher, who could well have joined his manager for an early bath when he elbowed Cowan during the second half, returned with Souness to the Norton House hotel in Edinburgh – owned by a certain David Murray at the time and host to Frank Bruno among other athletes who were there for the Commonwealth Games in the city – before deciding to go out and drown their sorrows. 'It was a nightmare,' according to Butcher, as Souness nearly got into a fight with someone who was enjoying the day's events rather more than he was. 'Fuck off' was all that he was allowed to respond with before Butcher bundled him in a taxi and they headed back to their rooms.

It was Holmes who provided the leadership on the Monday as he came into Ibrox to let them all know what was expected and that they were now a huge target in this country. Not for the last time Souness would apologise for his own individual actions but not for his team's, of which he was proud. It showed him that they were up for what was required that season. McCoist later remarked that the 'hostility worked in our favour. It totally united the squad in a them-against-us way. We had to stick together as a team – that was obvious – and the dressing-room atmosphere was quite simply superb … the big-name boys and the lads who had come up through the ranks mixed together perfectly.'

Later that season, and especially in future years, Souness would create a side that would win games and trophies by playing some beautiful football but it simply wasn't realistic for that to happen immediately. Rangers had been a laughing stock and a punchbag for years and now, because of their newfound ambition, they were an even bigger target for aggression. Souness said that weekend that Rangers would 'have to match that aggression because I cannot allow us to be trampled on and I won't as long as I am in charge at Ibrox'. The lines had been drawn from the very first battle. Like Souness's iconic Liverpool side, his new-look Rangers would have to be prepared to fight as much as they were programmed to play.

* * *

It was in early October – nearly six months to the day that he arrived at Ibrox – that Souness picked up a cheque for £250 and a small plaque for being September's manager of the month, such was the impressive nature of Rangers' recovery. Some in the media took the opportunity, with Souness being mandated to speak to them, to run a half-year report on the club's progress and ask him for his own reflections. One quote in particular was revealing as it spoke to his impetuosity, his inexperience and perhaps even his insecurity, 'Sometimes I think we are getting places, and then at other times I don't think we have made any progress at all. I still find it hard to grasp that I am a manager.' The inconsistency was a clear frustration to Souness – championships can rarely be won without a big run of wins after all – and he would often pass the post-match duties on to Walter Smith during that period, such was that simmering dissatisfaction at not being the finished article already. Even when able to affect the game on the field – when not suspended – the overall responsibility for results was a new feature of the game to him now and that lack of direct agency was clearly causing some early strain.

In retrospect, the expectations should not have been anything else. An initial period of 'one step forward, two steps back' is hardly unreasonable for a project that, although well-funded, was making such fundamental cultural and footballing changes. Cases of immediate impact on previously under-performing sides usually involve an exceptional man-manager who either doesn't seek to change the existing style too much or whose approach is simplistic and rudimentary in itself,[16] but wholesale change can often take time to bed in. Two of the greatest sides in modern football history, AC Milan under Arrigo Sacchi and Pep Guardiola's Barcelona, had some early struggles in their first season before there was complete trust and acceptance of the new methodology. There were always going to be early highs and lows for this new Rangers regime.

As is often the way with frustrating and inconsistent sides, the lows were silly and unnecessary rather than a case of being being outclassed and blown away. Although Rangers had managed to scrape past Falkirk at Ibrox on the first home game of the season, by virtue of a debatable McCoist penalty, the first big home test was seen as the visit of Dundee United on the Saturday, just seven days after the debacle at Easter Road. Pitched as a game of money versus youth development, it also contained other individual narratives with Smith coming up against his old side on the touchline, Ian Redford returning to Ibrox as well as Richard Gough, the subject of a much-publicised transfer wrangle, taking to the field as well. For an hour the 44,000 who were packed into Ibrox on another gorgeous, sunny day were treated to a quality of football that they hadn't seen from a Rangers team in years. A 2-0 lead at half-time was well-deserved and once again both goals came from McCoist, the second of which – a composed finish after a defence-splitting pass from Souness – was typical of the performance on display. Smith said afterwards that in all his years at Tannadice, he had never seen anybody play as well against them as Rangers did in that first half, before going on to add, 'We threw it away, as simple as that.'

After McCoist and West missed good second-half chances to make the lead unassailable, three late defensive errors gifted United three goals. Each were down to communication and evidence of relationships that were not yet established. Butcher and Munro found themselves in a mess and then McPherson and Jimmy Nicholl did likewise to present Kevin Gallacher with two opportunities that he would not pass up, such was the form and promise at that stage of his career. The injury-time winner was a complete failure of anyone to mark Redford in the box following a set piece. As was the case the previous weekend, the press had a field day with its hysterical overreaction. Questions were being asked again over the

---

16   Martin O'Neill's initial success at Celtic in 2000 would be a good example.

ability of Souness – described as a man leaving Ibrox that evening as if he had 'just been told his house had burned down' – to handle the pressure of both roles whereas the English imports 'didn't look tuppence worth' let alone the fees that were paid. Some fans were joining in too. A Mrs M. Robertson from Glasgow wrote to the Evening Times to complain that Souness was 'making it the English Rangers instead of the Glasgow Rangers … and at exorbitant prices. Take it from someone who has known Rangers longer than most that it will not work.'

Even after the ship was steadied from the crashing waves of that opening week, it would be Tayside again that would provide a reminder that not all was yet in place when Rangers lost 1-0 at Dens Park on 20 September, a solitary John Brown goal making the difference.[17] Once again, it would be Smith sent out to face the music as Rangers lay fifth in the table, albeit only four points from the peak, although perhaps it was best that he did. On the Wednesday evening before the trip to Dundee, Rangers had defeated the Finnish side Ilves of Tampere 4-0 at Ibrox in their first European game of the season, which included a Robert Fleck hat-trick and a famous piece of mastery from Davie Cooper. It was the fifth win in a row and eight undefeated since that loss to Dundee United. Instead of playing that up, Souness lambasted them, 'I was very disappointed. We were very sloppy…a better team could have given us big problems the way we played.' The tough love that may have lifted his battle-hardened Liverpool side to even higher levels was not what this fledgling Rangers team required at that point in time and it was further evidence of a man struggling to recalibrate his standards and understand the job ahead of him.

The lowest possible low was avoided only by the narrowest of margins. 'They had the smallest dressing rooms in the world and a hard, bumpy pitch with a slope. We were very poor on the night,' said Terry Butcher of East Fife's old Bayview Park ground and the Skol-sponsored League Cup third round match that is arguably one of the most significant 'sliding doors' moment in the club's history. Having already missed a penalty in normal time,[18] Rangers needed a shoot-out to get past East Fife after a 0-0 draw (Gordon Marshall was unable to save any Rangers penalties including a poor one from Butcher that led him to swear that he'd never take another) and the natural Berwick comparisons,[19] given the start to the season, had to be left untouched by the nation's hacks. It is impossible to measure the importance of that early trophy success in building confidence and having something in the memory bank as the league race took shape; however, given the calamitous August that had already been endured relative to the summer spend and weight of expectation, the pressure that Souness would have felt could have led to more league trouble that in turn could have derailed the whole season. Such are the margins in sport.

---

17   Terry Butcher missed this game through suspension, the only time he was banned for a league fixture.

18   Strangely by Ally McCoist, who was about to embark on a run of one goal in six games. This match also saw Colin West suffer a serious injury from a wild tackle by Stuart Burgess. It highlighted a concern about the goalscoring burden that McCoist alone carried.

19   The worst result in club's history (before Progrès Niederkorn in 2017), Rangers crashed out of the Scottish Cup to Berwick Rangers in 1967 and the subsequent panicked reaction would have consequences for decades.

And yet Souness really was worthy of his manager of the month award. There really was a recovery. There were a string of standard victories such as the two league wins away to Hamilton Accies and Motherwell and a 4-0 hammering of Clydebank at Ibrox which saw Robert Fleck – initially a name placed by Souness on the cut list following his behaviour during the previous season[20] but now proving his worth as a reliable replacement for the injured West – score the first of four hat-tricks that season. Even the 1-1 draw at Hearts in early October had its merits given the amount of players missing on Rangers' right-hand side and the fact that they came back to equalise with another piece of Cooper brilliance. The biggest highs really did hit the heights and provided enough early evidence that it could be a special year. Naturally, the first of those landmark wins came in the first Old Firm game of the season, a match that told us much about the future in more ways than one.

In 1985 television was the spark for a potential breakaway Scottish Super League. Unlike its 21st-century iterations, it was one motivated less by greed but by fear. Live coverage of football was something to be resisted in both Scotland and England in the mid-1980s. With attendances down, it was a natural position of resistance but there was a counterintuitive reality in that, with television becoming an increasingly important part of an expanding leisure society, its aspirational power was underestimated. As history would demonstrate, especially with the English Premier League in 1992, when football was packaged well enough and beamed into people's homes, it then became a more desirable event to be a part of. Then, however, it was one issue that both Rangers and Celtic could agree on. They didn't want live coverage of league games but, as Rangers chairman John Paton acknowledged during the summer of 1986, 'Television is not going to go away so we have compromised.' BBC Scotland would screen the first live Old Firm league match on Sunday, 31 August and it would not disappoint.

'As Roy and I emerged from the tunnel, the noise hit us like a wall. It was immense and I loved it,' was Terry Butcher's recollection of stepping out into his very first experience of the fixture, the most keenly anticipated one for seven years. The new champions coming to the home of the rejuvenated challengers. Despite the electric atmosphere – the BBC's microphones couldn't cope with the early exchanges from the stands – the game was noticeably different from the previous league match at Ibrox, the vastly overrated, cartoon 4-4 draw in March. There was control and poise but still allied with energy from the young Rangers midfield of Durrant, Ferguson and McMinn missing, as they were, their suspended player-manager. Quite how Rangers managed to be level until the 74th minute is anyone's guess. Glaring chances, disallowed goals and strong penalty claims came and went until a moment of genuine quality by two players whose Ibrox careers had been infused with new life by the revolution. Davie Cooper had movement that was balletic and a reverse path that was telepathic, matched only by the cool composure shown by the young Ian Durrant as he waited for Pat Bonner to shift his weight first before stroking the ball home. The wild scenes

---

20   Fleck dropped his shorts to show his bare behind at Parkhead in a reserve game on Boxing Day 1985. Rangers lowered their asking price to as low as £20,000 but Dundee couldn't do the deal.

in the Copland Road Stand and the East Enclosure were typical of a Rangers winner over Celtic. The nature of the goal, however, was not. There was something different about that day. A team of Rangers players, be they young or old, who wouldn't be drawn into the usual pandemonium. A performance, and especially a goal, that was somehow above it all.

With the Old Firm test passed in late August, Rangers then had a 'New Firm' cup and league double-header to navigate at the end of September. With the exception of East Fife, Rangers had managed to reach the semi-finals of the League Cup with comfort but at Hampden on Wednesday, 24 September they would meet the form team in the country, the undefeated league leaders Dundee United.

The pressure was on, given the defeat at Dens Park on the Saturday and the fact that Celtic had already booked their final place the previous evening, beating Motherwell on penalties. Once again Souness's side rose to the challenge and this time against United they sustained it for the entire 90 minutes. Cooper and Durrant were impressive yet again but it was Ted McMinn and Ally McCoist who made the difference. McCoist stole in front of his marker to clinically snatch the first half opportunity created by McMinn and then he poked home the second after great strength and perseverance on the right, early in the second. Former Rangers player Iain Ferguson would pull one back but this time Souness's men were able to see it though, leaving Jim McLean with no complaints as he remarked afterwards, 'the result flattered us. We were outclassed.' Once more it was the revitalised players who were stepping up for their new manager.

On the Saturday Alex Ferguson's Aberdeen visited Ibrox, a trip that had been successful for them throughout the decade. 'Souness's Revenge' was how this game was billed, a clear reference to Ferguson's decision to drop him for that final World Cup fixture in Mexico, however it would have little in the way of spice and needle. Instead it was a thoroughly enjoyable match with Rangers both impressive creatively and, finally, defensively as Butcher marshalled his line to see out a sustained period of Aberdeen pressure in the second half. Rangers were already one goal ahead by that point, scored by the boss himself. It was an underrated goal because the ball barely crossed the line after hitting the post, although it came from a left-footed shot from outside the box that had a beautiful arc and moved away from Jim Leighton, leaving him scrambling to keep it out. Fleck's late second goal became more famous for Leighton's incandescent charge over to the linesman to complain about the lack of an offside call. It was a symbolic victory, a changing of the guard, as both men were interviewed by STV at the same time afterwards. It was done deliberately to finally put the Mexico tension to rest but the pair were clearly at different positions in their journey. Ferguson sounded uncharacteristically phlegmatic about a defeat to Rangers including a controversial goal. He was waiting for another call. Souness, club blazer on but with an open collar, looked satisfied but only momentarily. He was eager and inpatient for more definite success to arrive.

On Sunday, 26 October, Souness had to make do with his seat in Hampden's Main Stand as the League Cup Final kicked off. He was injured this time, not suspended, and he had to ask his young midfield to do the same job against Celtic as they had done at Ibrox two months previously. Fast and frenetic, it was an

Old Firm game fit for all the clichés as both sides roared at each other from the outset, tempers never too far from boiling over. The yellow cards – all ten of them – mounted up at a pace in keeping with the football but led, in the end, to a final that could not be controlled by the referee David Syme. Its farcical zenith was reached with only two minutes remaining when he showed Celtic's Tony Shepherd a red card after mistakenly thinking that he was responsible for hitting him with a coin. Quite why he thought that a professional footballer would be carrying loose change on the off-chance that an opposing defender might need to break a fiver before a corner was unclear. The matter was rectified quickly and the card rescinded, but by then it was too late to salvage the mess. Celtic had lost the cup but were handed an opportunity, never knowingly missed, to wallow in paranoia. As Alan Davidson put it in his Evening Times match report, 'To the victors the spoils. To the losers a sense of injustice that has hovered over them, like some maiden aunt, for the best part of a century.'

Earlier that season, after his Celtic side had surrendered a 2-0 lead at Tannadice, Davie Hay had requested that Bob Valentine not referee another game involving Celtic. A minute before the Shepherd chaos Hay – sporting an outfit that may or may not have been the inspiration for the Shooting Stars character Angelos Epithemiou – stormed on to the field to pick up the match ball, suggesting that they should pack up and leave.[21] The reason for this particular moment of moral outrage was the dismissal of Maurice Johnston after an off-the-ball skirmish with Stuart Munro. Celtic had argued that Syme didn't make it clear whether it he was showing both players a yellow or just Munro and then Johnston the red but this was a redundant argument as, due to Johnston's earlier booking, he would have had to walk in either case. It was an entirely manufactured drama late in a game that had produced plenty of the proper stuff.

It was the first of three breathless League Cup finals, played at a pace and abandon that looks almost foreign to more modern eyes, shaped as they are by the cagey awareness that dominates 21st-century finals. Celtic shaded the overall play but both sides had periods of domination and troubled the woodwork on more than one occasion. It was Rangers who carved out the best chances, the best of all falling to Ian Durrant just after an hour. A Cammy Fraser free kick was glanced on by Butcher but it was Durrant's first touch with his thigh that made all the difference. Once again the manic chaos was permeated by a moment of simple calm, control. After that the finish was easy and Rangers were ahead, but not for long. An exquisite give-and-go between Johnston and Brian McClair left Woods helpless as the latter rifled the ball into the top corner from the edge of the box.

The moment that settled the final – and lit the fire of Celtic rage – yet again came from another foul on Davie Cooper on Rangers' right. Derek Ferguson, the teenage man of the match, floated one to the back of the box where Butcher was waiting. The ball was overhit – Butcher would have had no chance of getting an attacking header on it – but it didn't stop Aitken trying to make sure with a little too much force. While not a 'stonewaller,' it was a penalty – there was no doubt with Jim McLean in the commentary box – and with only a few minutes

---

21   This was developed further in the post-match briefing when he did say that Celtic should join the English Football League.

remaining the opportunity was presented to Cooper to win the cup for his team. 'There was never any doubt in my mind that, despite all the tension, Coop would score,' wrote Ian Durrant. 'I never saw him miss one and I always felt it was unfair on keepers that Davie was allowed to go one-on-one against them. That spell was the best two seasons of Coop's life because Souness understood him.'

The noise was different. Rangers had beaten Celtic in the same cup final in 1984 – a great 3-2 win with McCoist the hat-trick hero – but it was a salvage job at the end of another disappointing season. There was an overwhelming feeling throughout the support that this was just the start of something, which gives – in hindsight – more power to the two images that lived long in the memory: Cooper being lifted aloft by McCoist, two Rangers fans living the dream in sharp focus while in the background the rest lived it vicariously through them on the wild terracing and Souness, at the full-time whistle, looking up at David Holmes from the dugout with his clenched fist held up in assured celebration.

For Walter Smith, it was a trophy that provided the momentum required to power a title campaign and he was delighted that the two goalscorers were players who had been at Ibrox for some time. Their flourishing was the real evidence of the revolution. In Cooper specifically he saw the burden – worn by a man whom, for many years had been the only hope the fans had – suddenly lift from his shoulders. 'Too much was expected from one man,' said Smith, but now that the responsibility was shared it gave Cooper 'the freedom to play, it gave him the setting he needed'. More generally however, players were lifting their levels. 'It was as if the other players saw things happening at the club that they never believed would happen. They got the message that this was the start of something big and there was a response from all of them.'

Importantly, the post-match party that evening included every single member of staff back at Ibrox, a further indication of the family culture that Holmes was determined to embed in the club. The fans responded in turn and in doing so caused tension as the stadium turnstiles could no longer cope with the traditional ability to pay at the gate. Games were now becoming all-ticket affairs by necessity and even the AGM – never usually an event that interested ticket touts – had to be re-arranged for the Scottish Exhibition Centre after the original meeting was postponed due to shareholders being locked out. Something truly special was brewing at Ibrox and now, with the first trophy of the year in the bag, surely it was now inevitable that Rangers had clicked into a new gear and the much sought-after consistency would follow.

Alas, no. The next two league results were draws, although credible ones. A midweek 0-0 at Tannadice was followed up with a 1-1 tie at Parkhead, six days since the cup final and a game that was far better-natured but, in turn, somewhat more placid. It was the visit of Motherwell at Ibrox on Saturday, 8 November, however, that had fans re-assessing just how fresh this new world really was. Tommy McLean's side was severely hampered by illness and, as a result, dug into a firm defensive position for 88 minutes that a ponderous Rangers couldn't break. With the match drifting away to the third league draw in succession, a rare Motherwell break finished with Ray Farningham heading an Andy Walker cross past Chris Woods. Yet again it was Smith who took the press responsibilities after a defeat where he bemoaned the lack of full-back support in getting around the rearguard before saying, tantalisingly, 'It's something we will sort out.' That 1-0 defeat was the most blunt reminder that season of how toothless Rangers had been previously.

Perennial whipping boys Clydebank were timely opponents as Rangers bounced back with a 4-1 win but the 2-1 victory over Dundee was another late show – a very late Dave McPherson goal getting the points – and Souness had to reiterate that the supporters, as well as the players, had to be patient as they tried to work through stuffy opponents, 'We will not resort to swinging the high ball into the area in frustration. We will continue to play it from the back and even if it takes 80 minutes to crack a defence then that is the way it will have to be.'

There would be more late winners to come but not at that old bogey ground, Pittodrie, on 22 November as Rangers lost the match 1-0 and McPherson to a straight red card. The defender had elbowed Davie Dodds, who was supposedly Ibrox-bound just a month earlier before signing for Aberdeen instead. Terry Butcher's first response to another dismissal was to call foul and declare Dodds a diving cheat, 'The referee looked at me and said, "Before you say another word, look at him." I did. Poor Dodds had his nose splattered right across his face and it certainly wasn't self-inflicted.' The bus journey home from Aberdeen was a sombre one, with Rangers now eight points behind leaders Celtic. The next time they would take that trip would be very different but that seemed like a speck on the horizon at this point.

The UEFA Cup was still providing hope, however. A very fine double win over the Portuguese side Boavista – coming from behind to win the first leg at Ibrox 2-1 and then a brilliant Derek Ferguson goal the only mark made in Portugal – led to a third-round meeting with Borussia Mönchengladbach, then managed by Jupp Heynckes in his final season before leaving to commence his first spell in charge of Bayern Munich.

Rangers started the opening leg at home very brightly and were ahead inside 15 minutes with yet another Ian Durrant goal coming directly from a ghosted late run into the box, this time thundering in off the bar instead of the cultured placement of previous strikes. But, as was the case at Pittodrie on the Saturday, it was yet another self-inflicted wound, right before half-time, that halted the momentum. Derek Ferguson's loose pass out of defence allowed the Germans to spring a counter for which Rangers were ill-prepared. Munro was easily outpaced by André Winkhold before Uwe Rahn converted the cross amid statuesque defending. The 1-1 draw meant that Souness, by then sidelined with an achilles tendon operation, would travel to Germany behind the eight-ball.

Despite cup glory and some genuinely excellent performances, there always seemed to be that double-step backwards arriving soon. In that six-month review interview Souness acknowledged that his side wasn't yet the finished article, 'We still don't have a squad good enough to win the league, but we are on the hunt for another player.' One interested spectator at Hampden for that cup final was Graham Roberts of Tottenham Hotspur, the subject of a pursuit that would last until Christmas before Souness finally got his man, the missing piece of his defensive jigsaw. Rahn's goal may have been a source of yet more frustration but it would be the last time Rangers fans would see their backline breached for more than two months. The concrete of a title-winning foundation was beginning to set.

* * *

It was on a short walk from Porto's Sheraton Hotel, where the Rangers squad and media were staying, to Boavista's small Campo do Bessa home that Chris Woods spoke to Chick Young about his early frustrations at Ibrox, 'The Rangers fans have not seen what I can do. Believe me, I am about to show them. Only against Dundee United in the Skol Cup did I feel like I produced anything like the form I was showing in my days with Norwich. Now I am settled in and I know that I am ready to produce performances like my days in England on a more consistent basis … If any supporters are wondering about my inclusion in English international squads then I can only say to them, "Watch me go now."' Woods almost certainly didn't speak in that tabloid English but it was clear to all that the Rangers rearguard hadn't fully settled into place. He was brilliant in Portugal that night – the highlight being an almost impossible stop from Agatão – but it wasn't until that disappointing 1-1 draw against Mönchengladbach in the next round that something locked in.

Rangers didn't concede a goal for the remaining seven games of 1986 as the penny dropped metaphorically before many were spent literally to finish the job off. The only domestic blip in that sequence was a 0-0 draw at Easter Road, back at the scene of the opening day's crime, and yet again the source of that dropped point could arguably be found in the manager's use of the media during the run-up to a game that was always going to have its own difficulties. Rangers beat St Mirren 2-0 on Wednesday, 3 December in a very scrappy performance. What should have been a night for positivity – given that Celtic lost at Tynecastle meaning that the gap was cut to seven points with a game in hand – was seen by Souness as another opportunity to dish out some tough love. 'It was simply not good enough,' he moaned after the match, likening his players that night to a 'pub team'. The immediate setback in Leith at the weekend brought it back to eight points, moving Alex Cameron to write that the title 'seems out of reach', but the lapse was only momentary. Celtic would go on to have a very troubled December with three 1-1 draws in a row, the final one coming away to Clydebank, as Rangers continued to rack up wins without conceding. It was a grinding type of chase instead of an aggressive one, with the challengers looking more and more unstoppable, not because of spectacular and chaotic wins but with a run of shutouts that were now becoming routine.

The eventual arrival of Graham Roberts just before Christmas for £450,000 was seen by David Holmes – now the chairman following the departure of John Paton in the November – as a well-deserved festive gift for the fans and proved to be the final substantial outlay for the season. Roberts's well-deserved 'hard man' tag from his time in England was one reason why Souness pursued him so vigorously, still of the the belief that his side needed one more 'warrior', but Roberts was an excellent player too. The iron side of his character was evident on his debut, a 2-0 win over Dundee United at Ibrox two days after Christmas. The sound from his tackle on Paul Sturrock inside five minutes is something that Campbell Ogilvie, club secretary at the time, can still recall over 30 years later, and his work to set up Ally McCoist for the goal that broke the deadlock was full of endeavour and heart. The supporters fell for him instantly, such was the noise of their reception. Not only were Rangers unbeaten in seven league games without a single reply, but they had spent close to half a million pounds on yet another international defender.

With the calendar year drawing to a close, the gap – which had once been nine points – was now only five with Celtic having played one more game. The psychological impact of the Roberts signing on the champions should not be underestimated. This wasn't a panic buy from Rangers, trying to arrest a large slump in form, it was done at a time when they already looked impenetrable. Bringing in yet another proven quality defender, during a period of incredible defensive form, and for more money than Celtic had ever paid for any player, just cranked up the pressure even more.

It wasn't simply Woods, Butcher and now Roberts who comprised this wall, although every player recognised their influence. 'The big man gives everyone around him confidence,' said Dave McPherson at the time. 'You can get on with doing your own thing, knowing that Terry will be there to tidy up should anything go wrong. It's also the same when the boss plays. The fact that he is totally confident puts us all at ease.'

McPherson had talked earlier in the season about learning from Butcher but that Rangers had tried to play in a similar way under John Greig although the older players, maybe set in different ways, called the shots on the park. Now the senior players were guiding the club in a more progressive direction. Souness wrote later that Butcher 'got the other players organised from day one, he growled at them when it was necessary, he was perfect on the pitch and perfect off it in the PR department'. In the STV documentary The Rangers Revival, which was shown at the very end of the season, Souness, asked when he thought that he could win the league at the first attempt, said, 'When I signed certain players. Butcher and the goalkeeper. The lads already at the club responded. I could see the way they responded to them. And then I got Roberts who is in the same mould as those two and then again he brought the best out in certain individuals. All of a sudden you were going from players who had been at Rangers maybe too long, been in the company of bad professionals and all of a sudden they were winners.' All of this is further testimony to the twin influence that Souness and his high-profile signings had: the ability to pull others up with them and also the fact that they would take away the burden from those who couldn't carry it by themselves. The players were both inspired to push themselves to new heights but also free to concentrate more on their own job without the crippling fear of being ultimately responsible for others.

Not all the culture changes that Souness tried to embed at Rangers took root. 'Getting yourself full of drink two or three times a week is not going to make you a better player on a Saturday afternoon,' he would later lament. What was a professional prerequisite in Serie A was a foreign language in Scotland.

Second nature in Empoli, not so in East Kilbride. In the early hours of Friday, 5 December, Ally McCoist and Ian Durrant were charged with breach of the peace and assault after a fracas with an 18-year-old in a South Lanarkshire chip shop. Ted McMinn was also questioned[22]. Durrant was later cleared in court but McCoist was eventually convicted of minor assault and fined £150. 'Ally McCoist saved my life that night,' Durrant wrote later. He was on crutches, nursing an ankle injury, and fell for the bait set by a bar-room loudmouth when, by his own admission, he should have ignored the taunting. Before his injured friend could be assaulted, McCoist stepped in with a preemptive strike. 'Because of that he has a criminal record, which hurts me,' wrote Durrant. A similar incident happened in Airdrie the following season, leading to Durrant to suggest that he may be best leaving the city as there was a constant target on his back. For all the changes to diet and sleeping habits, Glasgow culture and its microscopic focus are always likely to provide substantial resistance.

None of this was ideal preparation for the second leg in Germany, where Rangers needed an away goal to provide any hope of progression to the quarter-finals. Souness decided to return to the fold following his operation in an attempt to give his side some much-needed experience but it was agonisingly to no avail in an incident-packed night in the Bökelbergstadion. It was a very impressive performance by Rangers but the quality in the final third was missing and the resulting blank meant that the moment of self-harm in the first leg made all the difference. As one journalist noted, 'It would of course be the game's unlikeliest transfer deal, but if the Ibrox club had Mo Johnston, they might still be in the competition.'

Or perhaps, a different referee. Rangers incredibly ended the match with nine men after Stuart Munro and Davie Cooper saw red. Munro was sent off for retaliation to being kicked by André Winkhold while he was lying on the floor and Cooper was sent packing for asking the Belgian referee Alexis Ponnet if he was allowed to send any Germans off, following a couple of dreadful tackles on himself and McMinn. It was perhaps not the most diplomatic mission as Ponnet confirmed later that the language used was bad enough to warrant a dismissal. The Rangers players – the captain in particular who was in tears at the final whistle – were furious with the handling of the tie but it was all impotent rage. Souness stood by his men and confirmed that there would be no internal fines[23] but it was another season where Rangers were out of Europe before Christmas. Overall, Rangers' European story is a difficult and ultimately underwhelming one but perhaps this campaign is one of the underrated near misses.

Borussia Mönchengladbach would beat Vitória de Guimarães in the quarter-finals and, although they were considerably better than Boavista, it would not have

---

22   This incident was arguably the beginning of the end for McMinn. Souness wasn't impressed with all three of them but two were irreplaceable at that time whereas McMinn, a maverick individual in a team that was being shaped to one of patience and controlled possession, was less so. He was sold to Sevilla and his old manager Jock Wallace in January following an internal club suspension in relation to yet another fracas.

23   The club was later fined £5,000 and both players received a substantial UEFA ban, Munro for four games.

been an impossible task. A similar path would have seen Rangers face Dundee United in a two-legged European semi-final before IFK Göteborg at their home ground in the final. It wouldn't have required a miracle but it may have drained resources later in the season when the league campaign needed that focus the most. By the turn of the year, that was hotting up nicely.

Rangers were magnificent on New Year's Day, especially Souness as he made his Old Firm debut. Both goals in the 2-0 win, by Fleck and McCoist, were scrappy close-range efforts, the latter coming from a dreadful Pat Bonner mistake in the falling snow,[24] but they don't tell the story of an absolutely imperious performance. The press recognised that the margin between the two sides on the day was greater than the two goals but were quick to point out that the profit margins were the biggest factor at play. 'Money Talks' and 'It's cheque-mate for Rangers Aces' were the headlines chosen in the first editions of 1987 which runs somewhat contrary to the late summer opinion pieces that warned that money couldn't buy success. The win left Rangers only three points behind, with a game in hand and the momentum shifting in only one direction. Speaking for a BBC Scotland retrospective on the season in 2007, both Smith and Souness recognised the importance of this match. 'That, as much as anything else gave us an enormous boost and then it led us to believe that we could go on and win the championship,' said Smith, with Souness adding, 'We knew that once we got on to their coattails that they wouldn't be able to handle the pressure. We just went from strength to strength.'

The freezing Scottish winter played havoc with the fixtures in January but Rangers seemed unaffected as the impressive form continued apace. A 35-yard wonder strike from Roberts was the only goal against Motherwell at Fir Park and Clydebank were made to suffer once again at Ibrox, this time 5-0 (this brought the season's total to 13 goals) and another Robert Fleck hat-trick. Celtic's 3-2 defeat to Dundee United that day brought Rangers within touching distance of the summit and a win over Hamilton Accies at Ibrox, in the only fixture to beat the snow that weekend, would finally see them top of the league for the first time at this stage of a campaign since 1978.

In many ways this fixture typified so much of the season. It was yet another sell-out crowd – the 13th time that Ibrox had to be all-ticket that season, something that was completely unheard of – and it was a win achieved both because of, and in spite of, the split personality of this Souness team. The 2-0 victory was commensurate with such a dominant display over a part-time side and the opener from Durrant was well in keeping with his growing repertoire however, it was the conclusion to the game that saw yet more unnecessary ill-discipline. Roberts was sent off for a second yellow card with just 15 minutes remaining and then Durrant followed him down the tunnel five minutes later after a dreadful tackle on Albert Craig. For the second time that season, Rangers had two players dismissed in the same game and it could have happened more often. Success seemed a real prospect for the first time in nearly a decade but it was balanced upon a razor's edge.

---

24   Bonner had suggested in the summer that Woods may be the most expensive goalkeeper in the world but he would still have to prove that he was the best in Scotland. At around this moment, the jury returned their verdict.

It was after five or six clean sheets that Chris Woods was in Walter Smith's ear, asking what the British record was and how far he still had to go. Smith dismissed him but promised him that he would come to him if he was ever close. By late January Woods was very close indeed and, although a dropped point at home to Aberdeen meant that Rangers fell back behind Celtic again, it took the shut-out run to 13 consecutive matches. Its significance stretched well beyond becoming a piece of sporting trivia and the chance to meet Roy Castle on Record Breakers, it provided the launchpad for a title chase over the most notoriously difficult period in the Scottish footballing calendar. 'We were all in it together,' Woods would later say with trademark modesty. 'If I missed a cross, someone would clear off the line and if they missed a header, I'd make a save. It kept the whole team going along.'

In the 44th minute of the Scottish Cup third round tie at Ibrox against Hamilton, the crowd roared their appreciation of Woods – who at that point had so little to do that he could well be classed as a spectator too – as he officially became a record holder for the second time that season (he was the world's most expensive goalkeeper) and a nice full stop was placed on any debate about the investment. Rangers had the best goalkeeper in Britain and, even if McCoist or Fleck popped up to score the goal to send them into the next round, it would be Woods who would get the headlines the next morning.

Only, they didn't and he wouldn't. Woods lasted for 1,196 minutes without being beaten. With 20 minutes of that cup tie remaining and Rangers, despite all the possession and attempts on Dave McKellar's goal, still searching for a breakthrough, Accies launched a long free kick forward which somehow got lost under the feet of Dave McPherson and presented Adrian Sprott with the chance to produce both a moment of glory and shame as he scored the only goal of the game to sensationally knock high-flying Rangers out of the cup. 'HUMILIATION!' was the headline in the Evening Times, a back page that was printed on to T-shirts by the Willie Malloy Celtic Supporters' Club. The result may have been on a par with Berwick Rangers 20 years before (although it should be said that Hamilton were a Premier Division side, unlike Berwick who were in the league below) but the reaction wasn't.

Internally, Souness's rage was as one would expect – his foot went through a television screen in the dressing room – but the message to the outside world was different. Given the shock and embarrassment of such an exit, and in light of recent media rants after victories, this was a week that could very easily have been mismanaged. At the end of the season he would describe it as the 'biggest shock' of his career, adding, 'It proved I knew nothing.' However, in the Monday papers Souness was measured and positive. The FA Cup in England was strangely absent from his glittering playing career at Liverpool and he suffered his share of shock defeats in that competition, so he knew all too well that this kind of result can be part and parcel of the British game. He knew that his forwards were off-form at the wrong time but, unlike the mass panic of 1967, he stuck by them and promised fans that McCoist and Fleck would both be in the side the following weekend. He maintained that the focus was on the league championship and that the players and fans shouldn't lose sight of that in the inevitable noise and smoke that follows such a result. He would have his moans of course – 'losing the goal was ridiculous. I have spent a lot of money getting the defence right.' – but he wouldn't cut McPherson adrift until the summer, in the meantime sticking by him, to good effect.

This appears to be evidence of a manager who had finally realised that his public messages had an impact on the inside and the tone with which he and Smith used, and their chosen subject matter, would be pitch perfect for the rest of the season. That week it simply had to be as, with Rangers back in the position of being two points behind but with a game spare, the title race was precariously poised. The following weekend saw Rangers visit Tynecastle, where they hadn't won a league match since 1977 and where Hearts hadn't suffered any kind of defeat for nearly two years. With Celtic at home to the always generous St Mirren, it looked exactly like the kind of situation where some of the ground that had been made up so well, would be handed back. Yet another step backwards after so many positive strides. It would be the biggest test of the season.

* * *

'What I am trying to do is create a situation where the players are always under pressure. That is, I believe, how to get the best out of people.,' said Graeme Souness in early January. 'If anyone can't handle that, then they aren't the type we want in any case.'

Pressure would be a word that Souness and Smith would continually refer to in the final three months of the season and it was certainly felt on 7 February with the visit to Hearts and a Scottish footballing community expecting dropped points. In what was possibly the finest all-round performance of the season, Rangers showed exactly the kind of characteristics champions possess. They dominated the game from the outset and were well worthy of the lead after half an hour from a goal finished superbly by Fleck but the result of some intelligent play by Souness and Munro down the left-hand side. Hearts were soon back level through a justified John Robertson penalty but, key to the growing sense of steely assurance within this side, the response came within a minute of that setback as a thunderous Souness free kick deflected past Henry Smith and into the Hearts goal.

Inexperienced challengers often feel the tension when so close to maximum points from a difficult venue but the second half was just wave after wave of Rangers attacks. Fleck converted a Cooper corner with a brilliant overhead kick, Durrant's defence-splitting pass and McCoist's movement forced an own goal from Kenny Black and finally the number nine got a goal of his own when he finished off a beautiful move to make it 5-1.[25] Hearts would get another penalty at the death but it was immaterial. This was a landmark win and as strong a signal as any other that theirs was a serious challenge, despite the pre-season and mid-season predictions that Rangers would certainly be an improved side in 1986/87 but surely they wouldn't have the necessary qualities to go all the way.

---

25   Bizarrely, Rangers won 5-1 away to Hearts on 4 February 1967, the next game after the Berwick debacle.

The scepticism wasn't entirely misplaced; £2m bought international quality and experience but not the kind that knew how to get over this particular line. The three big English buys each had a European medal (Butcher and Roberts had won the UEFA Cup with Ipswich Town and Tottenham Hotspur respectively and Woods was a young reserve in Nottingham Forest's famous European Cup success in 1978/79) but none had won a league title, a very different type of achievement. Only Souness and Cooper had that knowledge on the park and Smith, in an assistant role, off it. It speaks volumes for the influence of the management duo and the natural confidence of the new purchases, that Rangers negotiated the final part of this championship race so well. The captain's assurance was literally there in black and white when he did a series of four in-depth interviews for the Evening Times in late February. 'Rangers will win the Premier League this year – and you read it here first,' Butcher proclaimed. 'I am very confident the championship flag will be flying above Ibrox and there are a number of reasons why I say so now even though there are still a quarter of our season's games still to go.' Those reasons mainly being the rock solid defence of which he was the leader and the experience of Souness. To modern eyes this is a remarkable thing for any footballer to say in public even if his side had a healthy lead, but Rangers weren't even top of the table at this point. This, as well as the consistent references to pressure, was done to keep the Rangers players positive but focused and also to try and unsettle their rivals.

Perhaps it worked. Celtic had already slipped up, a 1-1 home draw with Hearts the week after Rangers had crushed them, as Souness's men marked up a routine 3-1 home win over St Mirren to go within one point of the top and a with game still in their pocket. Celtic then crashed out of the Scottish Cup on 21 February, once more to Hearts, before the most pivotal day of the league season the following Saturday, two days after Butcher's confident assertion was published. It didn't look that way at 4pm with Celtic one goal ahead at Dens Park and Rangers having another one of those of days where all the pressure and great football wasn't leading to goals and, even worse, they were 1-0 down thanks to a clever Eddie May goal for Hibs 15 minutes before the break. Eventually the resistance was broken when McPherson rose above every player in the crowed box to header home a beautifully flighted Cooper cross. It would finish 1-1 – in normal circumstances another dropped point that would have been held up as backfiring overconfidence yet again – but Celtic had suffered a massive second-half collapse. Dundee's four goals without reply meant that Rangers were now ahead on goal difference and with a game more to play. It was a pole position that would never be relinquished.

Souness tackled the issue of pressure as a manager in much the same way as he tackled anything that moved as a player: head on and with maximum force. There was no point in pretending that it didn't exist, as the crowd alone were reminding the players of that fact every week. With no other focus due to the Scottish Cup and European exits, every league game from that point onwards was a cup final. Only a win would suffice, no matter how it came. After going top of the table Rangers won their next five league matches, three of which by a solitary goal. Only in the middle fixture in that run, the game in hand up at Dens Park on Wednesday, 17 March, was there a degree of comfort with Rangers putting in an outstanding performance in a 4-0 win. Three up at half-time through goals from McCoist, McPherson and

Fleck, and with Souness yet again pulling the strings in midfield, it was another hurdle crossed. With Celtic losing at Aberdeen the weekend before, Rangers now had a four-point lead with eight games to go and, although those included trips to Tannadice, Parkhead and Pittodrie, the bookies made them 4/11 favourites with Celtic out at 4/1. Walter Smith could therefore allow himself to speak with a mixture of confidence and satisfaction after the game, 'Some of the stuff we produced was as good as anything I have seen in Scotland for a long time. Frankly we can only throw it away now.'

Managers rarely speak like that in the 21st century and indeed Smith would grow more cautious with his words as the years progressed, but his response spoke of what was becoming a sense of destiny within the squad. The pressure had become internalised. Training became more intense than matchdays ever could, especially on the Friday when Souness introduced an old trick from Liverpool – the Scotland v England five-a-side match where he continued his anglicisation by making up the English numbers. Some of the sessions were wild with Souness fighting off both Durrant and Ferguson simultaneously before Smith, the referee, picked the ball up and called a truce. 'But once we went out on that pitch,' said Graham Roberts, 'we knew that we were a family. We were one.'

It was a deliberate test of character that told Souness all that he needed to know about his players once the Saturday arrived. If they could deal with the pressure cooker of his own internal standards on a daily basis, they would deal with the need to find a way to two points, even when the supporters treated the first goal more like relief than joy. Never was this more in evidence than in the final two games of March where Rangers won 1-0 both at Tannadice against a Dundee United side fresh from UEFA Cup success at the Nou Camp, another crucial Dave McPherson goal making the difference, and at home to Motherwell, where it took until the 85th minute to find the breakthrough, McCoist managing to scramble the ball through the legs of Ally Maxwell from five yards out. With a lead of four points with six to play, Rangers could all but seal the championship with the visit to Parkhead on 4 April, a match so keenly anticipated that the 18,000 allocation wasn't enough for visiting fans who were now buying tickets for Celtic areas of the ground.

Although Davie Hay could be the subject of ridicule at times, Souness found him to be a very decent man as well as a championship-winning manager, but he was struggling by this point. Week after week he would make mention of the fact that Celtic needed to spend to match the Rangers challenge and that they too would be going into the English market – a young Steve Bruce from Norwich City was quoted – but his board didn't deliver. Confused and almost temporarily paralysed by the revolution that was happening around them, they did nothing, refusing to go beyond £300,000 for Steve Clarke in early 1987.

Hay also had to contend with a striker who was making as many front-page headlines as he was on the back. Maurice Johnston would go on to inflict further damage on Celtic in future seasons but he did his fair share throughout this one with altercations in nightclubs and his refusal to sign a new deal. Johnston knew that his true worth was more than Celtic were willing to match and the drawn out saga could not have helped a squad that required unity and cohesion now more than ever. He was booed by the Parkhead faithful with his first touch in the 3-1 win over Motherwell on 7 March and Hay seemed at a loss as to how he could grab hold of a situation that was spiralling out of control. Rangers crossed the city with a swagger befitting champions-elect, making the away dressing their own as always by carrying the two pictures of The Queen with them on every trip – 'they were our pride and joy' wrote Terry Butcher – and the manager and captain warming up in front of the 'Jungle'[26], hosting fans baying for blood as they stretched. Souness would later point to them to suggest that he had Johnston in his pocket but for the first time in months, it was a confidence that spilled over into complacent arrogance.

Celtic would have their last say of that season – and Hay's final hurrah in charge – with a 3-1 victory. Brian McClair scored two penalties in the space of five first-half minutes to put Celtic in control and, despite a McCoist response, Owen Archdeacon capitalised on a miscommunication between Woods and Nicholl to make certain. All of that could have been very different if the first goal of the game was allowed to stand by Bob Valentine. On a very windy day, Cooper's corner floated right over Bonner and into the goal but Valentine blew for an adjudged push by Fleck in the box, despite the Celtic goalkeeper being on his own in plenty of space. Alas, the man Hay wanted banned from controlling Celtic's fixtures thought differently and the gap was now only two points with five games to play.

It is important to note that Rangers responded strongly to every defeat during this season. With the exception of the 1-1 draw at home to Borussia Mönchengladbach, every other setback was immediately followed by a win. The individual blasts of turbulence created a great deal of noise but they were never allowed to develop into tailspins, from where crises are born. The loss at Parkhead was duly followed up with a 2-0 win at home to Dundee on 14 April. Not pretty, extremely tense in the stands and on the pitch, very fortunate – McCoist's first goal was originally flagged for offside before the referee Doug Yeats overruled it and his second broke to him in space by way of a wicked deflection – but it was another two points closer to the finish post as well as delivering a good psychological counter punch to Celtic.

Nothing helps those nerves like early goals and Robert Fleck got Rangers off and running within the first five minutes the following week at Clydebank. They then ran out 3-0 winners and a last-minute John Clark equaliser for Dundee United at Parkhead gave the fans leaving Kilbowie an extra sense of contentment. Nearly a year to the day since Rangers had lost there under Alex Totten – the defeat that forced David Holmes to bring in Walter Smith sooner than planned to try and safeguard fifth spot – the club was three points clear at the top of the league with only three games left to play. The sensational turnaround was nearly complete.

Another fast start against Hearts at Ibrox ensured that the by-now standard sell-out crowd were able to bask in the spring sunshine at the end of the Easter break, with a 3-0 win that symbolised another huge step forward. Fittingly it was McCoist who scored it, and the rest, to complete his hat-trick and close his record-breaking account for the season. His first goal that afternoon, a typical poacher's finish after

---

26   The section of terracing at parkhead that faces the main stand.

a powerful Roberts header was blocked into his path, broke Jim Forrest's league record of 30. It wouldn't be the last that he would smash in his Rangers career but there is such a sense of genuine, youthful glee in his celebrations later on, airplane gestures and all. The man whose boyhood dream came true in the middle of a nightmare[27] was now taking the adulation that he so richly deserved as 'Super Ally' echoed around the stadium. The championship title was so close that it could almost be touched and the hunt for Pittodrie tickets was now on.

Because the goal difference was so large, with Rangers having the advantage by ten, realistically a point in the final two games would be enough. Aberdeen away held obvious challenges with St Mirren, the eventual Scottish Cup winners, at Ibrox to close. Souness preached the virtues of calm in the media, as he had been doing for weeks, but privately the sense of achievement was getting the better of him, the most experienced and decorated player in the country. 'On the Thursday before he was on his toes buzzing at training,' wrote Ian Durrant. 'I knew he fancied it at Pittodrie.' His pre-match words again betrayed his feelings. 'The manager said, "Let's get out there, be a unit, be strong and let's not get anybody sent off,"' said Graham Roberts.

There are simply no excuses for Souness's performance that day. He had already received a warning for a high-footed challenge and a booking for a wild tackle on Irvine, all inside the opening half an hour. To commit an even worse tackle, on the same player, with both feet in mid-air, would be hard enough to fathom for a young tenacious midfielder eagerly awaiting their first league medal, but it was beyond belief for a manager days away from his 34th birthday, who already had five. A trip that was precarious enough at the best of times was not helped by having to play with ten men for the best part of an hour. Souness ran back to the dressing room, blanked by Smith, who had climbed down from the stand to take his place in the dugout. In the end, his powers of persuasion at the start of the season would make up for this moment of ill-discipline at the end of it.

'If you find me the money to sign Terry Butcher we will win the championship this year,' Souness reportedly said to David Holmes when he first arrived. It is almost impossible to conceive of this season being as successful without the almost ever-present, towering presence of Butcher. Fitting then, that the moment that marked this day involved both him and a player whose renaissance in the revolutionised Ibrox culture was just as vital. Five minutes before half-time Davie Cooper floated a free kick into the Aberdeen box where it was met with the crashing force of Butcher's head. 'It seemed as though I had the entire side on my back as all my team-mates jumped on me. It didn't matter: at that moment I could have lifted the world,' he later said. A fusion of deft craft and thunderous power involving a player whose own self-belief had reignited the other's, amid the struggle of a team playing a big match with ten men. Nothing could possibly crystallise this Rangers season more perfectly. Aberdeen would equalise just before the interval through Irvine, but it mattered little as, incredibly, Celtic were 1-0 down at home to Falkirk. Brian McClair would equalise from the penalty spot but there simply wasn't the heart left in that Celtic side to push Rangers all the way. Falkirk scored a comical long-range winner that bounced over a despairing Pat

---

27   McCost was signed by John Greig in 1983, one of the last decisions that he made as manager.

Bonner and, as news filtered up to Aberdeen that the chase was over, a monumental outpouring awaited the Rangers heroes.

There was something symbolic about Pittodrie Stadium – an impenetrable fortress that had been the source of so much heartache and embarrassment for a decade – being completely overwhelmed by Rangers supporters, some of whom had been let in at the very end to soak up the moment itself. From one end of the ground to the other, and on the pitch too, it was now owned by other fans, in red, white and blue. Colin West was the last Rangers player near the ball when the final whistle went and his naively understated, raised hand was soon swamped as the fans invaded the park, grabbing shirts, shorts, socks, even jewellery from the champions,[28] as well as the Pittodrie goalposts. It was a blissful moment of unity between fans and players. Many within that dressing room were both of course and in the words of Robert Fleck, he'd have been doing exactly the same if he wasn't partly responsible for causing the party. The English mercenaries who, it was written, wouldn't have the passion required, all singled this day out as the greatest of their professional lives. 'The bus journey on the way back to Glasgow was brilliant, as we sprayed each other with beer,' recalled Butcher. 'The boys were singing and jumping about so much the coach almost turned on its side. It was a great feeling, one of the best in my entire career … the punters wouldn't leave us alone: farmers in fields were waving wildly, the police were putting their thumbs up and every car was beeping its horn … No one realised how much it meant to our supporters to win this particular title.'

There was still business to be done for Souness, a touch sheepish now about his own role in the day's proceedings. Roberts was offered an increased deal on the bus and Durrant and McCoist were fined £1,500 each for that business in the chip shop.[29] Smith was always of the opinion that the emotional Souness reactions were far more calculated for effect than people ever realised. He could wait for the right moment to punish or, in the case of McPherson to sell on, but only after he had got what he needed from his players.

All that was left was for another Ibrox full house to see the Scottish Premier Division trophy lifted aloft in that final game, a 1-0 win against a St Mirren side with more than one eye on the upcoming Scottish Cup Final. Tradition was such that it would be presented pre-match but Rangers changed it around to ensure a fuller celebration could be enjoyed once all business had been concluded; this has remained the practice ever since. League bonuses weren't written into any of the contracts but the captain approached his manager and chairman and negotiated an agreement that every player would have an equal share of the takings from that final game against St Mirren, which worked out at around £10,000 each.[30] One man in attendance that day was Lawrence Marlborough, the individual ultimately responsible for it all. 'Just as in business you have to put the right men in the right positions and we have done that,' he said as he tried to quietly depart through the main doors. 'We are actually a bit ahead of our planning, but we won't kid ourselves there won't be setbacks in the future. But yes, my grandfather would have enjoyed all of this.'

---

28 A very sheepish phone call was made to arrange the safe return of Ally McCoist's gold chain.
29 They were told that they would get it back if they behaved for six months. They did.
30 Just under £30,000 adjusted for inflation.

* * *

There are countless examples in the history of British sport where individuals, clubs or even nations are so obsessed by one prize – their Holy Grail – that their thinking isn't wide enough to achieve it or, if they somehow do, their plunge off the cliff face of form is sudden. Instead of building a bigger infrastructure to support consistent success for the long term there are open-top buses and MBEs for winning that one solitary prize. There is a bit of both in the story of this season. The club, the players and the support really were driven to be league champions and end a decade of suffering. But it was clear to all that this wasn't ever to be a stand alone achievement. As celebrations raged up and down the country on 2 May, David Holmes quietly but firmly made assurances that the club weren't interested in having all this money that had flooded back into the coffers simply lie there, gaining interest. Holmes and Marlborough – men of construction who had built it and they had indeed come – were committed to this being just the start. 'You're only limited by your own ambitions,' said Holmes later that day, 'and this club has got ambitions.' Souness himself was reluctant to wallow too much after it was all over saying, 'This mustn't be a one-off success. Sure it has been a remarkable year but I don't particularly want to sit down and reflect. The party isn't over, it's just beginning.'

The long-term projections were not limited to those weaning blue-tinted glasses either. Alan Davidson, who had tipped Celtic throughout the season, wrote in the Evening Times on the Monday after the championship was sealed, 'Right now, any bookmaker prepared to offer any kind of odds against them retaining their championship is entitled to qualify as a philanthropist. Rangers are firmly back in the driving seat of the game and it might be no exaggeration to say that Scottish football could be in for a spell of one-club domination similar to that enjoyed by Celtic under the late Jock Stein.'

That would ultimately be true – a great old club had been truly reinvigorated – but it wouldn't prove to be quite as simple as that. With Celtic going into their centenary season and the expectations around Ibrox raised considerably, at least the same level of energy and drive would need to be found again. Souness was acutely aware of that as he surveyed, with a wry smile in the summer of 1987, the cultural revolution that he had created. From installing washing machines to installing winners, he had dragged a footballing culture from the abyss. One year earlier Rangers fans were desperately hoping that their club would stay in the top half of the league so that they could snatch the last remaining UEFA Cup place, now they were seriously considering whether the European Cup would be within reach this time 12 months further on.

'Now we've got the biggest problem, a nice problem,' Souness said. 'Now we have to follow on from that.'

2

THE IRON MAN
AND THE IRON LADY

'She was still more admired than loved, and still as hated as she was admired, but she sailed on regardless, untouched by those who refused to agree with her.'

Alwyn W. Turner, Rejoice! Rejoice! Britain in the 1980s

'I'm a professional footballer who plays for money.'

Graeme Souness, 1985

For someone who seemed to enjoy dominating the shot, there was something very different about Graeme Souness during this particular Ibrox photo op. He would have stood patiently on countless occasions to pose with an adoring fan, for that brief moment presenting a smile of calm assurance next to one who was more sheepish and self-conscious, if it could even be mustered at all beyond the nerves. On this day, however, in the front section of the Govan Stand, it was as if roles had been reversed momentarily as he stood next to a heroine of his own, a woman who even he would concede had more authority than he could ever possess. Prime ministerial visits to stadia or invitations to assist with cup draws were not especially unusual and nor was Margaret Thatcher's acceptance to visit Glasgow to draw the Scottish Cup semi-final pairings[31] an act of pure tokenism. Fresh from the publication of the Taylor Report[32], Thatcher was keen to use Ibrox as an example of what the future of football needed to look like, describing it as the 'best one I've ever seen' and saying that it was 'almost legendary in that it leads the whole of the United Kingdom in the excellence of its facilities'. Souness and David Murray looked on, beaming with pride.

They were very much in a minority. Some players, like Terry Butcher and John Brown, relished the opportunity but most of the squad felt that she should have been nowhere near the event including Mark Walters – the 'left-wing left-winger' according to his team-mates – and Stuart Munro, who deliberately cut himself adrift from the team photo with the PM at the bottom of the marble staircase, even to the point of looking the other way, such was his fury at her presence at his club. This was 10 March 1990, by which time the attitudes in Scotland towards Thatcherism – especially in Glasgow – were hardening to granite. Two years previously, she had been the SFA's guest of honour at the Scottish Cup Final between Dundee United and Celtic and she couldn't even perform the customary pre-match handshake with the players on the pitch such was the venom that

---

31   The draw was done the week before the quarter-finals had even been played. It would fit into her schedule and not the other way around.

32   The outcome of the Hillsborough Stadium Disaster Inquiry by Lord Justice Taylor.

would inevitably emanate from the Hampden terracing.[33] The United players met with her in the foyer and a collection of Celtic's squad were told to wait for her in an old snooker room in the bowels of the South Stand. Some players such as Mick McCarthy – the son of a Yorkshire miner – refused outright. Her visit was toxic.

A fortnight before that final, Thatcher had stoked those tensions with her speech at the Scottish Conservatives' conference in Perth. With a clear nod towards Adam Smith and the Scottish Enlightenment, she reminded her audience – both her supporters in the auditorium and more pointedly her detractors in their homes – that 'the Scots invented Thatcherism, long before I was thought of'. Scotland, she said, had been let down in the past by governments who promised too much rather than by doing too little and who had tried to inculcate the country from the reality of industrial change through the protection of bad management and tradition. 'But they couldn't – and they didn't …and the money that might have been invested in new industries, new opportunities, went instead in trying to keep yesterday's jobs alive.' Easier said that done when those jobs and those traditions were so often welded to real human communities but, as with so much of the tension in 1980s Scotland, it was still born from a hard truth.

And so it was true of Rangers during this era. It was fitting that Margaret Thatcher visited Ibrox Stadium and posed for those photographs with Graeme Souness – the Iron Lady and the Iron Man together – just as it was fitting that Stuart Munro, the unsung and underdog left-back, would do what he could to make a protest. The fault lines within that dressing room were the same ones running through the Rangers support, with so many open in their unease and indeed disgust for Thatcher's policies and style. There was, however, something of a dilemma inherent within that outrage. The ideas and attitudes for which thousands professed such a hatred had produced unprecedented success for an institution that they loved. Ironically, for all the initiatives and legislation that Thatcher and her government would try and spin as measures of success, arguably the best practical application of her philosophy took place on old Red Clydeside.

* * *

How on earth could this jarring juxtaposition possibly come to pass in one of the British cities least likely to share a sense of spirit with 'that bloody woman'? 'Last week, I took the first major step to putting Rangers on the road to the modern world,' wrote David Holmes in the Rangers News shortly after the arrival of Souness, before going on to say that there would be many more changes to come, 'The whole structure of the club has to be brought into line with the time we live in.' Again, it is the word 'modern' that dominates the Rangers narrative as it did many pronouncements throughout the decade on British industry, a deliberate distinction between the failures of the past and the new ideas of the future. 'It is the pure economics I was interested in,' said Holmes in STV's The Rangers Revival. His job, as he saw it, was to go in there and 'shake it up'.

---

33   The *Daily Record* included a cut-out 'red card' for fans on the morning of the game and they
      were waved with gusto.

The club had been underperforming as a business as well as football team and it needed ripping apart. The short, sharp shock that he delivered to the boardroom within months of taking control fuelled a commercial performance that had been unheard of in Scottish football. As the paint was still fresh on the new Waddell Suite for the pre-season friendly against Bayern Munich in August 1986, it set a tone for hospitality packages and sponsorship deals that would in turn fund a product which sent demand for season tickets through the roof. It was literally catering for a new clientele while enticing the normal punters back in ways that weren't traditional. The season ticket culture began there and then because it had simply had to. Fans couldn't guarantee seeing the game if they didn't splash out in advance during the summer and more than half in the summer of 1987 did so on credit. With the rise of home ownership – and therefore mortgages alongside credit cards – 1980s life in Britain was changed by a different attitude towards debt, and it was no different inside the Ibrox boardroom.

The Rangers revolution wasn't created by a sugar daddy or an oligarchical splurge; instead it was very much a product of its political time in that it was a perfect example of speculating to accumulate, with a more modern approach to risk. The ambition realised in the transfer market in 1986/87 and beyond was done so with a hefty overdraft but one that could be serviced by a huge increase in the turnover that it helped produce. The initial start-up cost of this success took the overdraft from £315,592 to £4.1m between 1986 and 1987, but turnover was over £4.2m in that year alone, a rise from £1.8m just prior to the Ibrox Big Bang. By 1992 that overdraft stood at around £7m but Rangers were, by then, bringing in over £11m a year,[34] had expanded the stadium and had just agreed a new five-year kit deal with Adidas worth over another £11m. From a couple of thousand season tickets prior to the arrival of Souness, by 1992 there were over 27,000 people who felt the need to secure their place at the biggest show in Scotland. Like most of the success stories of the era, it was a business risk that was backed up by confidence. A vision that was rooted in reality. It wasn't a fanciful daydream and nor was it one that was dimmed by the way things had always been done.

Much of that vision came from Souness himself. As we have already seen, he approached the footballing management practices recently seen at Ibrox in much the same way that Thatcher looked at those within traditional British industry: with complete disdain. From training and diet to style of play, Souness transformed the dressing room culture and would alter nothing even when criticism bombarded him during those early months. In common with the prime minister, he seemed to positively revel in conflict and sniping from the sidelines while pushing on regardless. Like the initial failures of Thatcher's economic reform early in her first term, they shared the same iron will and conviction in the ultimate value of their ideas, no matter the noise surrounding them.

Even the great moderniser had his limits, however. For all the flip-flops and new stretching regimes, Souness had a blind spot when it came to physical repair and recovery. Perhaps he projected his own individual experience on to others. A man who kept himself incredibly fit, his was a career not blighted by serious injury. Since breaking through at Middlesborough in 1973/74, Souness never played

---

34   A figure which didn't include the then lucrative Rangers Pools scheme.

fewer than 34 league games a season in his career in England and at Liverpool, never fewer than 50 games in total every year.[35] His expectations for his players may well have been shaped by a belief that injury won't be an issue if you work hard – except for freak incidents – and there was therefore no need to invest in modern physiotherapy. Instead he brought in his old Anfield team-mate Phil Boersma to fill that role, presumably solely on the basis that he owned his own sponge. It would arguably be a costly oversight, if a general exception to his rule.

On the whole though, it was unquestionably an application of Thatcherite ideology to the football operation as well as the business side of the club and that was best exemplified when it came to wages. The prime function of salary caps in team sports is one of frugal control but there is also the side benefit of establishing an esprit de corps within the club. A culture where no individual is allowed to stand out too far ahead of the rest. In other words, something of a socialist principle, which was clearly a non-starter for Souness. Ally McCoist's basic £15,000 per year was not too far removed from Rangers' reserves in 1986. His new contract, signed on the night of the first win over Celtic under the new regime, was significantly different. That year there was only one Rangers employee earning over £30,000 but by 1987 there were 15 including Souness, whose salary exceeded £110,000. The statement of intent was almost immediate and it signalled to the rest that they too would have to match that ambition lest they be left behind. Things were never going to be the same again. You would only get what you pay for.

The press were obsessed with Rangers' spending in those first few seasons but could never quite make up their mind as to what the rules were. Initially supporters were warned that money couldn't buy success but then, when it did come, the coverage of big results was always tempered with the caveat that the club had, in fact, bought success. There was some truth in the warnings. The history of sport is littered with examples of results not quite matching the receipts and club owners throwing more good money after bad. We will cover the extent of this in a later chapter but there is absolutely no doubt that Souness was a very successful operator in the transfer market – both in terms of buying and selling – in a way that would not be replicated throughout the rest of his post-Ibrox career. Most would argue that he had to be. If he relied on the players that he inherited, he would not have lasted and the same could be said for relying on the same kind of small-time transfer policy that had served the club so poorly before. Nor did he have the time – or patience – to wait for a youth system to deliver him a championship-winning side. And yet the contemporary reaction to the audacity of that ambition – by reversing the traditional movement of footballing labour in Britain – still sent shockwaves throughout footballing circles. Spending money is easy but exploiting the free market of football is anything but, even when there was an opportunity ready and waiting as there was for Rangers in the immediate post-Heysel years. Once again it was supreme confidence in a vision that changed the policy at Ibrox and in turn, the rest of Scottish football.

There was another signing policy that Souness had his sights on from day one but took him three years to tear up. Thatcherism paid a lot of lip service

---

35   This excludes 1977/78 when Souness arrived at Anfield in the January. He still made 18 appearances.

to the concept of tradition. Even when it came to morality or the monarchy there was a sense of saying the right things so as to keep the old Tory grandees on board rather than a fervent belief that nothing should ever change. When it came to economic policy however, there were sacred cows that the prime minister positively enjoyed sacrificing, no matter how hard those affected complained. If it was good for the United Kingdom PLC, then feelings didn't come into it. Souness was adamant from his first day inside the Blue Room that he would sign a Roman Catholic. It didn't appear to enter his head how that would impact on swathes of loyal supporters. To him, they all faced a choice between a sectarian team and a successful one and that wasn't remotely a dilemma for him in the way that it was throughout many communities in Scotland. He could have broken away from tradition gradually – as many fans expected – with an English player of that faith or even, more excitingly, a South American. But no, in a fashion typical of the prevailing political dogma, he detonated it in the most controversial way possible with the transfer of a former Celtic player who had previously professed a hatred of Rangers and had recently genuflected following being sent off in an Old Firm cup final. To Souness it was simple footballing science. Maurice Johnston was an excellent all-round forward who would benefit his team immediately and Rangers also needed to open the door to a wider market for their longer-term good. The feelings of supporters who felt that the fabric of the club was being irreparably damaged as a result, was of absolutely no concern to him. Like the implementation of monetarist policy or managed industrial decline, there was a cold ruthlessness about it in contrast with the passion that his decision created. The people would just have to deal with it. He was in the right.

Outside of the ideology, Souness the man embodied so much of the Thatcherite age and his strength of personality cannot be extricated from the project itself. A self-made man from a modest prefab in Edinburgh, he was never one to try and hide his wealth. The apotheosis of this came in November 1988 when he was appointed to the board of directors by investing a personal stake of £600,000, a remarkable sum of money at that time for a football manager to put into his club. Workaholic boss and part-owner of one of the biggest institutions in Britain, Souness personified the yuppie spirit of the age and the idealised shareholding democracy.[36] It was a sound investment as Rangers' share price rose by almost 300 per cent between that takeover and his departure and, even though David Murray had agreed a first option at a set rate, Souness still made over £1m in profit when he left. It was a practice increasingly common throughout British business by the end of the decade but not within British football. Present and former managers had often taken their seats on the board but not in this way.

The general Thatcherite trend in football had started earlier in the decade in England, especially in the south-east, where one might expect such a shared identity to occur. The First Division had its first sponsorship (with Canon) in 1982/83 and Tottenham became the first club to be floated on the stock market in October 1983 under the chairmanship of Irving Scholar, another man in keeping with the time. Manager Keith Burkinshaw left the following season, partly due to

---

36   By the end of the 1980s there were more shareholders than trade unionists in Britain, with that number trebling under Thatcher's reign.

a resentment at the business culture that was becoming all-pervasive. 'There used to be a football club over there,' he lamented. His counterpart at Arsenal, Terry Neill, complained bitterly about the rise in wages and bonuses, and that players had lost their 'hunger' for the simplicity of glory and goals. They were muttering into a gale, however. The fusion of the political spirit to the national game was beginning to take hold and would only strengthen over the next three decades. There is no doubt that Souness and Rangers were at the forefront of forging it.

His management style too was also perfectly in sync with Thatcher's: an arrogant, abrasive authoritarianism where very few, if any, alternative points of view would be considered, lest it display any hint of weakness. Sandy Jamieson, in his book on the subject, likened Souness to the famous Spitting Image sketch of Thatcher and her cabinet, in relation to his dealings with his players, most notably the ones in place when he arrived. In the short skit, the cabinet is having dinner together and the waiter serves the prime minister first, with her choice of meat and sauces. 'And what about the vegetables, Madam?' 'Oh, they'll have the same as me.' A little harsh perhaps – as lines exaggerated for comic effect tend to be – but, as some big-name players would find out, there was only one voice that would reverberate through the Ibrox corridors of power. The hierarchical lines were drawn unmistakably clear.

That shared style led both Souness and Thatcher into some similar battles with direct opponents, their own support and the media – with one football writer finding himself banned for questioning Souness's tactical nous in Europe and being branded a 'little socialist' who was just jealous of the money players were earning[37] – but perhaps the biggest of all was with the bureaucracy. If Whitehall was Thatcher's bête noire then for Souness it was the house on the hill at 6 Park Gardens, Glasgow: the official home of the Scottish Football Association. He often wouldn't even try to hide his contempt during the various visits in front of the Disciplinary and Referee Committee, where their proposed touchline bans would have exceeded a normal managerial career if their final judgement had come to pass before he finally left. The attitudes that held Scotland back, in his view, were typified by these little men with their red tape and rule books, something that goes back to his time as a Scotland player where he felt aggrieved at the SFA officials taking care of themselves ahead of the players when it came to flights and hotels. He had been a European champion three times over and these mandarins in blazers could barely run a bowling club. For him, it should be the individual talent who deserved the limelight and the rewards.

None of this was new to the footballing public by 1986. His style and attitude were long established at Liverpool – another industrial city with a deep hatred of Thatcherism – and as a Scotland player. Even those for whom he played admired him rather than loved him. One chapter of his first autobiography, No Half Measures, first published in 1985, was entitled 'Sometimes I wish I was English'. A joke, for sure, but one that had a grain of truth in it somewhere. In so many ways, Souness far better represented the south of England – where he would eventually settle – than Liverpool, Glasgow and Scotland. Easy then for fans of

Celtic and every other Scottish club to associate him with Thatcherite dogma and enjoy hating him even more than they normally would hate a rival manager who was delivering success. It was far harder for Rangers fans who shared that antipathy for a man who should instead have been looked upon as their saviour.

* * *

'I remember when the club's history was sacred and traditions were upheld. I remember when the players had to remember who they were and what they represented,' wrote Colin Fleming from Cumbernauld in only the ninth edition of the Rangers fanzine Follow, Follow in the autumn of 1989, on the back of a story that Rangers had unfairly dismissed their groundsman of 32 years. He continued, 'I remember feeling like part of a huge family at Ibrox, but most of all I remember the wonderful feelings of love and devotion that I used to have for the club and its players. I say used to because those feelings have disappeared along with the Rangers Football Club, or at least the Rangers that I used to know. I have watched the present management destroy everything that it used to stand for in the name of progress. Granted, championships and cups have come our way, but as far as I am concerned the price has been too high. Souness and especially Murray are making the mistake of running Rangers as a business rather than as a football club. In doing so they are causing thousands of true supporters to become disillusioned with the club and they will eventually be driven away from the club completely. In a few years an Ibrox season ticket will be an American Express Gold Card and the days of the terracing will be numbered. How much longer before the Enclosure is turned into a restaurant?'

The fanzine had only been going for just over a season but these tensions around the erosions of tradition and an increasing class divide were nothing new. From the very first issue, where there are complaints about the 'Johnnie-come-lately crew of fat cats who only appeared at Ibrox once Souness brought the glory days back', the cognitive dissonance between Thatcherism and titles was a constant theme in its pages but also in the stands. As the season ticket culture took root, the fans in the Copland Road Stand (where many early books were sold) were serenaded by those day-ticket supporters in the East Enclosure with, 'You can stick your season tickets up your arse!' By the second issue, one season ticket holder was compelled to respond with a letter saying, 'Most season ticket holders have had to make sacrifices to obtain their seats and don't take kindly to being portrayed as "elitist bastards" by anyone, especially fellow Bears.'

Over in the Govan Stand Rear, the Premier Club was opened in 1987 whereby season ticket holders with seats there were given a club tie as part of their package. It wasn't a nod to the 1930s and an era where most men wore a full suit to the game; instead it was a reference to the aspirational, white-collar future and it too was a source of derision and scepticism from some. Not unlike those early fans of bands who make it big, the resentment was more around the laws of supply and demand than the act losing their shine. When tickets were easy to come by, there was a guarantee that groups of friends could travel the country to watch their club, with the added Calvinist attraction of toil and suffering to boot. With newfound success, tickets became scarce and more expensive – in some cases the prices doubled within the space of a year – and the suspicions that 35,000 people must all have had contacts in high places for the Scottish Cup Final of 1989 became deep-rooted.

It is such a perfect distillation of the internal arguments that so many people in late-1980s Britain were dealing with. Moans and groans but – at some level at least – an appreciation for what had been created or what could be. For some Rangers fans, those conclusions were more than a little naive. When stadium expansion was proposed in the spring of 1989 – corporate boxes in the Govan Stand costing £3m and a new top deck on the Main Stand at a price of £11m and was announced in the Rangers News under the headline 'The People's Club' – fanzine editor Mark Dingwall wrote, 'Follow, Follow accepts that if we are to compete in Europe in future the club needs to take in more money than we have in the past … The money will be going to enable us to buy and pay better players, fair enough, but was does that matter if huge sections of the Stadium are populated not by Bears but by the camel coat mob?' This was an oft-used epithet for those 'new' faces at Ibrox whose only contribution towards the atmosphere was the 'clanging of their gold chains and half-sovereign rings'. 'To me,' Dingwall continued later in the same edition, 'Rangers should be run as a limited commercial company in the areas of finance only – in all other aspects it should be run as a club where each member has the same rights.' This is to have your cake and eat it, however. The genie was out of the bottle by this point and, in any case, the truth was that the majority of these supporters were very unlikely to be new faces at all, more likely returning ones whose refusal to pay for the fare they were being offered at the start of the decade was the main catalyst for Lawrence Marlborough's intervention in the first place. It was a harsh economic reality that ultimately produced sporting results for a football club.

The romantic value – what many are prone to call the 'soul of a club' – rather than the monetarist one was felt to be in danger from the outset of the revolution but the lid was kept on that angst as much-wanted silverware began to flow in. In the summer of 1989, however, no amount of cup wins could contain the reaction to the ultimate break with tradition in the name of progress. The 'treacherous fat cats on the board', wrote one furious fan who could only call himself 'MR UPSET', had overstepped the mark with the signing of Johnston, and Murray and Souness were firmly in the crosshairs, 'These two are not winners, they're Thatcherite money-grabbers who operate only with profit and a healthy bank balance in mind. They may be self-made men but they couldn't care a toss about anyone who doesn't line their pockets. Given half a chance these asset-strippers would sell Rangers tomorrow in order to make a financial killing. They may fool some of the people some of the time but they'll slip up sooner or later. Give them the cold shoulder meantime, they have no principles, no morals, no sense of tradition and no respect for Rangers supporters, to them money is God. Souness and Murray, barrow-boy spivs, give me a pair of dossers any day, they have better taste.' The emotional value that communities felt towards a management practice that was all many had ever known, being worth more than the cold decision to get one over rivals and open up a new market for the future, was so redolent of much of the decade's discourse. The past was over, no matter how painful it was for some to accept.

Although it was sensationalised and overplayed in the tabloids, there were some fans who took the decision to remove themselves, for a year or two at least, and who felt the club was no longer Rangers after 10 July. Andrew Cowie from Bellshill wrote before Christmas 1989, 'Although the soul has gone the body of the club still stumbles on, a giant soulless zombie devoid of any heart or feeling. Sadly the people who have vigorously supported the club do not realise that they have lost the one they love. Just like a corny Dracula movie when someone has been bitten by a vampire the Goodies think it is the same person because it looks the same and answers to the same name, but in reality the creature is something alien. Rangers are no longer about the vast legions of fans who have follow, followed all over the globe, it is now only about money for it has become just another subsidiary of Murray International Holdings PLC … If Murray, Souness and Co. are left to go unchecked they will destroy the whole of Scottish football not only Rangers FC. If you want to save the club, personally I think it is a lost cause, the time to do it is now before it is too late.'

One prominent fan, Drew Millar, refused to go back – he later would – and was interviewed by Dingwall ten months later. When asked, 'Do you still want to see them win or did Rangers die for you on 10 July 1989? he said, 'Rangers probably died before then, it probably died when Souness came and we didn't realise it. There's still a team that plays in Govan in red, white and blue and they still call themselves Rangers but I don't believe it's the Rangers I knew, that I've watched, grew up with and I don't believe it's the same Rangers support.'

The visit of Thatcher to Ibrox didn't reach those levels but there were enough for whom it represented everything that was going wrong at a time when everything was going right. One fan from Edinburgh felt the link between the prime minister and the club and its support was 'out of order', adding, 'Can anyone suggest to me a good reason as to why someone who does not give a shit about Rangers or anything to do with Scotland, Maggie Thatcher, was photographed alongside the players at Ibrox? Did it slip the mind of Murray and Co. that the majority of Scots did not vote Conservative at the last election and with the exception of the camel coat brigade are all suffering under the poll tax … The majority of supporters want fuck all to do with Thatcher, but because the directors support her because of the amount of money they've gained with her policies, we're now all tarred with the brush of supporting that cow.'

Language like that was not a rarity in Scotland at the time as Thatcher became more and more a figure of hate in the media and popular culture. Even 'safe' bands like Deacon Blue were moved to deliver an on-stage rant over Scotland's industrial decline at Glasgow's Big Day, a festival of free open-air music to celebrate the City of Culture in June 1990. Lead singer Ricky Ross included the weak Labour opposition at Westminster in his tirade, 'This concert is for the people of Glasgow who have no homes to go to, the people of Motherwell and Ravenscraig who soon won't be able to afford a home, and to the people of Scotland who have been lied to and sold down the river by the Labour Party who don't ask questions on their behalf in Westminster.' This was on the same bill as Bellshill-born Sheena Easton, whose mid-Atlantic accent and multimillion-pound success was greeted by boos and bottles. Evidently Rangers weren't the only Glasgow act who had sold out.

It hadn't always been this way, however. With a small 'c' and a massive 'U,' the combination of conservative and unionist parties never dipped below 24 per cent of the Scottish popular vote in 20th-century general elections until the wipeout in 1997, and were the last to win an overall majority, in 1955. With a loyalty on religious grounds, the protestant 'blue' vote held together throughout the depression and mythology of Red Clydeside in the interwar years and, with an appeal to postwar unity and consensus strength, lasted until the economic decline of the late 1970s where Scotland saw nearly a third of its manufacturing capacity disappear between 1976 and 1987, in addition to the loss of its heavy industry within a generation.

A post-industrial Scotland would eventually emerge in the late 1990s but in that interregnum it was Thatcher who wielded the axe, swinging the final blows to Scottish industry alongside the early introduction of the poll tax and something of a tin ear when it came to speaking to the nation. And yet, despite that dominant narrative, the ideas themselves were not as hated as the personification of them. In 1992, the Tory vote increased in Scotland, helping John Major to cling on to power and pursue much of the same agenda. In the midst of Thatcher's removal in November 1990, the Conservative MP and diarist Alan Clark remarked, 'People are sick of passion, they want reassurance.' Other than the silver hair, there are not many qualities that Major shared with Walter Smith, but there is perhaps something similar in the Rangers story when it too required a change at the top five months after the drama in Downing Street. Similar ideas but with a less-abrasive manner. It's simply easier for people to push any thoughts that create discomfort to the back of the mind when they're not being projected as forcibly and as often.

In Drew Millar's interview he talked about the end of the Rangers support as he knew it, 'The end of the greatest support that ever was. People that got Rangers to the top through protesting against bad turns that were done against them, protesting about bad management, protesting about bad directors, where are they now? They've disappeared. They protested to get Rangers where they are, I want to know where all these people are now, the great protesters.' Maybe it was the concerted effort to hammer home the protestant puns but the comments missed the point in more ways than one. The real protestors who got Rangers to where they were, were the silent ones who refused to turn up unless the club showed some ambition but even the call to arms for those who had continued to attend through the bad times was misguided. Some vented their spleen in fanzines, others were happily in sync with the new political age but the majority just shrugged at how it had all come about and enjoyed the party anyway. It was action that counted, not words.

And this, perhaps more than anything else, sums up the era best of all. It is hard to read any history of Britain in the 1980s without the words being automatically underscored by 'Ghost Town' or 'Two Tribes' in the back of one's mind. It was undoubtedly a time of discord rather than harmony for many but for millions of Britons, life continued onwards and upwards without any riot police in sight. The leading historian of modern Britain, Dominic Sandbrook, captured that complexity so well when he wrote, 'On any given street, one family might be struggling to come to terms with redundancy, another struggling to work their new video recorder. One brother might be heading out on a Right to Work march, another might be finishing the paperwork for the Right to Buy. Aspiration and anxiety often lived under the same roof: the same people who lamented the death of community and the decline of traditional morality might be looking forward to a night in with a rented film or a summer break in Yugoslavia.'

If we want to better understand the political dynamics in modern history, or indeed contemporary society, then we are best served by paying less attention to what people say, how they publicly identify themselves and even, to some extent, how they vote and place more emphasis on how they actually live their lives, their behaviour and their choices. Many in 1989 would bemoan the decline in British industry, manufacturing and jobs while driving home in their German car to watch American sitcoms on their Japanese television. Or indeed write, complain, march or strike against neoliberal economics while celebrating the goals and trophies that it produced with just as much passion.

That complexity and contradiction – the real story of 1980s Britain – was personified in different ways by the two men who drove the Rangers revolution forward. Souness was the obvious, unashamed living embodiment of Thatcherism in practice but David Holmes, the man who started it all with a ruthless boardroom coup, a vision of what was possible and a firm belief that Rangers had to stand on its own two feet and take responsibility for its own future, was ostensibly from the old Labour school and who had toyed in the recent past with standing for parliamentary election. Whether it was the obnoxious 'Loadsamoney' character by Harry Enfield or a stoic gentleman of the postwar political consensus, how they spoke and what they said mattered less and less. They knew what had to be done in order to move forward with the rushing current, which sweeps us all up in the end. Where it would eventually sweep Rangers is perhaps a study for another book. The coda to this story is that unfettered capitalism and irresponsible lending eventually led Rangers, and a global economy, into deep trouble. The freedom to realise ambition still requires pragmatism and both Souness and Thatcher, perhaps because of their upbringing, always knew the value of their money. The big danger was assuming that everyone else did. As Andrew Marr put it, 'Margaret Thatcher knew very clearly what she was freeing people from, but she was less sure what she was freeing people for.'

Mr Fleming of Cumbernauld, who feared exactly that kind of mayhem, didn't stop turning up and paying his money, 'Despite all my pessimism and sadness a stupid sense of loyalty will ensure that I will still follow on, and despite all their shortcomings I'll still cheer the lads on as I have been doing now for more years than I care to remember. I will always be saddened though by the knowledge that the youngsters who are seeing their first games now will never be able to feel the same intense devotion and pride in our team which I and so many others felt in the past. Some may disagree with this statement, but let me ask you this. How can you love a business as you would a football team? I, for one, cannot.'

One can only wonder if and how he enjoyed the decade that was about to follow but there isn't a football fan on the planet who has loved the business as they do the team and none are ever asked to. The generation who began their Rangers experience during this time seemed to have no issue showing devotion and pride in a side which produced constant success but perhaps, more importantly, it was a generation better able to understand the developing nuance around their club and the game itself. They understood that without the business being successful, there wouldn't be much of a football team left for them to love. For them, tradition had very little value at all if it stood in the way of progress and they seemed less inclined to believe in the infantile, monochrome interpretation of heroes and villains or be so tightly bound by rhetoric and dogma. As if life, politics and football were all a great deal more complicated than that.

Which they always are.

3

TURMOIL

SEASON 1987/88

'With a top club you cannot sit back and wallow in the celebrations which mark your trophy wins.'
Walter Smith

'I wouldn't mind losing four times to Celtic next year, if we won the league.'
Graeme Souness

There was a darker mood around The Hawthorns as winter descended in 1987. Situated on Kenilworth Road, this beautiful sandstone home was a little piece of England in Stirlingshire, its address matching perfectly with its owner. Terry Butcher had moved in a year before, with one medal already safely in the collection and the optimistic promise of more to come. Now he was anxious and depressed. The man who had carried his team-mates on his back – both literally and metaphorically – was in tears as he tried to hobble up the stairs, such was the pain from his broken tibia. The year before he had been a standout performer at the World Cup and now his European Championship ambitions – to be held in West Germany in seven months' time – were hanging in the balance.

Many visitors and well-wishers had come to the door, including Graeme Souness and some other Rangers players. A new, but expected, face arrived eventually. He was a Rangers fan but not one there to collect an autograph or to pass on his best wishes for a quick recovery. 'I hate having to do this,' he told Butcher as he arrested the Rangers captain and formally charged him with behaviour likely to cause breach of the peace. He confirmed this with his three other colleagues via radio. They were doing the same job at the homes of Chris Woods, Graham Roberts and Frank McAvennie.

The season of revolution that had promised – if not guaranteed – consistent success for a generation or more, seemed a long time ago now. On the face of it very little had changed. At the same stage of the previous season, Rangers had won the League Cup and were six points behind the league leaders. This was exactly their situation on 17 November 1987, with the added bonus of progression to the quarter-finals of the European Cup – after dispatching one of the favourites en route – as well as the addition of Richard Gough, the must sought-after transfer target of the previous summer. But that snapshot look at history is misleading, as it almost always is. All was not well at Ibrox. The arrogant swagger had turned into a complacent entropy. The manager's obsession with meeting the physical demands of the Scottish game was now leading, more and more often, to an unruly tumult, meaning that rivals knew they simply had to press buttons and stand back. And now Butcher, the almost ever-present totemic figure of that championship season, was out for months.

Souness's Rangers had won a title race at full throttle in 1986/87 but were always able to regain control when they hit bumps on the road. The manager's natural energy was harnessed to devastating effect but now it was becoming unbridled, and 1987/88 was a season when chaos ensued. When the three Bears got tangled up with Goldilocks and ended up in the dock. When brawn too often overshadowed beauty. When young talent was nearly extinguished at the whim of the manager. When a Rangers player suffered the worst racist abuse in the history of the Scottish game. When the big talent could have easily called it quits and gone home for a quieter life.

Perhaps this wild disparity is best explained by the fact that it was the season when Walter Smith felt that Rangers were almost back to square one and Ian Durrant thought that they should have won the European Cup. Incredibly, both men had a point.

* * *

Few things characterised the 12-year reign of Souness and Smith the Younger more than their annual summer statement of intent in the transfer market. The two most subdued years led to very different seasons. In 1992 some, correctly, believed that Rangers were so far ahead of their domestic competition that nothing dramatic was required. Although still at a cost of nearly £4m, Walter Smith banked on what he knew best as he brought a couple of former players back to the club. In 1987 some, wrongly, believed that Rangers had already created such a gap that, even if they didn't repeat the blockbuster spending of 1986, it wouldn't matter. They didn't and it would.

Years later, the explanation that Souness gave for such a light-touch summer spend in 1987 was that strong foundations were already in place, the money wasn't immediately there for another big spree and that he 'did not think it would be necessary anyway'. This was only partially true. Rangers would eventually spend over £3m during the season and, although over £1m was recouped on sales and that entire budget may not have been readily available in the close-season, the intent for another big name was certainly there from the outset. 'The main aim must always be to try and improve the team while you are still winning,' wrote Smith later. 'Our problem was that at the end of that season [1986/87] we did not get the quality of new signings we were looking for.' The foundations were indeed strong but there was always a hint that the success of that first year was evidence of overachievement rather than a cast-iron guarantee that happy days were here to stay.

Glenn Hoddle, Kerry Dixon, Trevor Steven, Steve Archibald and Graeme Sharp were all quoted as targets and, before the previous season had even formally closed, Souness was making familiar noises that Rangers were going to spend big in England once more. Speaking in the Rangers News in May, he made no apologies for shopping in a 'bigger marketplace' and without the 'ridiculously inflated prices' that Scotland presented. With Jim McLean's handling of the Richard Gough saga no doubt still fresh in the memory he said, 'The days of Rangers being in business to subsidise other Scottish clubs ended when I came here.' It was an understandable stubbornness but it wasn't realistic. Before the season was out, he would renege on that proclamation by spending over £1m on two Scottish players who would become mainstays for a decade, but they arrived too late to salvage 1987/88.

The transfer obsession that summer had started in the spring of 1987 when Souness, along with Smith and Holmes, made the trip to Italy to watch Milan lose 2-0 to Sampdoria in the San Siro. Mark Hateley, who had gone to the Rossonieri in 1984 and had become something of a cult hero there, had long been admired by Souness in the target man role that he so desperately loved. His original buy, Colin West, had suffered a disappointing season with form and injury,[38]and now Souness was back on the hunt for someone to fill that key position. With his contract coming to an end, it was clear that Hateley was going to leave that summer and Rangers were front runners for most of the race.[39] By 8 June Hateley confirmed that he would be moving to either Glasgow or Monaco and that he would make up his mind in the next 48 hours. Rangers could offer the excitement of a project that was just under way, the chance of playing in the European Cup and the noise and exhilaration of playing in front of 40,000 people instead of just 4,000.[40] Monaco, however, could offer £7,000 a week[41] and, well, Monaco. Hateley ultimately opted for the latter and at that moment, the initial momentum that the Souness revolution had generated started to slow down. Even once the title celebrations had dissipated, any achievement and any signing had seemed possible. Missing out on Richard Gough in 1986 had been annoying but was soon forgotten once Terry Butcher was landed. This was different. Souness felt that he had his man and he knew that there weren't many like him available. Hateley would have an incredible season with Arsène Wenger in Monte Carlo, scoring 14 goals on the way to winning the club's fifth Ligue 1 title. As time would tell, those goals and that power could have made a huge difference to Rangers' season.

Instead of laying out the £2m that would have been required to get Hateley, Rangers were effectively net spenders in the summer of 1987 as Souness turned to old friends. John McGregor's Liverpool contract was taken over and another former Anfield team-mate, the defender Avi Cohen, was finally signed from Maccabi Tel Aviv after an ongoing wrangle from the previous season. Trevor Francis was the last name in the door before the season began – a close friend of Souness at Sampdoria before moving to Atalanta – coming in on a short-term deal due to concerns about his long-term knee injury, while the choice for the

---

38   West would eventually move on to Sheffield Wednesday in September 1987.

39   Silvio Berlusconi was not just adamant that Hateley would leave Milan but that he would leave Italy. No rivals were allowed to purchase him which made Rangers such a strong suitor.

40   Hateley has said many times that he thrives on a close relationship with a big crowd. It would have been a genuine consideration.

41   Graeme Souness was the highest paid player in Scotland at this time and earned just over £2,000 per week.

target man role for this season was another of Tottenham Hotspur's UEFA Cup-winning side of 1984, Mark Falco, who was signed from Watford. Rangers could cover all of those transfers with change to spare from the £500,000 they received from Hearts for Hugh Burns and Dave McPherson, the latter being the most high-profile departure of the summer. Any sense that Souness had marked that particular card after the Hamilton Scottish Cup debacle rang true when a deal was done quickly and without so much as a personal heads-up for McPherson. This wasn't a summer in keeping with the profile of the last one. Even the pre-season tour of Switzerland was low-key, with Souness replacing the traditional high-intensity training schedule with more matches and some light training in between. The players didn't enjoy it – the results were mixed to say the least, a 5-0 drubbing from FC Zürich being the nadir – and it just added to the increasing sense of inertia following the incredible highs of May.

Nevertheless, the supporters were excited at the prospect of a title defence and a tilt at the European Cup, all with a new, modern-style, shadow check strip and a large new £1m sponsorship deal with brewers McEwan's. They were, however, beginning to realise that this newfound success would have to be paid for and mainly by them. Season tickets had doubled in price in some cases for the forthcoming season, such as the new Premier Club in the Govan Rear which had gone from £80 to £160, or indeed a rise of £100 if fans chose to pay with credit, of which more and more were availing themselves. David Miller, general secretary of the Rangers Supporters' Association, called it a 'bloody disgrace' and added, 'A lot of loyal Rangers fans are not going to be at all happy.' All 6,000 Premier Club season tickets had sold out by 15 June, half of them through the credit facility. With 1986/87 dominated by both cups and queues, many were unwilling to risk missing out again.

It was a residual optimism shared by bookmakers and pundits alike with Rangers being odds-on favourites to retain the championship and most of the country's football writers agreeing. Alan Davidson said in the Evening Times that it was 'impossible to predict anything other than continued success' while Graham Clark, covering Rangers in pre-season, suggested that the real question was, 'Who is going to be second?'

Perhaps Souness had an intuitive sense that it wasn't going to be anywhere near as easy as that. Still stung by a disappointing close-season in the market and knowing that the squad dynamic wasn't where it should be, he gave a bizarre interview on the eve of the new campaign that should have triggered an alarm for anyone paying attention. When the confidence of the support and the bookies was put to him in the final pre-season press conference he seemed to resist the position of overwhelming favourites rather than relish it, 'Theirs is a typical Scottish reaction. Because we won the league title and the Skol Cup last season they seem to believe that we will not only repeat those triumphs but collect the Scottish Cup as well. It is all nonsense. Everyone has to realise that Rangers have no rights to anything. It's time they changed their way of thinking.' Lowering expectations at the beginning of the season so as to oversell at the end is nothing new of course, but there is a degree of edge to that response that was in stark contrast to the confident assurance of the young challenger 12 months before.

Not everyone backed Rangers. Ian Archer thought that Hearts would win the title – they would go on to have a good season but not quite that good – but even he couldn't find room in his top four for Celtic. It was summer of change at Parkhead too with Davie Hay losing his job as a consequence of the revival at Ibrox. A repeat of this failure – in this, their centenary season – was not an option so they elected for the emotional choice of bringing back Billy McNeil. McNeill had already brought success to Celtic as manager earlier in the decade, winning three titles and two cups, but by 1987 he was not a manager in form having led Manchester City and Aston Villa during the previous season, both of whom were relegated. He was immediately faced with the problem of having four of Celtic's best players – the attacking trident of Maurice Johnston, Brian McClair and Alan McInally, as well as the midfielder Murdo McLeod – wanting away as their contracts ran out. The departure of all four would bring in nearly £1.6m[42] but would leave a big hole to fill in Celtic's attack. McNeill spent just over £1m on the promise of Andy Walker and the experience of Billy Stark while finally adopting the new transfer model by going to England and dropping £625,000 on Mick McCarthy and Chris Morris to shore up his defence. Celtic were net spenders as well but had delivered a significantly bigger outlay than Rangers, including more on one player – McCarthy – than Rangers had spent in total. But then, they really had no other option.

The random fixture generator had thrown up an awkward August for the defending champions with trips to Hibs, Aberdeen and Celtic all included in the first five games. This was made all the more difficult by the fact that Souness, Roberts and Butcher were all suspended for the first two matches. The season's curtain was raised along with the Scottish league championship flag[43] with the visit of Dundee United to Ibrox. Rangers started poorly; the makeshift central defensive partnership of Avi Cohen and John McGregor was badly exposed by a simple through pass by Eamonn Bannon and Dave Beaumont was given two opportunities to force the ball beyond Woods. The introduction of Ian Durrant from the bench at half-time – his failure to be selected from the start an indication of the growing tension between him and the manager – sparked Rangers into life with McCoist equalising from a thoroughly deserved penalty after good link-up with Mark Falco and only the post denying him a winner, but it was a point dropped immediately. After the following two matches away at Easter Road and Pittodrie, Rangers' points total was no better off, they were third bottom of the table and were already five points behind Celtic. Form finally returned when Souness could call on all of his big names, with the exception of Trevor Francis who wasn't yet match fit. Progress in the comfortable familiarity of the League Cup included a fine 4-1 away win to the in-form Dunfermline, who had beaten Celtic in the league the weekend before. That match saw Ally McCoist score his second hat-trick in the space of five days, his first coming in the 4-0 league win over Falkirk. Evidence that at least someone's game had been lifted by the new arrivals.

---

42   Over £1m of this was brought in by the sales of Johnston and McClair, both of which were decided by a tribunal, a pre-Bosman institution set up to judge the transfer fee when clubs couldn't agree one and the player involved was out of contract.

43   It was unfurled by Betty Holmes, wife of the Rangers chairman and chief executive.

Rangers approached the first Old Firm match of this season from a position that was seemingly identical to the previous campaign: three points behind and having already lost two games. Much was different in reality. Unlike the first week of 1986/87, where the losses to Hibs and Dundee United at least showed some degree of quality, the nature of these two defeats was utterly insipid and, for the first time under Souness, they happened back-to-back, suggesting already that a sense of control was slipping. Rangers dipped into the market before the trip to Parkhead but it wasn't the kind of psychological blow that the signing of Roberts had dealt to Celtic in the build-up to the new year fixture of the previous season; instead it was the £200,000 capture of Dunfermline Athletic youngster Ian McCall. There was in fact an attempted double signing that week but a £300,000 bid for Robert Connor of Aberdeen failed. Rangers' financial flex was suddenly looking less impressive.

If the 1-0 win over Celtic in August 1986 was a model performance of cool composure under pressure, with Butcher, Cooper and Durrant the absolute standout individuals, then the 1-0 defeat in August 1987 was ragged and unchecked, with Durrant hardly able to find a pass, Cooper half fit and Butcher missing completely, due to a back injury. Celtic were by far the better side with McNeill singling out the significance of this performance at the end of the season. Discipline was the key word for them all week, the implication being that Rangers would lose theirs first. Billy Stark's goal inside five minutes was a nice finish but came from a Jimmy Nicholl error. The tone had been set from the start.

It was a tone that the manager couldn't change, try as he did in a predictable manner. Souness would often complain about the target that was on his back in Scotland and point to his exemplary disciplinary record during his long career in England but his sending off at Parkhead was as legitimate as the two from the season before. He could point to many other players who could have been booked for dissent that day – indeed, Walter Smith made that case after the match – but, with the knowledge of that first booking in mind, he still needlessly crashed through the back of Stark, who at the time was wearing only one boot. It was an extremely late tackle and perhaps signified the real reason for the sudden change in his conduct record; for all the class that Souness could still exude on the ball, he had lost a yard of pace off it. By his own admission, he wasn't listening to his body and was continually rushing himself back to play again. 'Rangers always came first in my book,' he later wrote, 'and I was prepared to take any personal risk to keep them in the chase for honours.' While this intent was undoubtedly true, it was now starting to become counterproductive. The muscular presence that Souness knew was required in Scotland still needed to be matched with a nimbleness and wit, otherwise the cautions would rise in step with the injuries. His frustrations with the rest of the footballing world – he reportedly caught up with referee David Syme outside the ground after the game, calling him a 'big fucking poof' and later that night told Holmes that he had had enough – were perhaps more internal. Graeme Souness the world-class footballer – an identity that he had carried for most of his adult life – was nearing its end.

* * *

The summer was just an overture before an autumnal first act, two months that perfectly encapsulated this Rangers season in that it was chaos disguised by the veneer of stability. After that defeat at Parkhead, Rangers won 18 points from the next 22, scoring 26 league goals in the process, including seven without reply at home to Morton with McCoist and Falco scoring a hat-trick apiece. It was a benevolent run of fixtures where the wins were expected and some of the dropped points – a draw at Tynecastle and a defeat at Tannadice – ultimately feared but it left Rangers only three points behind Celtic and with a game in hand. Woven throughout this period, however, was an almost violent volatility. In the space of eight weeks, between the middle of September to the middle of November, Rangers would have their manager banned for five games, their most precocious midfield talent hand in a transfer request, their star striker found guilty of assault, their three big English imports charged by the police and their captain ruled out for the season, while breaking the Scottish transfer record on a player who would become a club legend, qualify for the quarter-finals of the European Cup and play three matches which, more than 30 years on, fans still regard as among their greatest games of all time.

As soon as the title had been secured in May, fans and management alike were looking towards the club's first European Cup campaign in almost ten years. From the top the language was now about building a side that could compete in Europe, not just one that would be the best in Scotland. With the right draw and a bit of luck there was even a chance that Rangers could still be in the competition after Christmas and then, who knows what was possible? All that optimism was punctured on 9 July when Rangers were handed one of the toughest first-round draws imaginable. It would be a pivotal moment in European football history although no one knew that at the time. With 32 sides all tossed into an open, completely unseeded draw it had the ability to throw up ties such as AGF Aarhus v Jeunesse Esch and Real Madrid v Napoli, the latter of which prompted the first serious conversations around the possibility of a group format in the future to try and ensure that the tournament didn't lose its biggest names at the first hurdle. Although lacking the glamour of the champions of Spain and Italy, Dynamo Kiev were equally as feared. Having won the European Cup Winners' Cup in 1986 they were then defeated only by the eventual winners Porto in the semi-finals of the European Cup in 1987 and were a national team in all but name, with Dynamo players dominating the USSR squad that had impressed in Mexico and would go on to the final of the European Championship the following summer. With the legendary Valeriy Lobanovskyi in dual charge of both club and country, it was a stern early test for Souness the manager in his attempt to make a similar mark in the competition that he had as a player.

Even in defeat, the first leg, on 16 September, provided hope that the journey wouldn't terminate at its first stop. Souness played five in midfield – himself, Ferguson, Durrant, McGregor and Cohen – with Durrant being the one to support McCoist on those rare attacks, the first of which provided the number nine with a great opportunity to put Rangers into an incredible lead. The resistance – under the gaze of the 100,000 crowd including a band of Rangers fans numbering just fewer than 100[44] – was finally broken with just over 15 minutes to go when the Austrian referee Franz Wöhrer adjudged a tackle by Graham Roberts on Alexei Mikhailichenko to be illegal and the Soviet playmaker converted the penalty himself. It was a brave performance in intimidating circumstances, with McCoist especially bearing the brunt of the closest attention, mostly from Oleg Kusnetzov, but more guile would be required to overturn the deficit at home.

It was pouring with rain in Glasgow a fortnight later as the Dynamo players had their customary training session on the away ground the night before the game. Souness had noticed the amount of long passes that were being sprayed out wide, especially on the left to Ivan Yaremchuk. It was nothing revolutionary – Kiev's success had been built upon stretching the play so as to provide more space for their technical prowess to shine – but it forced him into making some last-minute alterations before kick-off. 'I arrived at 4pm on the day of the game and noticed it straight away,' said Campbell Ogilvie. 'It was between Graeme and the groundsmen, I'm not sure anyone else knew.' Even the Rangers players were unaware, until they turned up for duty, that the dimensions of their home turf had been narrowed by four yards at either side. Even during the delirium that followed the match, Ogilvie couldn't revel in the celebrations. Mikhail Oshenkov, his Kiev equivalent who later declared that there were 'no gentlemen at Glasgow Rangers', was pointing in his face just before half-time, demanding that the pitch be measured after the match. 'We went down with the UEFA delegate and when I went to pick up the tape that the groundsman had left on the ground he grabbed it off me. He wouldn't let me touch the tape! This was an hour after the match because he was adamant that the television cameras be packed away before it took place. Fortunately it was right on the limit.'[45]

It was a famous night on home turf. The ethereal quality of an Ibrox atmosphere has ever since been measured against the noise that was produced against Kiev. Being back in the big cup after so long was just a natural next step in the revolution and the Rangers support provided an electric charge that seemed to transform the ground – an inanimate structure both stately and modern – into a living, breathing organism. The 2-0 win was not without fortune as both goals carried more than their fair share of luck. The first came from a goalkeeping error when Viktor Chanov tried some gentle off spin instead of kicking it long and McCoist and Falco were alert as the former laid it on a plate for the latter before the Kiev defence could fully appreciate the danger. Roles were reversed in the making of the decisive second, with Falco heading on a Trevor Francis cross into the danger area where McCoist had expertly managed to find space. Although he maintained that he was just testing Chanov out with his eyes, it was a mis-timed header but an extremely valuable one. Rangers were great value for their timely blessings, however, as they took the game to Kiev in an all-too-rare example that season of controlled aggression. Ian Durrant later acknowledged that the club would build

---

44   Thousands were back at Ibrox watching on a big screen placed in front of the Govan Stand. With a 4pm kick-off in Glasgow, the lowering autumn sunlight meant that staying at home with the radio might have been a better option.

45   Rangers would get a taste of their own medicine when they visited Falkirk in November but managed to cope and get a 1-0 win.

more talented teams but that it would take 'five years to find one that blended together as well as this line-up'.

McCoist, Falco, Durrant, Francis and Nicholl all had good chances and McCoist should certainly have had a penalty in the first half. It was an exhilarating game where both sides played their part, Kiev being more and more dangerous as time ticked by, knowing that an away goal was all that they needed, and Rangers rode their luck more than once in that final quarter. But it was Souness's cunning, from the pre-match landscaping to one of the final kicks of the ball, that dominated the story. With seconds remaining he had possession in the Kiev half and, with the back-pass rule still years away, launched the ball all the way back to Woods in the Rangers box. His name rang around all four stands as the players took their applause. Rangers were now very much back in the big time and, although Souness was still in the infancy of his managerial career, how many understood this competition better than him?

The second round provided a relatively more straightforward task with the visit of Polish champions Górnik Zabrze to Ibrox on 21 October. For reasons that we shall come to shortly, the momentum that Rangers brought to the first leg ensured that the tie was all but done by the interval. A rampant display saw them 3-0 up with goals from McCoist, Durrant and Falco all worthy of commendation but it was the overall performance, especially from a midfield of Souness, Ferguson, Durrant and Francis, that seemed so well suited to that level of competition. The Poles got an away goal in the second half as the Rangers adrenaline finally subsided but McCoist's penalty in the return leg – another 4-5-1 smothering job – extinguished any faint hope that they had of progressing. Rangers were in the last eight of the European Cup for only the fifth time and at Souness's first attempt. Some of the play and poise in both ties was genuinely excellent.

And yet, despite the sparkle and sophistication that this team were capable of producing, discipline – both inside and outside the professional arena – was a growing concern and, as much as Souness would lament his players' behaviour at times, he was hardly setting the best example. On 24 September he was banned for five matches following his sending off inside Parkhead and his tirade at David Syme outside it. Only the day before, McCoist had been found guilty of assaulting a 19-year-old during 'that business in the chippy' that Souness had fined both he and Ian Durrant for on the bus home from Pittodrie in May.[46] Durrant escaped the wrath of the courts but his feud with Souness was approaching breaking point. There was yet another nightclub fight, this time in Airdrie with Robert Fleck and John McGregor in tow following the recording of a team single 'The Glasgow Rangers Boys'. Souness hit the roof and fined all three £1,000. This frustration of feeling trapped in public life, combined with a professional frustration of being forced to play wide on the right of midfield, led Durrant to demand a transfer. Souness called his bluff. Durrant admitted, 'He threw the Rothmans at me and told me to "go and pick a fucking team"!'[47]

---

46   McCoist was fined £150 in court. Unlike the club fine, he wasn't allowed it back after six
       months of good behaviour.

47   The *Rothmans Football Yearbook* was an annual guide to British football clubs.

Days later, during the weekly Scotland-England five-a-side match at training, Durrant flew into a tackle and Souness bit back. 'Is that your best shot?' was all Durrant could offer and he regretted it immediately, 'He was gone by now, roaring about how he was going to punch my head off until the whole squad tore in to break it all up. My last image as I ran away is big Terry being pulled along as the Gaffer chased me.' Durrant had accepted that, during those formative years, he could be a 'naughty boy' and that some mornings he would wake up in a foul mood but Souness, ultimately responsible for setting all standards, could hardly complain for too long about his players when he was charging around a training ground threatening blood from one of his most naturally gifted talents. He was dropped for the trip to Tannadice at the start of October – a 1-0 defeat that was the first domestic loss since Parkhead – but the bad blood was short-lived. Celtic were coming to Ibrox the following weekend, with a lead of four points and Hearts a further two in front of them. A big performance was required and so Durrant was back.

There are surely few better 90-minute distillations of this Rangers season than the derby on 17 October. Brief moments of class were drowned by raucous mayhem, wild sensationalism and poor judgement. It was a match where both sides were showcasing expensive new recruits, instead of just Rangers. When Richard Gough's wife felt that she couldn't stay in London for much longer, despite him being made Spurs' captain and signing a new longer-term deal in the summer, Souness was alert. A first bid of £800,000 at the end of September failed, but the second offer was sensational. On 2 October Gough became Scotland's first seven-figure signing when Rangers doubled the £750,000 that Spurs had originally paid Dundee United for him. Finally, the Ibrox muscle was back but their rivals were flexing their own at the same time as Celtic secured Frank McAvennie from West Ham for £750,000. The Tottenham captain and the top goalscorer in the English First Division coming back north on the same day. They would both feature heavily at Ibrox.

'Undoubtedly Britain's match of the day,' said Jock Brown on commentary at a time when Scotland could regularly make such boasts with confidence. McAvennie soon set about fulfilling his role of the agent provocateur by bundling into Chris Woods whenever Celtic sent up a big 'up-and-under' ball into the box. It was deliberate and it was working. After Woods himself ended up in the net, his team-mates started to lose their cool. 'We were all angry,' recalled Butcher. 'His [McAvennie's] strong-arm tactics were over the top even for an Old Firm game.' It only took 17 minutes before the top blew off. A tame Chris Morris cross was eased back to Woods by Jimmy Philips. McAvennie, at least five yards away at the time the cross was blocked, decided to continue his run into Woods who, mindful of what had already happened, shaped himself defensively for the striker's charge. McAvennie took a swipe, Woods held his neck before swiping back and then Butcher intervened with a shove that knocked McAvennie off balance before Graham Roberts provided the final punch which left him on the floor.[48] Referee Jim Duncan had no choice but to send Woods and McAvennie off and Butcher

---

48   In his autobiography Butcher, with perfect innocence said, 'Graham Roberts followed up, and though I didn't see it, apparently a punch was thrown, or some sort of contact was made.'

was booked, more for his protestations at the red card for his team-mate than the shove on McAvennie.

Roberts donned the red jersey – in the days before substitute goalkeepers were a thing – and play raged on. Souness made a change at half-time, withdrawing Falco and getting another defender in Cohen on, but he would have been far better served doing that immediately as by the break Rangers were in big trouble. With a three-man defence that called upon McGregor to drop back from midfield when needed, Rangers were a shambles and Celtic were able to break through the lines at will. Andy Walker struck first from a very simple long ball from McCarthy and then Butcher helped them to a second before the interval when, under pressure as Celtic flooded forward, he lobbed the ball over Roberts instead of dealing with the onrushing Peter Grant. The early season issues of control and clear thinking were re-surfacing and continued to harm Rangers in the second half when Butcher saw a second yellow card following a completely unnecessary scuffle with the Celtic goalkeeper Alan McKnight. It was perhaps apt that, in the anarchy that now ensued, Rangers grew in stature. Derek Ferguson, the man of the match, showed excellent power and control before playing in Gough – the right-back, now popping up in a number ten role – who laid it off to McCoist to thunder home in off the post with his left foot. Celtic were content to sit back, even though Rangers had a novice in goal, as both sides became punch drunk. That weariness was typified when not even Ferguson and Grant could be bothered squaring up after a thunderous 50/50 tackle.

Somehow Rangers found enough energy to muster one final attack. Ferguson, naturally, was in the middle of it as he sent a beautiful ball down the right to Durrant who breezed past Anton Rogan. His first fizzing effort was blocked but his second, a high hanging ball, caught out everyone including McKnight, and Gough, now seemingly playing as a penalty box poacher, was there to stab it home. The noise was sensational, almost breaking the STV microphones. Back in the dressing room a disconsolate Rangers captain likened it to an aeroplane taking off. There was still room for more controversy when Owen Archdeacon followed through into Roberts. The stand-in stopper made the most of it, the crowd responded and he then conducted them in a boisterous rendition of 'The Billy Boys'.

Players and fans alike felt that it was more than just one point. Souness coaxed Butcher out of his dressing room sulk to act like their captain as the team celebrated. However, it was just one point in a home match that provided the ideal opportunity to cut the gap and regain momentum. For all the incredible drama and thrill of the comeback, it was the second Old Firm game in succession where Rangers players had taken the bait and lost all sense of discipline. The media went to town on the violence and sectarian behaviour, more of which in a later chapter, and the Procurator Fiscal wasn't long in getting involved but the immediate footballing concern was the fact that Rangers would be without their captain and goalkeeper for the next weekend's match, which just happened to be the League Cup Final against Aberdeen.

At around the same time that Woods was walking off at Ibrox, Nicky Walker, Rangers' reserve goalkeeper, was getting treatment on an injured knee at

Parkhead.[49] He was quickly withdrawn. 'Woodsy's just been sent off,' said coach and former Barcelona Bear Peter McCloy. Would he be able to play in the cup final? 'I should have said no but you might never get a chance like that again so I said I was OK,' Walker lated admitted. Walker had been Jock Wallace's number one and had faced Aberdeen often. He had, however, not yet experienced the feeling of beating them. In front of him would be a brand new central defensive partnership as Gough moved over into the middle to replace Butcher. Not an ideal base then from which to combat a good Aberdeen side, now managed by Ian Porterfield, who were three points ahead in the league and had also enjoyed a good European result in midweek with a 2-1 win over Feyenoord.[50] With the passage of time and the advancements in fitness and organisation, there may well have been technically better cup finals in Scottish football history but arguably none that were as much fun as this one. Two fine sides went at each other from the first whistle and didn't stop until the final penalty was scored in the shoot-out. Rangers' defensive frailties were predictably exposed in the first 15 minutes as Aberdeen could have scored twice before Jim Bett's eighth-minute penalty broke the deadlock, and once more again after it. As with Celtic in the first half the previous weekend, the roof could have easily fallen in.

'I had the wind behind me and just blasted it,' said Davie Cooper. He had barely touched the ball in that first 20 minutes. When he did – an Exocet missile launched from his left foot that Jim Leighton was lucky to touch on the way back out – it was the first of many big momentum swings as he ran to embrace the wild celebrations on the north terracing, on which he would have been standing if he hadn't been a genius. Rangers' second, a move of opportunism and intelligence involving Nicholl, Robert Fleck, McCoist and finally Durrant, should be more affectionately remembered and surely would be, if it hadn't been for Cooper's brilliance.

After that, the interval was just a welcome breather in an end-to-end slugfest and the next punch landed square with 18 minutes remaining. Souness had spent the previous day at Nottingham Forest's City Ground watching the English international left-back Stuart Pearce, and it was down that side that Rangers were exposed when Joe Miller's cross wasn't adequately dealt with and John Hewitt punished them for it. Ten minutes later – after a very strong penalty claim against Willie Miller who was seemingly playing with full impunity from the law – it was down that left-hand side that Aberdeen tried again and, with the lack of central defensive cohesion, Willie Falconer rose to head his team into a late lead. Rangers continued to probe away in the final minutes but it was a more agricultural ball by Nicholl, met fiercely by the head of Roberts that was pounced on by Durrant and swept away by Fleck to equalise.

Extra time produced sitters for Falconer and McCoist, cramp for Joe Miller which would rule him out of penalties and Trevor Francis strolling around the Hampden turf as if he was helping out with the kids' game at a Sunday school trip. The sheer insouciance of his penalty in the shoot-out – taking only one step after having to re-spot the ball – is but one in a huge collection of memorable moments

49   The reserve league fixtures were mirrored at that time with the first team fixtures.
50   They would succumb to a late goal in Rotterdam in the second leg.

from that day. The other penalties were nearly as impressive except the Aberdeen second, blasted off the bar by Peter Nicholas, who had missed two spot-kicks for Luton Town the previous season and was only on the list because of Joe Miller's difficulty in standing up. The scene was eventually set for Durrant, a decisive presence in this final for the second year in a row, to slot his kick away and settle an incredible Sunday afternoon's football.

After the shame of the previous weekend, this showcase was welcomed by the nation's football literati but it was Durrant's contractual volte-face that was welcomed most of all around Ibrox, save of course for more silverware. Storm clouds were still visible but there was no sense of panic, instead an increasing optimism that Rangers would build on this cup success and hunt down the leaders in the league as they had done the year before. The next major test of that resurgence would involve Aberdeen once more, when they visited Ibrox on 17 November. Only six minutes had gone when Terry Butcher swung his trusted left leg at an arrowed Davie Cooper cross before Alex McLeish could get to the ball first. Butcher, and everyone connected with Rangers, would very quickly wish that McLeish had.

* * *

'Physio Phil Boersma came on and even then I told him I was fine. He helped me to my feet,' wrote Butcher. 'I thought it was easing, so I stamped my foot to check. Bad mistake. I knew then it was broken because I felt my tibia move. I collapsed to the floor again.'

It is completely unfathomable that Butcher was allowed to test that out and even more so that he, like the major Rangers injury the following season, was not securely placed on a stretcher but instead was carried off by Boersma, around the side of the pitch, in excruciating pain. He would receive an injection for that of course, as he felt every movement inside his leg when the inflatable yellow sock was pumped up around it, before being rushed to Ross Hall Hospital to get plastered up. The initial prognosis was encouraging as it was just the tibia and not the fibula that had been broken, with Butcher talking about returning for the European Cup quarter-final second leg or by the end of the season at least, so he could be back for England duty. Although he worked tirelessly in rehab at Lilleshall, it would be to no avail. The bone hadn't bonded well enough and there was still a sign of a crack that would not withstand that kind of pressure. Butcher's season was over and, according to management and fans of that vintage, so it was true of Rangers. Whenever asked about 1987/88 in later years, Souness references this injury quickly and it is what Smith referred to when he believed that they had almost gone back to square one. Richard Gough was all of a sudden no longer a prize addition that strengthened the defence – he was now an expensive replacement. Not only had they been unable to build upon strong foundations, the key stone has been taken away.

It really was a seismic loss. It could be argued that he was an even more totemic figure than Souness due to his consistent influence on the pitch. As the League

Cup Final had shown, Gough and Roberts were not a comfortable pairing and, although Roberts did a fine stand-in role and Gough would go on to be the most decorated Rangers captain of all time, neither had the leadership stature that Butcher could command at the time. Rangers would lose 1-0 that night – a very cheap Willie Miller header that you can't help but feel was inextricably related to the loss of Butcher 25 minutes before – which left them further behind in the title race. However, their response was strong with just one point dropped in the next eight games, a careless 2-2 draw at home to Dunfermline. There were good wins away at Hibs and Motherwell as well as victories over Dundee United and league leaders Hearts at Ibrox, the latter a very entertaining 3-2 win.[51]

Once again the superficial similarities with the previous campaign were in evidence as Rangers responded to a November loss to Aberdeen with six wins and a draw before heading into the new year Old Firm match five points behind and with a game in hand. Those stats were just an eerie quirk. Rangers were at full strength a year ago whereas, in addition to the obvious loss of Butcher, Ferguson was missing, Cooper started but was unfit and came off after 26 minutes and Woods had to go off in the second half with a broken rib. Souness, imperious before, was a shadow of his usual self on this occasion, giving the ball away twice in the first half that could have easily led to Celtic goals. And this match was to be played at Parkhead, where Rangers had not won since 1980. It was a somewhat predictable display, overwhelmed from the off, and the two goals from McAvennie – one before half-time and then a late header when Roberts was in goal – simply rubber-stamped a dominant Celtic performance. Once more it was possible that Souness's frustration at his own performance was externalised in the dressing room. 'We lost 2-0 but we were fortunate to escape with that. It was a shocking performance,' wrote Ally McCoist. 'I hadn't played well. The team hadn't played well and Souness was not a happy man. I was soon receiving the sharp end of his tongue. "You were the worst man out there," he barked at me. "No I wasn't," I hit back. "You were." Well I've never seen him so angry, and he had every right to be. I shouldn't have said that. I was so sick at the way that the game had gone that I just couldn't bite my tongue … The manager and Walter Smith tore my game to shreds, and I was left to reflect that sometimes silence is golden.' However bad the performance was and however bleak the league aspirations now looked, shamefully it wasn't even the worst part about the day.

On the team bus that made the short journey to the east end of Glasgow that day was a new signing who was just about to be pitched in to make the most hostile debut imaginable. In order to pass the time Mark Walters flicked through the newspapers where he found a message, just for him. A Celtic fan was pictured with boxes of fruit with the accompanying message 'This is for Mark'. 'We had a good laugh about it on the back of the bus on route [sic] to Celtic Park,' Walters wrote in his autobiography, 'but the reality was this clown had just spent 30 quid on fruit just to throw at me. Instead of feeding his family, he'd spend all that money on boxes of bananas to throw at a black guy! Pathetic.'

---

51   Rangers also won the Dubai Challenge Cup in December, against English champions Everton. An unofficial British Championship, Rangers scored two late goals from Fleck and McCoist to draw 2-2 and then won 8-7 on penalties.

Walters was the first black player to play in the Scottish Premier Division and the reception he got at Parkhead was febrile. Boos echoed around the ground from his first touch to his last and the bananas, and much worse, went his way whenever he took his place on the left wing. 'I expected the bananas, but there was also a pig's foot, darts and golf balls. They absolutely crossed the line when they started throwing objects like that,' Walters reflected. The preemptive support from the Rangers end could also hardly be classed as politically correct as they chanted 'I'd rather be a darkie than a Tim!' before the match kicked off.

The media coverage, however, was remarkably silent. BBC Scotland showed the bananas and Archie Macpherson merely commented that the second half was 'slightly held up while some assortment of fruit was removed from the pitch' without ever providing the context. There was still no mention of it in Macpherson's post-match piece to camera but years later, in 2021, he apologised for failing to grasp the racial significance on the day, 'I missed the implication of the banana throwing. Yes, I looked down and I saw them lying on the edge of the pitch, but no more than that. It didn't grab me, it didn't make any impact on me and I regret it to this day. I'm not sure how long after the game I reflected on what it meant for Scottish football. It took me by surprise. Celtic has a great tradition of being open to everybody and they were shocked by it.'

The press reports weren't much better. The incidents barely got a mention in the match reports and when they did elsewhere, the levels were downplayed. 'Only a few stupid fans greeted him with chants and fruit throwing,' one report said. 'But Walters cooly lobbed a piece of fruit back over the touchline.' The Sunday Mail, in a six-sentence piece, attributed the fruit and monkey chants to 'a handful of childish fans' with the implication being that the acoustics at Parkhead must provide sensational levels of natural amplification.[52] There is also a degree of Scottish exceptionalism about the short note, comparing this with the wider levels of thuggery and abuse in England. In the same piece, the Mail said, 'Lets's hope all Scottish fans live up to their boast. That they're better behaved than their counterparts down south.' The fact was that the assumed levels of tolerance and respect hadn't yet been tested in Scotland and the early signs were not good.

Walters wrote about the warm response that he received at his first home match at Ibrox – where he set up two goals in a 3-0 win over Morton – but even then a Rangers fan was removed and banned for life for racial abuse. The matter really came to a head on 16 January when Rangers made the trip to Tynecastle. Walters was exceptional throughout. Pacy, skilful and direct, he won a subsequently converted penalty in a tight 1-1 draw and was unfortunate not to grab a decisive second after some incredible control from a long Nicky Walker ball that took out his marker, Hugh Burns, with breathtaking ease. Years later Burns admitted using racist language as he was given an absolute chasing by Walters but he was merely fitting in with the Hearts crowd as yet again more fruit rained down on the winger whenever he went to take corners. Deputy

---

52   Plenty of space was made available days later to expose the fact that Souness earned £2,500 per week and that he, Butcher, Gough, Woods and Roberts were the top five earners in Scottish football.

captain Graham Roberts came out publicly to protect Walters but he shrugged it off at the time and made mention that part of it was simply footballing rivalry as Souness was also booed whenever he touched the ball. Later, however, he revealed that this was an attempt at self-preservation, 'I would be lying if I said I didn't have second thoughts. Rangers are a massive institution but were they worth losing an eye for? When I look back and recall seeing the darts lying at the side of the park, it still scares me.'

It was only now that the media started to find the courage to be introspective. An Evening Times editorial said, 'That was a disgraceful display of racism that shames Scotland. At Burns Suppers up and down the country just now, Scots are extolling the brotherhood of man. Yet yobbos unfit to lace his boots pillory Walters because of the colour of his skin.' Macpherson, too, found it easier in his post-match monologue at Tynecastle than at Parkhead, to hold up one of the bananas that was still trackside and ask, 'Do we really want a piece of fruit to become a blot on Scottish football? Give it up huh?'

Walters' talent alone made him an instant hit with the Rangers support and his £500,000 move from Aston Villa on Hogmanay was just one of several that saw players come and go over the course of that winter as the realisation began to dawn that an influx of better quality could not simply be done every two or three years, it needed to be constant. On the morning of 28 November Ian Durrant arrived at Ibrox for a late fitness test ahead of the 3-2 win over Hearts when he suddenly saw Ray Wilkins getting changed in the dressing room. He'd arrived only that day from Paris Saint-Germain for £250,000. Durrant really shouldn't have played but the injection of fresh competition forced his hand. 'I patched myself up, played and scored the winner,' he said years later. He joined a midfield of Wilkins, Derek Ferguson and Davie Cooper that day, perhaps a sign of where this Rangers team was slowly heading.

John Brown came in from Dundee for £350,000 in January in the same week that Danish left-back Jan Bartram arrived for £180,000. And then finally, after three months of brinksmanship and soap-opera drama, Souness did what he promised he wouldn't do in the summer by paying big money to a Scottish club when Ian Ferguson realised his life's ambition by signing from St Mirren for £800,000. The hero of the 1987 Scottish Cup Final, Ferguson promised more dynamism and skill in the middle of the park and a genuine goal threat from deep. The signings of Gough, Walters and Wilkins were genuine mid-season opportunism but the deals for Ferguson and Brown could arguably have been done in the summer, for the same money,[53] and provided more depth in defence and midfield as the inevitable suspensions and injuries mounted up.

It was the players who left Ibrox during the winter that caused the real questions later on. After just nine goals in four months Souness decided that he had seen enough of Mark Falco to know that he wasn't going to fill the Hateley-shaped hole in his heart and he was sold to Queens Park Rangers in early December. Less than two weeks later saw another striker depart in a move that

---

53   It could well have been cheaper had Rangers acted in the summer. Celtic's signing of Joe Miller from Aberdeen in November 1987 for £650,000 established the Old Firm premium in the domestic market.

was considerably more damaging. Speculation about Robert Fleck's future had been rumbling on for more than a month while he was scoring five goals in eight league games but, with the exit of Falco, all looked settled. On 15 December, before Rangers threw away that point at home to Dunfermline, Fleck told the Evening Times, 'All that transfer stuff is firmly behind me and I'm sure I can go on from here and score a few more … I have re-established the partnership with Ally and there's more to come.' The following day's headline read 'Why Fleck Had To Go' as he finalised a £600,000 transfer with Norwich City. Souness was clear that this was not his intention, he offered the player a new deal worth more than Norwich could match but that Fleck 'wanted to leave Glasgow, not Glasgow Rangers, for personal reasons and he insisted it was best for everyone if he went'.

The problem now was that, when the European Cup returned in March, Rangers would be far too heavily reliant on Ally McCoist and could not register another player for the competition even if they signed three new forwards. Souness would receive a lot of criticism over the years for creating this exposure. Given that Falco had played well and scored in the two rounds already, it is fair to say that this sale was an unnecessary risk but his hands were tied with Fleck and, given that it was just over a year since he was trying to sell him to Dundee for £20,000, it was undeniably great business.

The draw at Tynecastle in January was the only point dropped in the seven league games after the new year defeat. There was some flickering of the previous season's quality with the hammerings of Morton and St Mirren at Ibrox and the rarely spotted win away to Aberdeen. The 2-1 victory there on 6 February showcased much of this side's strengths and weaknesses. The predatory instincts of McCoist and the aerial prowess of Gough gave Rangers a 2-0 lead within 35 minutes but the latter saw red in the second half as Aberdeen came back into the game, and it required an almighty rearguard effort to see out the win. The title race wasn't entirely over – Celtic were three ahead with a game in hand and there was the final Old Firm game at Ibrox still to come – but it was an uphill struggle that involved both Hearts and Aberdeen, both of whom were also right in the mix.

If the league form wasn't the same as in the last campaign, sadly the Scottish Cup form was. The much-delayed third-round tie with Raith Rovers was a struggle – a 0-0 draw where it was Rangers hanging on for much of the later period – but was followed very quickly by a more routine 4-1 win in the Ibrox replay.[54] Dunfermline lay in wait on 20 February. They had been generous opponents for Rangers that season, with three wins and a draw already and four goals being scored in each of those victories. Perhaps it was the familiar face of Dave McKellar in goal, who had such an outstanding afternoon for Hamilton on that fateful day at Ibrox, that generated some nerves. The Fife side were ahead after only five minutes and it came through a freak goal. Former Celtic winger Mark Smith beat Bartram down the right and, before the ball could bobble out of play, he swung in a high, looping cross. Chris Woods, not long back from injury, should have done better as it sailed over his head and into the corner.

---

54   Eventually. Rangers were pegged back to 1-1 after 51 minutes, and Ian Durrant then missed a penalty before eventually scoring following a nice move and the floodgates opened.

Like the infamous Hamilton match, Rangers bombarded Dunfermline with Roberts, Durrant and Gough all going close. Already under some degree of pressure, once again it would be a lack of discipline that would simply create more of it as John Brown was sent off for a needless off-the-ball charge on Smith right before half-time. It was the 12th red card in Souness's 18-month reign and it would take four years for Rangers to chalk up that number again. A clever corner left John Watson with a simple header to make it two soon after the break and Rangers toiled thereafter, Gough being launched up front as an auxiliary target man to no avail. Rangers were once more out of the cup before the clocks changed but, with the league looking like an outside bet at best, at least there was Europe.

***

For the third time in succession, the European Cup draw sent Rangers behind the Iron Curtain when they were paired with Steaua Bucharest in the quarter-finals. Champions of Europe in 1986, defeating Barcelona via one of the worst penalty competitions in history at the end of that Seville final, and on a roll of three successive domestic titles, this was a strong side that had recently added one of the most promising young players in Europe, Gheroghe Hagi.[55] Real Madrid and Bayern Munich were the two superclubs paired together and perhaps only Benfica would have been a more daunting prospect than Steaua with Anderlecht, Bordeaux and PSV Eindhoven the others left in the competition.

The side that had beaten Kiev and had sailed past Górnik in the autumn would have relished this opportunity but Rangers in the springtime was a different proposition. Wilkins had been signed in time and Gough was also eligible to play but the new recruits – Walters, Brown, Bartram and Ian Ferguson – would have to wait until a possible semi-final, Butcher was still missing and now, three weeks before the first leg in Romania, the major fear around Souness's winter market trading was realised. After 40 goals in 128 consecutive appearances, Rangers' attacking reliance on Ally McCoist finally took its toll as he suffered a knee injury which ruled him out of the 4-0 home win over St Mirren and then the cup exit at East End Park. When the recovery didn't happen as hoped, McCoist was put under the knife on Tuesday, 23 February (just over a week before the first leg) and then sent off to Lilleshall for the best rehabilitation possible. Microscopic keyhole surgery was revolutionary in 1988 as, instead of removing cartilage from his knee, they simply trimmed off the parts that were causing the problem. There were even some feint hopes that he would be able to make a comeback for the second leg in Glasgow on 16 March. He would travel to Bucharest anyway, just for morale.

Even when the team sheets were shared an hour before the game, Steaua coach Anghel Iordănescu believed that there had been a mistake. They, like everyone else, had assumed that McCoist had as much chance of playing as

<hr />

55   He had scored the only goal to win the subsequent European Super Cup against Dynamo
       Kiev.

those who weren't yet registered. But there he was, the irrepressible talisman, taking his place as the lone striker – a job that requires great physical effort and more than a little bravery given the close attention of defenders – eight days after after undergoing knee surgery. His performance was a valiant one, he took his knocks and worked extremely hard to press the Romanians back but there was an understandable sharpness missing, especially with the one decent chance that was passed up midway through the first half after some delightful work by Cooper, Wilkins and finally Souness to send him into space. By then, however, much of the damage had already been done.

'It's a cardinal rule in these games away from home that you try and frustrate the opposition as much as possible in the early stages,' wrote Richard Gough. 'Our hopes of achieving any kind of frustration disappeared after a couple of minutes. That's how long it took them to score on a pitch which was a mud heap because of torrential rain.'

It was a sunny afternoon in Bucharest – the live STV coverage of the early kick-off bringing much stress to school teachers and office managers all around Scotland – but the night before had seen horrendous weather. 'It was the most surreal moment I've ever experienced in football,' said Campbell Ogilvie. 'They had brought in two army helicopters to hover over each half in order to try and dry it out.' It created a mud bath, especially in the penalty box, and Rangers were to suffer the consequences almost immediately. Steaua had pressed Rangers in from kick-off and despite many opportunities the lines could not be cleared, the last attempt – by Gough – weakly holding up on the floor before being rattled home by Victor Pitruca after only two minutes. Although the pressure continued, Woods was excellent and Rangers saw out that early storm well. Steaua's recent success had been mainly built around a good home record – they were not excellent away from home – so a 1-0 deficit, like Kiev, would have felt perfectly manageable. The killer blow came in the 66th minute when Ștefan Iovan's free kick deflected wickedly off Cooper and past Woods after Gough was thrown to the ground from the Rangers wall by Adrian Bumbescu, who had sprinted 50 yards to take his place in it. It was desperately bad luck just as it looked as if Rangers were doing the type of containing job that they had managed well on their previous trips east.

Although the mood on the plane home was tense,[56] Souness and later Roberts and McCoist, provided the usual frontier gibberish in the press so as to generate another special Ibrox atmosphere for the return and it didn't fail, with the pre-match noise reaching those famous Kiev levels. All that energy was unplugged by yet another early sting from a more experienced and canny side. It was a good ball from the captain Tudorel Stoica, and the finish by Marius Lăcătuș was sublime, but the defence were caught cold and square inside three minutes of a match where one away goal would likely be fatal. Ibrox responded quickly and

---

56   Souness had to be held back from attacking Gerry McNee of the *Daily Express* who was complaining vehemently about the fact that the manager had kept McCoist's fitness test from the Scottish press pack but an English writer had seen it while turning up at training the night before. According to Ian Durrant, Souness's eyes were bulging and he shouted, 'Don't you ever fucking speak to me like that again!'

so did the players, with the ball spending most of its time in and around the Steaua box. Gough powered home a header from a Roberts flick on 16 minutes and then McCoist buried a penalty after Durrant was hauled down. Souness's control on the ball wasn't in question as he directed so much of this counter pressure but yet again his lack of it in the tackle was scandalous, with an assault on Iosif Rotariu the best-remembered incident from the whole match. Souness was lucky to escape with a booking, his gesture of innocence, pointing to his ruffled sock, perhaps making all the difference. The Romanians were dangerous on the break and really should have grabbed another in the second half but Rangers too squandered some great chances to get a third goal that would really have made it interesting with Durrant going close twice and McCoist with the best chance, just 18 minutes from the end, which he blazed over in plenty of space inside the box after a brilliant back-heel by Wilkins. It wasn't to be.

But it could and arguably should have been. The sales of Falco and Fleck weren't as relevant in Romania, a lone role for which neither were particularly suited, but the support of either for a better-rested McCoist in the return leg would have been significant, especially if it meant Durrant could have moved over into the midfield role that was instead filled in both ties by a young Scott Nisbet. Ultimately both games were undone by unforced defensive errors, not failures in attack and, even with Terry Butcher watching a special BBC Pebble Mill feed of the second leg while in recovery, the players who were fit should have been more than capable of starting both matches in less comedic fashion.

PSV Eindhoven would go on to win that season's European Cup. From the nine matches they played in order to do so they won only three, none of those coming from the quarter-finals onwards, with two ties being settled on away goals and the final on penalties. This, more than the more famous near-miss in 1992/93, was arguably the best opportunity that Rangers had for European success in this period, bearing in mind the addition of the players who would have been eligible in the next round, especially Mark Walters. There was no opposition remotely close to the quality of Milan or Marseille that would follow five years later. Rangers played most of their best football of the season in Europe, a stage that seemed to suit them and provide a welcome and exciting break from the domestic drudgery with which they never quite got to grips. Individual defensive errors and bad luck with injuries cost most but the loss of Fleck and Falco has perhaps been a touch overstated over time. The failure to land Mark Hateley in the summer was a far bigger factor in this competition and the season as a whole. It could have been a transfer that led to the ultimate glory.

There wasn't much time for Rangers to mope as Celtic were heading to Ibrox on the Sunday, live on STV, and billed as something of a title decider with four hours of coverage dedicated to it, including helicopter shots of the Rangers bus coming up from their Turnberry hotel and the Celtic camp in Erskine. A Celtic win would effectively seal the championship – putting them six clear with a game in hand – whereas a Rangers victory would only intensify the pressure with eight games remaining. It was a tense but clean Old Firm game[57] with a frenetic pace and few clear-cut chances, especially in the first half with the

---

57   Souness elected not to start himself.

best falling to Ian Ferguson – a die-hard Rangers fan who was brought up in Parkhead – but he snatched at it and dragged it wide.

During the interval, both Sandy Clark and Willie Miller had noticed the lack of aerial dominance that Rangers had shown when defending crosses and in the second half this frailty was exposed. A Paul McStay delivery from the right was so badly dealt with – Roberts had two failed attempts to clear – that he had time to get himself to the edge of the box to volley home and put Celtic in front. Just seven minutes later Rangers, through Jan Bartram, equalised in a similar fashion as Celtic could only clear Cooper's cross to the periphery of the penalty area, where the Dane volleyed superbly into the corner of Pat Bonner's net. With Rangers tiring late in the game, Celtic squeezed in that crucial winner with just over ten minutes to go and yet again it was down to a calamitous lack of defensive organisation. Anton Rogan was presented with a free header from a Tommy Burns corner which was, typically, going well wide of the target until it was diverted quickly off the chest of the unmarked Andy Walker and in.

Overall, it wasn't a particularly poor Rangers performance at all. They enjoyed the better of the first half and had their moments in the second but, once more, it was a case of individual problems, especially the enforced central defensive partnership of Gough and Roberts, who were now a liability under better quality pressure. Their half-time dressing room argument at home to Steaua was the third of such fights when each player blamed the other for losing their man for an important goal. It was an enforced partnership that just didn't work and, according to Gough, the midweek bust-up left him 'unhappy and unsettled' in his relationship with Roberts. The loss of Butcher was also a matter of height – at 6ft 4in, he was considerably taller than both Gough and Roberts – and there was a never a settled back four with both full-back spots never being consistent.[58] Neither Souness nor Smith attended the post-match press conference – which was becoming something of a trend – and, now that the season was effectively over, the internal Ibrox pressure cooker was about to burst once more as the final seven weeks descended into even deeper levels of chaos.

The first impressions of Bartram were of a mild-mannered pro with an eye for a goal but who was perhaps not cut out for the physical nature of the Scottish game. No one could have imagined the repercussions of his trip to Italy in the midweek following the Old Firm defeat, on Olympic warm-up duty for Denmark. He talked in an open press conference about his experience at Rangers and the story was subsequently run by the Danish daily newspaper Ekstra Bladet under the headline 'My boss is a hooligan'. It wasn't an 1980s version of tabloid clickbait. Bartram's account was perhaps naive and ill-advised – he struggled to sleep later that night – but it was open, both in opinion and in fact. 'I didn't go to Scotland to risk breaking other players' legs. I'm very much against that style,' he said. 'Souness wants us to be hard when we're in trouble. He is a bastard. I will not follow orders and deliberately kick people. He should have been shown the red card against Steaua. He likes to get the ball and slaughter other players and I don't

---

58   Munro, Cohen and Bartram all made a substantial amount of appearances at left-back and, aware that he had increased the age of his side considerably, Souness felt that he had to bring in some youth so Nisbet was given a great deal of game time over Nicholl.

think I can learn this type of play. I like to see the beautiful things in the game so I am prepared to be fired … I am glad to be back among my Danish countrymen so I can play real football again.'

With more tales of television sets being smashed up in defeat, Bartram said the Souness 'behaves like a madman when we lose. He has threatened to hit a journalist so hard that he wouldn't get up again.' Bartram denied it all upon returning to Glasgow – despite three separate Danish sources, not a country known for sensationalist media, confirming it all to be true – and he and Souness went on television to provide a united, if well-rehearsed, front.[59] Few people seriously believed it. With each passing month of this season, Ibrox was further characterised as an environment of simmering tension and self-destructive turbulence.

Now, with no prizes left to play for, the results really did suffer as a consequence of a disharmonious dressing room. Rangers were fortunate to beat Dundee 3-2 at Dens Park thanks to a late Durrant penalty but lost 2-1 at home by Hearts, who were also chasing second place, despite being 1-0 up through Bartram, and then, as the Glasgow Garden Festival bloomed into life on Easter weekend, there was the embarrassment of a 3-2 defeat away to relegated Morton. Even with an Ian Ferguson scissor-kick goal – a promise of things to come – it was a performance typical of a tired season with Roberts going off injured and even Chris Woods looking very suspect for two of the Morton goals. Souness was curt but fair about the situation, 'Last year I spent a lot of money on the defence and they won us the Premier League championship. This year they have lost us the title.' He didn't however, place the entire blame on the loss of Butcher, 'We have internationalists at the back and shouldn't have to rely on one man. The attitude will need to change and some of the players will need to remember that they are playing for Rangers.'

On 12 April it was time for the most chaotic episode in this melodramatic season to come to its conclusion, as the trial began for the Old Firm Four. Four days were spent on the case at Glasgow Sheriff Court, most of which was spent on the behaviour of the crowd rather than the kind of 'handbags' incident that could be seen at grounds up and down the country every weekend. It all seemed to be much ado about nothing as Frank McAvennie – the one who started the whole thing – was found not guilty and Roberts not proven. Butcher was thus feeling quite relieved when it was his turn to stand and listen to Sheriff Archibald McKay's judgement. '"Guilty." I couldn't believe what I had heard. I didn't hear how much I was fined, I was so stunned.'[60] It was Butcher's decision to get involved, not to protect Woods but to deliver a 'deliberate, violent push' that could 'reasonably have been expected to upset other Celtic players and their supporters' that led to that judgment. Disregarding completely the reality of the football field and goalkeeping self-preservation, Woods was also found guilty of jabbing McAvennie sharply on the chin with his forearm. 'It was an assault which constituted a breach of the peace.'

The potential consequences of pitch invasions and riots were at the forefront of the judgement but both the players and the club felt that it was ridiculously

---

59   Bartram would reaffirm a lot of these comments in his autobiography ten years later.
60   He would be fined £250 and Woods £500.

harsh when far worse physical acts had been carried out in Old Firm games. This was, in Butcher's mind at least, a deliberate decision to make an example of the two most high-profile English players – 'it was completely rigged as far as I was concerned' – even going to the top of Thatcher's government. Souness was worried that this would lead to his prized assets calling it a day and it would have been the ultimate finale to the narrative of this season. 'Souness was in a flap because he was really worried we were going to say enough was enough' wrote Butcher. 'David Holmes also said if we decided we had had our fill of Scottish football and Scottish justice, the club wouldn't stand in the way of our leaving. But I told them immediately I wouldn't be forced away. It was a sick joke as far as I was concerned.' Woods did contemplate the impact of this on his England career but decided to stay. Roberts was also resolute that he wouldn't be going anywhere. In a somewhat fitting coda to this tempestuous tale, it would be a choice that would be taken out of his control.

'Frankly,' wrote Souness in his programme notes for the final home match of the season against Aberdeen, 'I hope I never have to go through another season like it.' He had already dropped Ian Durrant for the final few games, the midfielder being yet again the subject of a nightclub scuffle, saying, 'If a footballer chooses to do things away from training in his social life which prevent him from giving 100 per cent on a Saturday then he is in the wrong business.'

The 1-0 defeat was a typical way to close it off, a late Brian Irvine goal coming from another defensive failure to deal with a long ball. It was the type of goal that Rangers had been guilty of conceding in big moments all season and it was Walter Smith who had a go at Roberts for his positioning. 'He refused to accept any of the blame when it was clear to everyone in the dressing room that he had been at fault,' said Smith some time later. It wasn't a goal that had an obvious culprit, more a general organisational deficiency, but Roberts, being a centre-half and the captain, would have been expected to shoulder that responsibility. It was just as he was disputing his culpability that Souness arrived and immediately backed his assistant, saying, 'Some strong words were exchanged and his [Roberts's] response was along the lines of, "If that is the way you feel about it you'd better sell me." This was a direct challenge to my authority as manager and there was no way I was going to back down. I told him to "consider it done".' Souness has since then conceded that there was another way to handle it, to bring Roberts out of the dressing room quietly and give him the opportunity to apologise in front of the squad, but that this would have needed a different, more mature manager, who wasn't still kicking every ball.

Roberts by then was a massive cult hero among the Rangers support and some may argue that there is an underlying theme that runs through some of Souness's clashes with those types of characters. That he has to be the ultimate messiah. The reaction at the final game of the season at Brockville – a fine 5-0 win over Falkirk – was tense to say the least as Roberts took his place in the ground and fans chanted his name throughout alongside banners saying 'Robbo Must Stay!' Manager, assistant and chairman took an awful lot of stick that afternoon. Souness was a huge fan of Roberts, an ideal player for the kind of team he knew must be built first to make the original mark on the Scottish game. Souness loved that he was going to get the same kind of player at Parkhead as he would at a lower-league side in the cup. He was aware, however, of a feeling within the camp that Roberts was perhaps becoming too big an influence and a critical one when it came to the younger Scottish players and, by his own admission, he was looking for something with which to curb that. It would have made no difference here. Souness was always going to respond that way and the fans weren't likely to change his mind. Smith was in full support. 'Managers cannot afford to walk away from difficult or unpopular judgments,' he later wrote. 'Often things happen away from the public gaze which determine the direction you take. But if you bottle a tough disciplinary matter then you can lose all the players, not just the one who brought the trouble to a head.'

Graham Roberts would eventually leave, at a profit, to Chelsea for £475,000.

***

It was a pertinent way in which to bring a very difficult season to a close. The title had been handed over – Rangers could only finish third behind Hearts and Celtic – and another European opportunity passed up a little too easily in a year that seriously lacked order and professionalism. A week later Celtic would produce yet another late escape to come from behind to win the Scottish Cup Final against Dundee United and in doing so, secure the double in their centenary year. It was a tough summer for everyone who had Rangers at heart. There were some historical parallels; in the summer of 1976, Rangers looked ready to dominate Scotland again. After a long barren spell they had finally won the title in 1975 and then followed that up with a treble in 1975/76 but that summer they did very little, so sure they were of the gap which they had created whereas Celtic roared back and Rangers were left with nothing.

The mistakes of inactivity were learned and instead, the summer of 1988 proved to be the start of something very special. A period of real dominance, unparalleled in the history of the club. The physical point had been proven and by now Rangers were really only fighting themselves. It was time to focus more on the football and for Souness to build a classier side that couldn't be touched by any other team in the land. The signings of Ray Wilkins and Mark Walters were the first creative players he brought through the door and there would be more. Yes, the signing of John Brown would be paralleled in the future by Nigel Spackman and Terry Hurlock – Souness was never going to give up that particular principle entirely – but they would be surrounded more and more by players of genuine inventive talent. And Souness himself – for so many years the perfect blend of steel and silk – would now have to let go. Although a couple of years older, Kenny Dalglish could only do both jobs to full capacity for one season before happily becoming a bit-part cameo at Anfield.[61] Souness played 30 games in 1987/88. He would play 11 more for Rangers in the next two seasons before hanging up the boots for good. At a club of this size, a player-

[61] Admittedly easier when he suddenly had the attacking options of John Barnes, John Aldridge and Peter Beardsley after that first season.

manager can only ever be a short-term option and more detachment would ultimately lead to better control.

The complacency that he had shown in the 1986/87 official video had now been well and truly banished. Although technically true – Rangers fans would always favour a title without an Old Firm victory over four great games and no trophy – it completely ignored the reality of league arithmetic. Beating Celtic, and beating them often, was key to winning the flag. Ultimately that final argument with Roberts, after a season full of recrimination, perhaps drew a line in the sand. 'Is this how it is going to be?' an emotional Souness challenged his players that afternoon. 'We win one, they win one, we win one, they win one? Because I'm not fucking interested in that.'

As it would turn out, neither were they.

4

A WHOLE NEW BALL GAME

'So far the Premier League has failed to capture the imagination of an English football public not fooled by a change of label and the accompanying hype.'
David Lacey, The Guardian, October 1992

'Just make it fucking good.'
Dave Hill, executive producer, Sky Sports, 1992

It is unclear whether or not he was booked by BBC Scotland to do the job in advance but either way, Andy Gray was at a loose end on Sunday, 26 October 1986, the day of the League Cup Final. He had been injured for Aston Villa two weeks earlier in a 3-1 win over Southampton and, in fact, he had been missing for the first two months of the season, in which time he also managed to fit in another date for his new venture. For both the first Old Firm league game of the season at the end of August and now at Hampden for the final – wearing a quite phenomenal jumper in a caravan with Dougie Donnelly – Gray was present to give his thoughts and analysis at the interval and at the close of play. The same passion for the game that characterised his broadcasting career was evident then as it would be 30 years later but there were only brief hints of the ability to explain and dissect the action, the talent that would later change the whole picture for those watching at home. Gray was almost wholly descriptive in those early forays into television and so often used that well-worn trope of the senior professional approaching retirement – 'the boy Ferguson' or 'the kid Durrant'. He would improve markedly, however, and in doing so would help change the way an entire generation consumed their sporting obsession and, as a result, change the way they looked at their first footballing love.

In 1986, Scottish football's fraught and distrustful relationship with live television ensured one thing: the game and its success stories were protected from the reality of the outside world. As a result it felt that touch more special and meaningful, with no live action being beamed into houses every weekend which consistently highlighted a very different standard on show elsewhere. In a way the League Cup Final, taking place as it did on the last weekend in October – when the clocks go back in Britain – was a perfect example of that sense of exceptionalism. No other country was handing out silverware at this time of year, with the drama of the final always concluding under floodlights as the Glasgow skies darkened around them. With little with which to compare, it meant the world to fans at home, especially young ones for whom it was deemed too soon to enter the fray of the national stadium.

On the very same afternoon in Rome, Diego Maradona scored the only goal of the game to secure Napoli a win over Roma and put them top of Serie A, where they would not be replaced for the rest of the season. Before the match, those famous warm-up ball-juggling skills were on dazzling show but viewers in the United Kingdom would only see them later in the 1989 film on the man, Live is Life. On that Sunday he might as well have been playing on the moon. For all the snippets of action that would find their way up here and even the summer festivals of international contests that would be shown every two years, this was where the footballing world began and ended and therefore the results meant so much more.

The doors to this world were only open late on a Saturday night and early on a Sunday evening as BBC Scotland and STV shared highlights on those respective slots, ensuring an interminable wait for fans whose side were covered by STV's Scotsport that weekend. The only regular live action was exclusively for the ears and for that, most fans tuned into Radio Clyde, which had the rights to broadcast the final five minutes of the first half and the second half live. With the increased use of portable transistor radios, fans were kept up to date with action elsewhere while they were at their own team's match, in the days when almost all games were played at the same time. In addition to that was Open Line which became a fixture of journeys home from the game in the car. Introduced by Richard Park and Paul Cooney in the mid-1980s, it was another feature that the former had brought to the station from his time in the USA, as well as background music to goals in a post-match round-up. It ensued rampaging arguments but ones which were mostly entertaining. Its 21st-century iteration may have become a haven for opposition fans to feast on the misery of their rivals and their crackpot theories but, for several years, that hour between 5pm and 6pm on a Saturday was the home of some genuine debate and good humour, and all of that simply bound this closed community even tighter. Before social media ensured that public debate never ended – and so could only get worse – here was a defined time and place for it all to take place live and, as such, it was almost a national appointment.

With three outlets came three voices. There were others in a supporting cast but the trifecta of Archie Macpherson, Jock Brown and Gerry McNee was unsurpassed as the chief narrators of our national game throughout this period. Macpherson was the elder statesman of the three, a school teacher by profession and, via his early broadcasting the career with the BBC he had the bigger international distinction.[62] Taking the lead from David Coleman and Brian Moore – the doyens of 1970s commentary – Macpherson's narration was often a case of 'less is more' but no less authoritative with it. 'It's there' or '2-1' is often all you would get, in calm tones as Macpherson would allow the match atmosphere to escape through the television set and into millions of homes. Even when the words were dramatic, the voice rarely seemed to rise, always keeping things in scholarly check. In the future he would be parodied on the BBC's Only An Excuse comedy sketch show with his famous, excitable 'Woof!', but that was perhaps only relevant later in his career as he moved with the times as the production of live football reached heightened levels of sensationalism.

Jock Brown was already there. The practising solicitor and partner at law was far more verbose on STV than his BBC counterpart. The big-match moments

---

62   His commentary of Archie Gemmill's goal against the Netherlands in the 1978 World Cup gained even greater fame following the release of *Trainspotting*.

were matched by his excitement and quickfire levels of description but his real talent, perhaps understandably, was in his summing up. 'A goal made in England' was the perfect response, in the moment, to capture Ray Wilkins' volley against Celtic at Ibrox in August 1988 as the match and the balance of power in Scotland swung sharply. It was an iconic moment – he knew it – and his words made as indelible a mark on the minds of those who watched those highlights as the goal itself. Like so many moments in television coverage of sport, when the words match the pictures so perfectly, immortality often beckons.

Originally on Radio Clyde, Gerry McNee didn't have pictures with which to work. The self-appointed 'Voice of Football' was the journalist and columnist made manifest on the airwaves. His tone had more than a little hint of pomposity about it and describing the action was never enough. Opinion had to be part of the narrative, especially when there was a phone-in to excite the masses about. This meant that he had to take sides more obviously than his colleagues on other stations and the man who had grown up supporting Celtic – who had written books about them – perhaps felt an acute need to poke and provoke his boyhood club on air and in print. Later, as the 1990s unfolded, he would manage to deal with the cognitive dissonance of his weekly criticism of Rangers midfielder Paul Gascoigne – which reached the almost dehumanising stage of McNee refusing to call him by his name and instead using the moniker 'Number Eight' – and his energised and passionate commentary of the Englishman's title-winning hat-trick in 1996. It was almost as if this was all an act.

All three men swapped microphones in 1990, with Macpherson making the move to radio, McNeee to television and Brown the jump from STV to BBC. It was also a summer that was a significant plot point in the quickening development of football coverage throughout the country. Before then, exposure to live football in Scotland was very limited. In 1986/87 Scottish fans were treated to eight live matches and five of those were due only to Dundee United's run to the two-legged UEFA Cup Final. European finals were only live if there was a British interest – which extended to Terry Venables managing Barcelona in the 1986 European Cup Final against Steaua Bucharest – but between 1987 and 1991 there was very little in the way of live coverage. This meant that in Scotland, unless you had some nascent satellite technology, the great AC Milan side of 1988 to 1990 were only accessible in snapshots, with their two European Cup finals coming to us via Sportsnight highlights.

English football was also restricted. Live FA Cup finals in the 1980s were only shown if there was a replay due to the clash of dates with the Scottish Cup Final[63] and even when the Football League finally saw the full opportunities that television had when it sold the rights to ITV for £44m in exchange for live Sunday matches from October 1988 to May 1992,[64] it still didn't apply north of the border apart from the odd exception, such as the incredible Friday night denouement of the 1988/89 season at Anfield. Manchester United drew 1-1 with Everton at Goodison Park on Sunday, 30 October 1988 – the first live Sunday match in this

---

63   Only six FA Cup finals were seen live in Scotland before 1992 and four of those were replays.

64   There had been live Sunday fixtures since 1983 but not on this level and relationships were fractious, as exemplified by the blackout strike during 1985/86.

new deal – but viewers in Scotland had to make do with Broadway Serenade from 1939. It was all done deliberately to protect the mystique of the domestic story, like some kind of Soviet sporting paradise. It wouldn't be long, however, until our own wall came crashing down.

With the World Cup being held in Italy in the summer of 1990, the floodgates opened and everything began to change. Live football was now on every day for a whole month and crucially with ideal kick-off times[65]. Arguably the only World Cup to have ever taken place in a country that was the sport's epicentre at the time of the tournament, there can be criticism over the quality of attacking football but absolutely none about the sheer drama that seemed to unfold on a daily basis and it was the coverage of this that changed the game in broadcasting. The BBC's touch was operatic as Luciano Pavarotti's version of 'Nessun Dorma' became the soundtrack to the summer. It was not, however, overdone and – for the 1990s at least – this balance was struck perfectly with Puccini, Bernstein and Faure before the tipping point was reached in the 21st century and Bolton v West Ham would be sold as the imminent apocalypse. Then, however, there was an understanding that sport produces a kind of tension that no writer possibly can. Pavarotti's contribution simply amplified the action and, with Toto Schillachi's eyes and Paul Gascoigne's tears, they engaged the middle classes and made football executives realise that the solution to the carnage and violence of the 1970s and 1980s had been staring them in the face from the corner of the living room all along. Make the event an attractive one and people will want to be a part of it. In England they did, and soon enough the draw that Rangers had enjoyed since the revolution started would quickly weaken.

Our understanding of the game was changing too. Because the main feed came from the Italian broadcaster RAI, there was more emphasis on statistics and the tactical shape of a side was represented on screen. Every live game in Scotland until the Scottish Cup Final of 1990 had shown the team line-ups in either a vertical or horizontal line but on the first day of the 1990/91 season, the BBC highlights of Rangers v Dunfermline had the teams shown in formation. Even before the big bang of 1992, Sky could go into depth that terrestrial television couldn't do simply because it had the space to fill. Law changes – a feature of the game that would gather pace – were better discussed and as a result, left the audience better informed. In September 1991 there was a perfect example when the Scottish football media were up in arms about a red card that Pieter Huistra did not receive in a recent Old Firm game at Parkhead. The Footballer's Football Show – a panel discussion format on Sky – was able to easily explain how the new FIFA directives meant that, as Gary Stevens was sweeping up behind, it wasn't a sending-off offence. Small steps perhaps, but it was the start of an acceptance that fans could cope with more detail. It wouldn't be slow in coming.

For things to get better for those watching at home, they first had to become horrific for those who dared to enter the grounds. The Hillsborough disaster in April 1989 was finally English football's nadir, the moment whereby it couldn't ignore

---

65   Eurosport was still the only channel to screen every game of the tournament, as it would be in 1994. It wasn't until 1998 that BBC and ITV combined to provide access to the whole finals.

its decay any longer. Most of the requirements to changes in stadia contained in Lord Justice Taylor's report would no doubt have happened gradually without the tragedy, but it ensured that the pace of change had to be more rapid. The Taylor Report shaped how English football would look by the end of the 1990s but there was now a sudden need to pay for that renovation. English clubs, especially the 'Big Five' of Liverpool, Manchester United, Arsenal, Tottenham Hotspur and Everton, were forced to realise the market potential that their product had always had. Encouraged by Greg Dyke at ITV, who wanted to ensure the biggest sides were playing if he was paying, talks of a breakaway started soon after the World Cup but there was an initial challenge in bringing along the rest. The Football Association, at the time no great friends of the Football League, produced a document in April 1991 that recommended a Premier League in the best interests of English football but it wasn't until the spring of 1992 the split finally happened and the English Premier League would be born the following season. News of this announcement sparked panic in the Ibrox boardroom as frantic phone calls were made to the Football League, asking, 'What happened to the British Super League that we had talked about?' That ship had sailed, leaving Rangers high and dry.

The race to win the broadcasting contract was almost as dramatic as the coverage they would provide as Sky gazumped ITV at the 11th hour with a massive £304m bid. It was alleged by Dyke that Sky had been tipped off about ITV's bid by the then Tottenham chairman Alan Sugar, whose company Amstrad happened to make the satellite receivers for Rupert Murdoch's enterprise, when he was overheard on his mobile phone encouraging the person at the other end to 'blow them out the water'.[66] It all paved the way for 1992 being the year of lift-off, where that shelter that Scottish football enjoyed was blown away by the introduction of four different game-changers in the way a new generation of supporters would consume the game.

On Sunday, 16 August 1992, the first Super Sunday was broadcast on Sky, with Monday Night Football – fireworks, cheerleaders, live half-time music and all – following on the next evening.[67] The television ideas, like much of the new stadium redevelopment and matchday experience, were drawn from the success of NFL in the UK throughout the 1980s. Sky were always likely to market the new Premier League well and with little modesty but, crucially, they added depth and Andy Gray, now out of the ridiculous knitwear and into a suit or polo shirt, was the man who provided it. Andy Melvin was the deputy head of Sky Sports and was tasked with producing the new Premier League coverage. He recalled a conversation a few years before with Gray and David Livingstone – who at the time was presenting football and golf for Sky – in a Glasgow pub, where he asked the former international footballer what the difference really was between playing with a back three and back four. Gray moved around the empty beer bottles on the table to graphically demonstrate it in a way that Melvin would understand. When

---

66   Tottenham were only club in the 'Big Five' to vote for the Sky deal, the rest staying loyal to Dyke and ITV.

67   Teddy Sheringham scored the only goal of *Super Sunday*, his last for Nottingham Forest before his move to Spurs, as Liverpool lost at the City Ground. Manchester City then drew 1-1 with QPR on the Monday night at Maine Road.

the new deal commenced, he was asked to do that on television, but this time using a Subbuteo pitch pinned to a table and black and white draught checkers while talking to a current player in their club's kit room about what went right and wrong the previous week. Andy Gray's Boot Room was at 30-minute weekly show about football tactics in a time where the subject barely received a passing mention. Rudimentary production values perhaps, but it was the start of a much-needed revolution in how the British media talked about their game.

The rest of Sky's production values were ground-breaking, however, such as multi-angle instant replays in the gantry as well as for the viewers and the permanent clock and live score box in the top-right corner of the screen. It was a huge gamble for Sky – already haemorrhaging £1m a week for the Murdoch empire, they were 500,000 subscribers away from breaking even and were now forced to bid £30m more than planned for this new football league – but it paid off handsomely and millions flocked to watch the regular coverage. Even for those without a dish, the renewed Match of the Day on BBC1 every Saturday night gave viewers a better and quicker highlights package than the previous wait for Saint and Greavsie the following Saturday lunchtime as it had been under the ITV deal. Fans north of the border were effectively drawn towards a new television drama and, as such, were forced to choose their own heroes and villains. Scottish fans having a soft spot for an English club was nothing new but those numbers increased dramatically – especially among casual supporters – as did the replica kits on show. Kids at school in the 1990s had to have an English team.

They also had to have an Italian one. Serie A coverage wasn't new – it had been available to viewers in Wales on SC4 since 1988 and BSB and Sky had shown games sporadically before 1992 as well – but Channel 4's decision to buy the rights for live coverage was another huge moment in how the sport was shown in this country. Originally Michael Grade, chief executive of the channel between 1988 and 1997, had wanted to show only Lazio games, following the transfer for Paul Gascoigne from Tottenham, but that wasn't contractually possible so, with the success and impact of the World Cup still fresh in the mind, he decided to take the lot. It was, by some considerable distance, the best league on the planet, and from Sunday, 6 September 1992, when Lazio drew 3-3 away to Sampdoria, the greatest players in the world were on display every weekend on terrestrial television. The live Sunday match would often get ratings of three million and the highlights package Gazzetta – presented by James Richardson – would get 800,000 viewers on a Saturday morning, usually the preserve of children's programming. It was a surprise hit and the footballing public would further quench their burgeoning thirst for continental knowledge and appreciation that year when ITV spent some of what it had earmarked for the Premier League on the new UEFA Champions League. Viewers had felt lucky just to see the European Cup Final live in recent seasons and now there would be live coverage of the top level of European club football from the autumn through to the spring. Foreign superstars were no longer only accessible every four years at a World Cup or on selected highlights here and there. They were now a fixture of the living room and a deeper part of the footballing conversation.

This was also the season where the new back-pass law was introduced, meaning that goalkeepers would have to use their feet if the ball was passed to them. This was done to curb time-wasting, the most egregious of which happened in the World Cup where the Republic of Ireland drew 0-0 with Egypt and Pat Bonner had the ball in his hands for six minutes in total. Even the laws of the game were being changed for the sake of entertainment, just as football effectively became one big television series.

The final revolutionary introduction into the football media in 1992 helped to broaden that conversation even further. Prior to this footballing Year Zero, the beautiful game's adaptation to the computer screen had been basic at best. Management simulations that allowed users to make an unenforced substitution were considered futuristic but the release of Championship Manager was the start of a phenomenon. Written by two brothers – Paul and Oliver Collyer – from their bedroom, it became more than just a wildly popular and addictive computer game. As the series developed, it ensured that a generation needed to have a grasp of the more abstract elements of the game as well as going through the emotional highs and lows for 36 hours on end when they should have been studying for exams. Formational tweaks soon became established parts of the lexicon and, even at its most basic level, fans started to associate numbers with performance and attributes. The general information that could be gained of players from leagues further afield than those shown live on a Sunday afternoon was so prevalent that some clubs used the game engine as a basic scouting platform. Ordinary supporters had more knowledge about the game of football than they had ever had before and it is hard to conceive of such a welcome reaction to the more in-depth analytical writing of Jonathan Wilson and Michael Cox in the late 2000s had it not been for the rise of the manager games in the 1990s. From the terracing to the car, the living room to the bedroom, the television to the computer monitor, football consumption was becoming all-pervasive.

Rangers fans have always known who the greatest players in the world were and what wider trends were taking place in the game. It is not as if there was a complete blackout before 1992. However, the impact of consistent live football and quality highlights from different leagues cannot be underestimated. From having eight live matches in Scotland in 1986/87, all involving a Scottish club, and rarely reaching double figures throughout the next five seasons, to reaching over 80 in 1992/93 – where the best the world had to offer were on show on a regular basis – is an incredible jump.

All of sudden Rangers faced competition for a generation with only so much bandwidth with which to download all of this football. It wasn't direct competition – even those with two or three teams and all their replica strips would still prioritise the Ibrox club in their affections – but often it is the indirect competition that can be more significant in the longer run. The success of the Rangers revolution was arguably amplified in the imagination of those who savoured it because it took place behind this curtain of protection. But in the 1990s, the footballing world would suddenly seem a lot wider. Yes, Rangers were kings, but of a smaller castle now that more and more were looking at it through a new lens. A generation of supporters would now grow up being all too aware of the real benchmarks of success. Scotland wasn't enough now that they had seen what else was on offer and, in turn, Rangers would be held to different standards and with less patience than ever before. It was a generation who also grew up believing that they knew best when it came to who Rangers should be signing or the formational adjustments that the manager simply needed to make, solely off the back of a good cup run on a computer simulation. If they knew all about the anticipation and flair of a new Algerian forward, then why the hell didn't Walter Smith?

It wasn't just the younger generation, however. The success of football's new dawn was based on huge audiences tuning in and subscribing. In the summer of 1995, one contributor to Follow, Follow wrote to say that not even the arrival of Paul Gascoigne would tempt him to renew his season ticket, 'It's not enough to beat poor opposition by the odd goal. Entertainment is the name of the game, with the trophies being won in style. I have succumbed to the temptations of Sky TV and now have the power to watch games with more verve or simply switch channels if they show the lack of interest like that in the recent Old Firm game.'

After years of grainy footage and miserly access to the main events, we gorged ourselves silly on what was suddenly on offer and in so doing, helped feed the monster that would keep Rangers, and Scottish football, in the shadows for the foreseeable future.

5

A JOY TO BEHOLD

SEASON 1988/89

'Celtic are still basking in the glory of their centenary season success, but I can assure you all that we intend to make their joy as short-lived as possible.'
Graeme Souness, July 1988

'It's launched in-field by Stevens, there's Butcher. Back with Wilkins …'
Jock Brown

So much had changed and yet, as Joe Miller placed the ball on the penalty spot, thousands at the other end of the ground could have been forgiven for feeling that nothing had. With only seven minutes remaining of a game that Rangers had dominated for so long, Celtic had the chance to equalise and continue their long unbeaten Old Firm run at home. Richard Gough, on his way to becoming Scotland's player of the year, had presented them with the opportunity when his outstretched hand made contact with a ball that had bobbled wildly on the Parkhead surface all afternoon. The jinx – one of a few that a strangely superstitious Graeme Souness lamented in the diary that he kept that season – looked certain to provide the chasing pack with the slip that they had expected. Second-placed Aberdeen were best-suited to take advantage. Four points behind on that morning, a defeat of fellow chasers Dundee United at Pittodrie would surely bring them back into contention, with Rangers' record in the east end being as poor as it was.

Miller's penalty, however, like Celtic's title defence that season, was weak and devoid of the necessary energy and belief. Chris Woods stopped it and Gary Stevens was quickest to clear the danger completely. The last chance to catch Rangers had been snuffed out. 'This was a decisive day as far as the title is concerned,' Souness wrote later. 'I'm sure that EVERYONE, but EVERYONE, from Aberdeen right down through the whole country will realise it,' he added. His emphasis encapsulated the extent to which he was proud of his side's response to the disappointment from the previous year. Front-runners from the start, it was a display of power and prowess that set it apart from the first two seasons of the Souness era. There was no long, chaotic game of catch-up following a shambolic start and, although significant injury would strike again, Rangers now had a squad with the depth that could absorb the blows and respond strongly.

It was a season that resonated far beyond the one footballing calendar. On and off the pitch, the pace of modernisation at Ibrox outstripped Scottish football by some distance which in turn would create a chasm that had not been seen in the country for a generation. Rangers landed big victories in 1988/89 – both in terms of margin and importance – that acted as a bellwether for the impending new decade. During those first two years questions persisted about Souness's long-term commitment, the hunger of the English mercenaries to bounce back from setbacks and the impact that the wild temperament within the squad had on consistency. By the end of the third season, that noise had subsided.

This is a tale of transition from an inconsistent and immature impertinence to a more measured and balanced team that was now playing for keeps. The campaign would have setbacks – as would those that followed – but by its conclusion all of Scottish football had started to realise that it would now take more than a few bad results to knock Rangers off course in achieving their number one aim. Before 1 April 1989, Rangers hadn't beaten Celtic away from home in nine years. After that day, 12 years would pass before they would fail to go through a season without such a victory again. Rangers had only retained the league title twice in the previous 30 years. By the time they next lost out there would be teenage fans unable to recall how that once felt.

What was exceptional would soon become customary, the transformation from rarity to routine. Far from being flaky and unreliable, Rangers were now becoming a machine.

* * *

High up in the hills of northern Tuscany, minutes from the Medici palaces of Barga, lies the 'Living Mountain', a 600-hectare-long vista marked by olive groves, terraced vineyards and picturesque villages. It also plays host to the luxury Il Ciocco resort, a sprawling network of hotels, chalets, restaurants and sports facilities 3,600ft above sea level, and it was from this base that Graeme Souness launched his championship fightback. After three days of running to, from and around Bellahouston Park, the Rangers players were given beautiful weather and food in exchange for ten days of the most punishing pre-season training that any of them could remember. Three sessions every day – morning, noon and night – focusing on ball work and stamina provided the kind of modern, professional framework that had been badly missing the year before. 'By the evening we were too tired to do anything else other than have dinner,' wrote Terry Butcher. 'Even if we went to the bar it was for water, because we were there for one reason only – to get fit.'[68] The impact of the work at altitude was not lost on the players upon their return home, via a full health and technical assessment at Lilleshall, most of whom raved about how fit they now felt. Il Ciocco borders the Garfagnana – the green lung of Tuscany – and it was a trip that would breathe new life into the Rangers revolution.

Something had to do it. While the players were in Italy, the club's annual report was released with a clear message from David Holmes. Referring to the previous

---

68   The squad were allowed one night out for bonding which ended with Butcher and Woods challenging their team-mates to a fight on the bus back to the hotel. No headshots, body only.

season's 'traumatic' experience, the chairman drew a line that was visible from space, 'It has always been an honour to pull on the blue shirt of Rangers. There follows from that certain responsibilities to maintain the high standards of the club both on and off the field. If a player's on- or off-the-field behaviour brings the club into disrepute he becomes a liability. If a player cannot accept the discipline imposed by an officer of the club then he cannot stay with us.' However, both he and Souness, writing in the club's accompanying yearbook, were adamant that there would be no continuation of the debilitating inconsistency and turmoil that eroded the morale of that dressing room. 'The only team who can stop us regaining the title are ourselves,' the manager asserted.

Privately, before the squad met up, Souness was less bombastic. In his diary he shared concerns about how his squad would respond and that he was 'beginning to wonder what the season will hold for us'. His sense of apprehension wasn't confined to his players, 'I have a feeling that the chairman has lost some of his enthusiasm. I would never have believed that possible. During my first season David Holmes was a tower of strength to myself and Walter Smith – maybe now he has had enough. He took a buffeting on all sides last season. Perhaps that explains why he is not quite as bouncy as he was before.' His inkling would have more relevance later in the season but that summer Holmes delivered for Souness once again. He finished his report address in an upbeat fashion by reassuring shareholders that the management team had 'assembled a squad of players who have the ability to put this club where it belongs – at the top'.

The traditional summer dance to land Mark Hateley ended quickly – the player was keen but Monaco wouldn't budge – and so Souness opted for Norwich City's Kevin Drinkell as his target man. Rangers had been keen to sign Drinkell during the previous season – his 12 goals went a long way to keeping Norwich in the First Division – but due to the dogfight that they found themselves in at the bottom of the table, they were unwilling to let him go. Once their safety had been secured, £500,000 and the Ibrox lure now becoming very familiar to English footballers was enough to fight off Manchester United and Spurs yet again to a prized asset. Six feet tall and full of power, Drinkell would prove popular with fans and team-mates alike, providing not only great link-up play but plenty of goals to boot.

With Graham Roberts certain to be on his way out[69], Souness needed to address the gap at the other end of the pitch. A bid for the Derby County centre-half Mark Wright was rejected and rumours linking Rangers to the promising young Gary Pallister from Middlesborough came to nothing, but it suggests that Souness's initial thought was to bring in another established central defender and move Richard Gough back to his original position at right-back. That plan changed when it became known that the best player in that position in Britain was restless.

After seven years at Everton, where he had won two league championships, an FA Cup and a European Cup Winners' Cup, Gary Stevens felt that it was time for a move. His performances had started to dip and his relationship with his manager Colin Harvey was not as fruitful as it had been under Howard Kendall, who had left Goodison in the summer of 1987. England's calamity at the European

---

69   In the end a protracted affair until Rangers got the £475,000 they were after from Chelsea
      on 7 August.

Championship – where Stevens had started all three defeats – had only soured his mood further. Change was needed and Rangers were only too happy to help, as they spent another £1m to try and bring some much-needed stability at the back.[70]

Souness had often lamented the constant need to chop and change in that vital area of the field the previous season and believed that Stevens would be a key component in locking that back door. 'He [Stevens] is the ideal modern defender,' the manager wrote. 'Quick. Athletic. Strong. He gets tight on his opponent, he can get across to cover and he is the best at reading a situation.' On the odd occasion that any opponent got past Stevens, Souness was sure that he had 'the pace to get back at them'. This energy and fitness – he was by far the best player on the post-Italy beep test – would provide Souness with the reliability he wanted as Stevens missed only one game throughout the entire season.

The signing of Stevens brought the spending to just over £7m in two years but, with the previous campaign's five mid-term new faces already settled in and Derek Ferguson and Ally McCoist tied up on new long-term deals, it was now an established squad filled with quality. Rangers started the new season with arguably the best goalkeeper and right-back in the Britain alongside two of its finest central defenders, three very promising young Scottish midfielders, a winger who would end up in the World Soccer top 20 players of 1988 and, of course, Scotland's sharpest striker. In stark contrast to the spiky, irritable interview he gave on the eve of the previous season where he appeared to resist the pressure of going for multiple titles, Souness was full of confidence this time around. Delighted with the work that had been done, he was comfortable when saying that Rangers would be 'going all out to win everything we enter. That's the way it has to be at this club.' For all the bitterness of 1987/88, there was still reason for Rangers fans to be positive and, for all the new arrivals, there was only one player they wanted to see back in action.

Those first glimpses of Terry Butcher's return were difficult to catch. An SFA ruling that prohibited fans from attending games before 30 July meant that many Rangers supporters had to clamber on the gates and walls of Lesser Hampden to see Rangers take on Queen's Park. Souness had rejected a £1m bid for Butcher that week, the second of that value in the space of a year[71], which showed a remarkable amount of faith in his captain's recovery untested as it was by a competitive contest. He came through that first match well as Rangers ramped up their pre-season games against Scotland's lower-league sides[72] before the showpiece match at Ibrox four days prior to the league getting under way. It was a special August evening as

---

70   Everton initially wanted £1.4m but it was quickly sorted out between Souness and Harvey.

71   Manchester United had tried to buy him just before the match with Aberdeen in November 1987 where his season ended and now it was Tottenham who were back in the hunt.

72   Kilmarnock, Raith Rovers, Ayr United and Clydebank were all used in a short space of time upon returning from Tuscany, where they only played one game against a side of local amateurs. This approach was far more structured and considered than the previous tours which mixed both training and games too much. Light Sunday training sessions were also introduced instead of allowing that gap before recovering on the Monday. It was an early example of the sports science advances that were being taken on board.

thousands of fans were locked out, such was the interest. Bordeaux, runners-up to Monaco in Ligue 1 the season before[73], provided quality opposition with the likes of Jean Tigana, Clive Allen and Enzo Scifo and the 43,000 were treated to a 3-1 win with Butcher and Drinkell marking their return and debut respectively with a goal before McCoist made sure with a beautiful strike near the end.

As good as the entertainment was, it wasn't why fans were trying to bribe their way into the ground. After 11 years of service, Davie Cooper was entering his testimonial year at Rangers and, as it would turn out, his last. This night belonged to him, an ideal way for a support to pay homage to the one remaining hero whose career touched two eras of glory and who had provided them with one of their rare lights during the darker years in between.[74] A Rangers fan who could have played almost anywhere but was happy to play for the club he loved, he was perhaps only fully appreciated as his time began to draw to a close, although it was a swansong that was packed full of high notes. Fittingly for a player who spent too many years carrying team-mates who were not fit to play in the same team as him, he was lifted shoulder-high by a side brimming with talent and who were all desperate to go again.

It was a seamless transition from a promising pre-season to a realisation of results. From a Stevens goal at Douglas Park against Hamilton on the opening day, Rangers ripped though the opening eight league games, dropping only one point along the way. That 2-0 victory against the Accies was matched by expected wins at home to St Mirren and Dundee but the three away victories at Motherwell, Hearts and Dundee United – traditionally difficult trips – showed an early resolve in this side coupled with, in the case of the 1-0 win at Tannadice, some excellent football. Ian Ferguson's header seven minutes from time was the least that his side deserved that night with a showing that left even Jim McLean compelled to remark, 'There was just one team on the park … Rangers were miles ahead and, I thought, tactically brilliant.' For the first time under Souness, there was no fumbling around at the starting line and although this run – the best that Rangers had enjoyed since 1974/75 – had its roots in Tuscany, it was jet-propelled by one afternoon in Govan.

In contrast to so many iterations of this old encounter when he had been manager, Souness had near enough a full squad from which to choose when Celtic visited Ibrox on 27 August. Only Stuart Munro was missing but would be covered more than adequately by John Brown at left-back. His opposite number Billy McNeill, however, had some headaches as the constant summer speculation regarding Frank McAvennie's return to London showed no signs of abating. In a stunning statement of prescient accuracy, McNeill told the press the day before the game, 'There's as much chance of McAvennie moving as there is of Rangers beating us 5-1 tomorrow.'

With Pat Bonner injured and Alan McKnight sold, McNeill's more pressing concern was who to throw in for their Old Firm goalkeeping debut. In the end he chose his recent £250,000 signing from Leicester City, Ian Andrews, over the

---

73   Monaco were the original opponents for the match before pulling out. Ironically Rangers
       played in their new away strip that was a copy of the Monaco red and white diagonal design.

74   Cooper's first season at Ibrox, in 1977/78, was the last title-winning side before the arrival of
       Souness.

veteran Alan Rough but the Englishman didn't sound fazed in the build-up to the big game, 'I've not seen very much of Rangers but that doesn't worry me. If we do our job properly we'll beat them. I know nerves will come into it at some point … it all helps to keep you on your toes.' By the time the teams lined up in the tunnel, things had changed for Andrews. 'I looked at him and saw his eyes were glazed,' wrote Butcher. 'I turned to Woodsy and told him his opposite number was all over the place and we would win this one.'

In many ways the early exchanges were typical fare for this fixture – blustery conditions, frantic pace, bad tackles and poor passes – with an early goal apiece owing as much to slapstick defending as it did to the clinical awareness and execution of McAvennie and McCoist. And yet, there was always something extra in the air that day as a mixture of sporting intrigue and political tension ensured that it wasn't going to follow the normal pattern of draws or victories by the odd goal or two.[75] The new champions visiting the challengers, stung by the loss of the crown they assumed would be theirs for the foreseeable future and aching to regain it, in a fixture that had recently seen players end up in court was added to the darker strain of current affairs that summer. An IRA campaign of violence had reached its crescendo that week when seven British soldiers were killed by a bomb attack on their bus and, if former players on the after-dinner circuit are to be believed, it was a story opportunistically included in the dressing room motivation for a starting XI that contained six Englishmen. This was also the day that Rangers kitman Jimmy Bell decided to permanently fix a picture of Queen Elizabeth II on the dressing room wall, under which it was decided the team's captain should sit. It was no coincidence.

As the clouds parted and the sun shone on the righteous, it was one of those Englishmen who turned the game on a new course in the most spectacular fashion. The constant jibes in those early years that the revolving door of English mercenaries wouldn't provide Rangers with what they needed when it really mattered were finally silenced that afternoon but there was no question that with so many players at Ibrox for such short spells, most would never make a big impact. Ray Wilkins spent just under two years as a Rangers player but the resonance of that spell is stronger for some who could triple the length of his contract. The 'goal made in England', as Jock Brown described it on commentary, started with a throw-in from Stevens, and was concluded after a header by Butcher which eventually sat up for Wilkins to stun Celtic with a perfect volley from the edge of the box. Where McCoist's equaliser was celebrated with faces of adrenaline-fuelled tension, this strike saw Rangers players react with pure joy.

Tommy Burns was removed at half-time due to injury and McNeill replaced him with a defender in Derek Whyte instead of the more attack-minded option of Joe Miller but any plans for establishing a second-half period of calm were shattered within a minute as Andrews flapped at a looping McCoist header. The floodgates were opening. Mark Walters, who had done an excellent defensive job on limiting the threat of Chris Morris on the Celtic right, was now given the freedom to turn up anywhere he wished and his movement, speed of feet and

---

75   Only three times in the last 40 Old Firm league games had there been a margin of three
      goals.

excellent cross presented Drinkell with the opportunity for an Old Firm debut goal which he took with a thunderous header. The fifth could have easily been a penalty when McCoist was bundled over by Roy Aitken but Walters didn't wait to ask as he rolled the ball home as Ibrox moved from tension to delirium.

With just under half an hour to go it could have been more and the chance to set new records was very much on the mind of Brown, Durrant, McCoist and Ian Ferguson. Such trivia was lost on Souness, never having been completely immersed in the city's obsession, and he came on as a substitute to calm the hysteria and complete Celtic's humiliation in a very different way: by hardly allowing them a touch of the ball. It was a truly remarkable victory – a margin that hadn't been seen in the fixture for 22 years – and thus, easy for the immediate reaction to be hyperbolic. Tommy Burns felt compelled to do an interview on Scotsport the following day to apologise and followed it up in the press by saying, 'In all my years with Celtic I have never been involved in anything so humiliating. However, it won't happen again.' Except, of course, that it would. This result was a strong signal and some of media reaction on the Monday grasped it. The two-year period of adjustment was now over. Those Rangers players who weren't 'dyed in the wool' now knew enough about what was required and could power on with their demonstration of quality. Stunned and bewildered, Celtic went on to lose three of their next five league games and crashed out of the League Cup. Rangers went top of the Scottish Premier Division that afternoon, in its third week, and would not be removed from that spot for the rest of the season.

While the League Cup was the familiar early season cruise, scoring 13 goals in the first three rounds, the UEFA Cup draw sent Rangers behind the Iron Curtain for the fourth time in a row. Katowice were the first-round opponents and the first leg at Ibrox was a scrappy affair that Rangers were fortunate to get out of with a 1-0 win. Walters eased the nerves with his second-half goal but the Poles could have easily been ahead before half-time, with Stevens being forced to clear off the goal line on one occasion. Those familiar frustrations and moments of ill-discipline crept back in a little when Brown was given a ban for throwing the Polish physio's medical bag off the pitch, with its contents spilling out all over the track. That loss of concentration that was becoming in endemic in Europe was evident at the start of the second leg, with Rangers one down within four minutes as Woods slipped when diving to stop a Jan Furtok free kick.

From there, however, it was an almost perfect European away performance. Rangers peppered the Polish box with corners before Butcher powered one home on 12 minutes and then added another from a free kick four minutes later. Woods atoned for the early error with some great stops early in the second before he was finally beaten by Mirosław Kubisztal to level things up on the night. There was no Rangers retreat, however, as Durrant and Ian Ferguson scored two more to put it all well out of sight. Souness felt the two final goals were 'fitting because I thought they were the best players on the park'. For Durrant especially, it was just another step on an upward career trajectory that was reaching for the stars. Beside Davie Cooper, he was the most natural creative force in the Rangers team and was the obvious heir to his role as the homegrown genius who loved his club as much as the sport itself. In a game where simply wanting it isn't enough, the resonance of players who can match supreme talent with an instinctive appreciation for those who pay to watch is incalculable.

Cooper started alongside Durrant in Poland that night. The two men would never line up together for Rangers again.

* * *

Although satisfied with the work done in pre-season, there was one concern gnawing at Souness as matters got under way for real. 'The only worry on the horizon is the constant fear of injuries to key players,' he wrote on 12 August. 'Last season was a nightmare for us. And, since I came here as manager, I have found it hard to come to terms with the amount of injuries we pick up.' For understandable reasons, Souness compared so much of his Rangers experience with his time at Anfield and initially was amazed at how that Liverpool side could win a title using only 14 players when he had used 26 and 29 in his first two seasons as manager respectively. Eventually he realised that the reality of being a Rangers player is that every week is someone's cup final. He relayed a story about Bill Struth, told to him by the veteran football writer Jim Rodger, where he used to say to potential signings, 'I hear you are a great player, son, but can you play for Rangers?' That, according to Souness, was what it was all about: the ability to face up to the unrelenting physical and mental pressure of the small pond.

On 8 October, his side's unbeaten start to the season would face its biggest threat. Aberdeen v Rangers is not a fixture that needed any extra spice but Souness, never totally at peace with the make-up of his squad, added some anyway by bringing former Dons hero Neale Cooper to Ibrox in order to strengthen his midfield options after yet another falling-out with Derek Ferguson, who failed to make the squad 16 times in the first 20 games. Cooper would score the opening goal, and celebrated wildly, but Aberdeen came roaring back in the second half and, after Jim Bett had equalised from the penalty spot, Charlie Nicholas grabbed a winner with a looping header only five minutes from time. A disappointment but a result that Souness wrote 'did not matter to any of us'. Walters called it 'one of the dirtiest matches I had ever played in' and he failed to come back out for the second half due to injury, McCoist needed stitches in the head and Brown suffered a bad leg injury. All were trivial in comparison to the game's main incident.

It took only eight minutes for those simmering pre-match tensions to erupt. Cooper had won the ball from John Hewitt and, as he got back to his feet, was clattered by Robert Connor. Referee Louis Thow blew the whistle for a free kick as the ball ran into space near Durrant. Normally so aware of what was happening around him he uncharacteristically relaxed as he slowed down to control the ball and try a quick free kick. Despite being the player closest to the referee's whistle, Neil Simpson's rage carried him through regardless and a young career was left hanging in the balance. The images of Durrant being carried off on the back of Phil Boersma, weeping as his shattered right leg dangled limply, were burned on any fan who saw them later that evening. He has always refused to blame Boersma and insisted that he screamed at him to get him off the field when it was clear that no stretcher was being made available. Either way the whole incident was a sad incitement of where Scottish football was as the sport in general was developing far beyond it. The lack of medical support, the viciousness of the assault itself and the tribal reaction from the home support that saw Durrant as the villain then and since[76] were all indicative of a game still lost in a backwater.

The damage – the medial, anterior and posterior ligament all ruptured and the lateral stretched – was likened by his surgeon to something from a serious car crash. It would have to be entirely rebuilt as would a career that many, including his manager, felt had few limits. The severity wasn't fully appreciated by the Rangers players or management at the time nor at the interval, as Durrant lay sedated in the medical room with David Holmes throughout the match where he was told by the chairman that the club would stand by him, 'I promise you that.' By the time they were back on the bus, with Durrant strapped in at the back, they were dumbstruck with Souness feeling an acute sense of guilt that he wasn't the one out there taking that blow during the final act of his career.[77] Durrant likened the reaction of Souness, Smith and Holmes to mourners at his bedside when his surgeon delivered the post-op message that he may never play again. Aged just 21, his club's most prized asset and the potential to carry his country to levels they had never reached, and it could all have been just switched off. The club were true to Holmes's word in their investment and dedication to his long recovery but the more immediate term shock was visceral. Yet again the autumn had brought Rangers a major injury.

The defeat at Pittodrie left Rangers only two points clear at the top with a midweek visit to Hibs, the only other side to take anything in that opening run of games, following close on the heels. What could have been precarious was comfortable and assured; McCoist's excellent strike in the 23rd minute all that was required as the gap was extended by a further point. If the theme of the first two months of the league season was strong front-runners then the next three months – which would not be without difficulty – was one of using that buffer to ride out the storms. A 1-1 draw at St Mirren would follow at the end of October but the only damage done was to McCoist who went down with another hamstring injury that, despite some early positive noises, would keep him out until January. Most likely the consequence of over-reliance throughout the last few years, it was yet another gap that was filled with a short-term experienced replacement in the form of lifelong fan Andy Gray. He had been brought up in September when both McCoist and Drinkell were out with short-term hamstring problems, to provide exactly the kind of cover that had been missing the previous season and popped up at the death in Paisley to keep the momentum going with a late equaliser and would continue his streak at Ibrox the following week with a 3-0 win over Hearts.

It was Hearts who Rangers had faced in the week that Gray arrived, Souness sending his team out in the League Cup semi-final at Hampden with no recognised

---

76   Aberdeen fans screamed abuse at Durrant as he left the ground on a stretcher and that was just the start of a decade and more of hate mail.

77   Bizarrely, despite facing more potential police action for kicking the referee's door in after the game, Terry Butcher wasn't present on that journey but instead having dinner and staying with the Aberdeen captain Willie Miller that evening. There was no court case this time.

striker on the field. He used Scott Nisbet and Mark Walters in an improvised front two and both scored, the latter twice, in a comfortable 3-0 win that saw them meet Aberdeen once again in the final. Taking place just two weeks after the infamous league game, concerns were high about such a showpiece event becoming a revenge match. The BBC, as part of their studio guest line-up, had former grade one referee Alan Ferguson in to speculate on the job that the match referee George Smith had in store. He wasn't ambiguous in his thoughts on Simpson's selection for the final, 'I'm absolutely astonished at the naivety of the Aberdeen management and Aberdeen as a club, that Simpson is actually on the park today. I think that if you're trying to stop vendettas happening then you have to remove the source of that vendetta in the first place.' It was something that weighed on Souness's mind too as he tried to find a balance between avoiding mayhem and curbing the natural aggression required to win a big game. Not easy when the impact of Durrant's injury was still so raw. 'Durrant was one of the most popular players in the dressing room. Everyone had been upset about the injury,' wrote the boss. In the end all those fears were misplaced as both sides, even with their rivalry starting to rise to preeminence in the country, played out another fantastic final.

While it was almost impossible to top the previous season's showpiece, it was a fine effort that came alive in its final third. Rangers had taken the lead through a McCoist penalty, the result of a scrappy bit of play in the Aberdeen defence between David Robertson and Theo Snelders – both future Rangers players – before the latter had to haul down the alert Drinkell just inside the box but the leaders returned the favour soon after when they failed to clear their lines and presented David Dodds with the chance to nudge Aberdeen level. The explosion that defined this particular fixture was a moment of beauty rather than violence. With just over 30 minutes remaining, a Stevens throw was nudged away from Drinkell but only as far as Ian Ferguson, whose bicycle kick smashed the ball into the top corner and the game ignited into a classic end-to-end drama. Walters and McCoist went close from great Rangers moves before Dodds equalised in a sequence that left both Butcher and Woods looking anything but pretty. Woods atoned by preventing the ultimate nightmare scenario when he tipped Simpson's chip over the bar and Bett and McCoist both missed great chances as the game headed for extra time. In the end it wasn't required. The final two minutes produced two moments of pinball wizardry in the respective penalty areas but McCoist capitalised where Dodds couldn't and Rangers won the cup once again. It was a win that signified so much about the changes that had occurred at Ibrox since that last final. Only two Rangers players – Gough and McCoist – played in both matches and, just when a valuable piece of midfield dynamite was removed, Rangers were able to call on another star to stand up. Souness, who felt that Ferguson was maligned during his start because of the need to play him up front at the end of 1987/88, took him over to the supporters where he raised his player's hand to a more appropriate acclaim. A new hero was born.

It was genuinely a new Rangers but there were still some old, familiar failures, especially in Europe. 'For 75 minutes we played the perfect European away leg in the Müngersdorfer Stadion,' said Souness. Butcher had a good chance in the first half and McCoist missed a sitter in the second but it was a strangely comfortable display against 1. FC Köln, a difficult challenge including five members of the West German side that would win the World Cup in 1990 including Bodo Illgner, Pierre Littbarksi, Thomas Häßler and Jürgen Kohler whom Walters said never gave him a touch of the ball. And then, after an even contest the concentration issue returned. Gary Stevens misjudged the bounce of a cross and, while Olaf Janßen's lob was expertly executed, Woods was a long way off his line and was thus rendered helpless. Trailing 1-0 was not the end of the world but within ten minutes, the whole complexion of the tie was changed with a smart Köln move that dragged both Butcher and Gough out of position before Thomas Allofs poked it home. Perhaps it was fatigue – the League Cup Final had been played only three days earlier and Souness didn't make a single substitute, making only two changes for this game – but it was then that the old Rangers really did come through when McCoist, in the final minute, launched a wild challenge on Paul Steiner that fully justified his red card. Drinkell finally found a Rangers goal at Ibrox in the second leg but it was too late on the night to launch a proper assault and the gaps left were exploited when Köln equalised with the last kick of the ball. Europe remained a mystery to a manager who had conquered it so often as a player.

It was a European game that was now on a different path to the one that Souness had dominated as part of that Liverpool midfield. The source of that diversion can be traced back to the Old Course at St Andrews where UEFA had met on 3 May 1988 to implement new rules that would shape European football for the 1990s. As of the following season – 1988/89 – any club side involved in one of Europe's three competitions would only be allowed to field up to four 'foreigners' in those ties. The principle wasn't new – Italy and Spain had league limits of two but were about to raise that to three – and the same rules were in place in the British league systems too. The only difference on these islands was that all home nations were counted as one and the same for that purpose whereas UEFA's plan would involve demarcation by individual association.

It is probably no coincidence that this change to the laws came about in tandem with a renewed debate on when to let English clubs back into the fold. Talks were held throughout the first half of 1988 about a potential re-entry the following season but much would depend on the behaviour of English fans at that summer's European Championship in West Germany. The results were predictably awful and the ban would remain in place for another two years. Jacques Georges, the French president of UEFA, justified the decision to limit foreign players in European competition by saying that it was done 'to help national teams with their build-ups, encourage young players, and give more clubs an equal chance'. All very noble but a more cynical view would be that it was a blunt attempt to limit the power of English clubs upon their eventual return. When Liverpool took to field on that fateful night in Belgium, nine of their players weren't English and of their team that won the FA Cup to complete the double in 1986, only Craig Johnston would have qualified to play at Wembley on another occasion in an England shirt. The grip that English clubs had wielded on the Big Cup was traditionally strengthened from all corners of the United Kingdom and the Republic of Ireland. Never again, if UEFA had their way.

For Rangers – with the revolution being so dependent on English internationals – this presented an immediate problem although UEFA were kind enough to provide three years of grace. Any 'foreign' player on the books of a club at the end of the 1987/88 season – from Mark Hateley at Monaco to Diego Maradona at Napoli – would be naturalised for three years if they stayed at that club. Only new signings would count and then all bets were off at the start of the 1991/92 season. That was all for another day.

By the time Rangers faced Celtic again, at Parkhead on 12 November, both were out of continental competition. Once again the side who took the lead first were soundly defeated but this time it was Rangers who were on the receiving end. An early Walters penalty was cancelled out by his captain – Butcher scored more goals past Woods than any Premier Division striker – and a hungrier Celtic went on to a deserved 3-1 win. A 0-0 draw at Dundee left Rangers only two points ahead of Aberdeen at the top, although six ahead of Celtic, but the pressure was beginning to build. McCoist's absence was exacerbated when, following the Celtic game, Woods came down with what was believed to be a flu but would in fact transpire to be labyrinthitis. In addition to the loss of Durrant, Rangers would now be without two other key players for the difficult Scottish winter. The injury jinx had returned. Talks were had with Newcastle United to try and bring John Robertson back home to Scotland following a short spell away from Hearts, but it wasn't a deal that could be done in the end. Very few realised that Souness was currently involved in another deal that would change the pace of Rangers' modernisation significantly.

* * *

In the late 1980s, if you were ever fortunate enough to spend a Friday evening dining at Raffaelli's in Edinburgh, just around the corner from Charlotte Square, you would most likely see Graeme Souness, sat at his usual table, keeping a regular dinner date with a friend. The pair had been introduced shortly after Souness's arrival back in Scotland when he was a guest for some time at the hotel owned by his new acquaintance. Despite personal tragedy he was a rising star in Scottish business, mainly in steel but had dabbled in the world of sport with an attempt to create a wider interest in British basketball and an unsuccessful bid to buy his hometown football club, Ayr United. Souness had often told them that, if he really wanted to get into football, then it should be at the top. By the summer of 1988, with his observations about the change in energy in David Holmes fresh in his mind, he started to suggest that Rangers might well be a possibility. David Murray told him to keep him updated should the opportunity arise.

Three days after the defeat at Pittodrie, on 11 October, Souness took the plunge and approached his chairman about the possibility of a change in ownership. His hunch was right. Lawrence Marlborough's attention was becoming more and more concentrated on his building projects in Nevada and he was keen to invest further.[78] Marlborough, with his long family links to club, wanted out and a new

---

78   It was not a success and the losses of John Lawrence (Nevada) Inc eventually brought down the entire John Lawrence Group in 1997.

brand of 1980s self-made man wanted in. Their first meeting took place on 21 October and was immediately promising, leading to more over the following four weeks resulting in a final signing meeting, in the boardroom at Ibrox, on Tuesday, 22 November. It wasn't a completely smooth process at the end. A deal of £6m for 75 per cent of a club with the market position that Rangers had, despite an overdraft of several million pounds, was considered something of a bargain. Tottenham had been recently valued at £13m and did not have the exposure of European football. When it became known within the family that a deal was close and for the figure discussed, it caused alarm. Marlborough's brother, Norman, felt that it vastly undervalued the club and sought to try and block it or attract another bidder. Through another family member, media tycoon Robert Maxwell was approached and expressed an interest in buying Rangers. When this was relayed to Holmes, the Murray deal went into overdrive, with changes to contract being made up until three minutes to midnight when it was finally signed. The following day the new owner was introduced to the media, flanked in the Blue Room by Souness, Holmes, Marlborough and Gillespie. It would be a life-changing decision for Murray and an era-defining one for Rangers.

Any assessment of the reign of David Murray – and part of that will feature later in this book – will naturally be a damning one in the end. However, given the sales that Maxwell had to make in 1989 to offset his debt and the discovery of the vast fraud he had committed, subsequent to his mysterious death in 1991, there is no question that, of the two interested parties, Murray was the better option. The initial reaction from those who would later pillory him, was favourable. Mark Dingawall, editor of the Follow, Follow fanzine, then in only its fourth edition, was wary but hopeful when he wrote, 'We would all like to see Rangers achieve the sort of dominance we once enjoyed in Scottish football and the sort of dominance in Europe that Real Madrid had in the late 1950s. To do so requires money and we'll support any schemes that raise that dosh short of seeing the club taken over by a soulless multi-national or seeing the ordinary fan ripped off.' The price of success would be a tension that would run through the decade that was to follow.

The shock change in ownership was made more palatable by the new director and now second-largest shareholder in the club, Graeme Souness. Not only had he helped broker this deal but he had put his money where his mouth was with a £600,000 stake, ten per cent of Murray's purchase. It was an absolutely remarkable level of personal investment for a manager to make – there really wasn't anything remotely comparable elsewhere in Britain – but Souness loved his job so much that he needed what he called 'total involvement' and his diary was brimming with excitement as the deal approached fruition. He saw Murray – still only 37 at the time of this deal – very much like he saw himself: an ambitious winner who had already achieved much but would go on to achieve much more, 'The whole deal excites me. The future always did look bright with this club – now I see it as even brighter. I doubt if David Murray's ambitions know any limits. We are probably well matched in that way. I feel the same and I know that the players I have brought here feel the same. What we have achieved so far may only be the beginning. Watch this space.'

Player, manager and director at an all-consuming club, it was an incredible burden to take on but, for a workaholic who defined himself by success in a Gordon Gekko world, it was simply part of an insatiable appetite. Naturally, it would have an impact on the human being behind the image. On 11 August 1988 the Souness family were the subject of a warm tabloid feature on the life behind the mania. On 17 March 1989, the exact same photo was used in a story about divorce proceedings and a custody battle.

It didn't take long for the football itself to get under the new owners's skin. As the two met for dinner as normal on Friday, 25 November, the following day's match at home to Aberdeen – Murray's first in his new seat in the directors' box[79] – was the main topic of conversation. Souness recounted how Murray started the meal by saying 'it would be good to get a win tomorrow', before expressing 'how much we need to win' and finishing up by telling his manager, 'We have to win tomorrow.' With Aberdeen unbeaten in the league, only two points behind and the mounting injuries at Ibrox[80], his urgency was merited. Rangers responded in a way that would characterise the winter period. Never at full strength, they would simply keep challengers at arm's length with some big results when needed and the Murray era got off to a winning start with a Richard Gough goal being all that separated the sides as the lead at the top extended to four points going into December.

There were setbacks, of course. Dundee United, so often a troublesome visitor to Ibrox, enjoyed a shock 1-0 win and that was compounded the following Saturday with a 2-0 defeat at Tynecastle on 10 December, which saw Walters receive a red card following two unnecessary yellows. A small echo of the past perhaps, but it was the second and final dismissal of the season and it still left Rangers with a lead of two points. Fir Park on 7 January was the scene of the last of these winter losses, a Gough own goal making the difference in a 2-1 defeat. In between, Rangers had ground out two late 1-0 wins at home to Hibs and away to Hamilton to see out 1988 before the visit of Celtic at new year. With Rangers in an attritional mood and having not scored more than one goal in a match in seven weeks, there was surely no threat of another high-scoring evisceration of their old rivals.

All the talk within the Celtic camp after the August fixture had been about a freak aberration, never to be repeated. There appeared to be merit in that defiance when Chris Morris rifled in a low free kick after only two minutes but it would prove to be the third game in a row whereby that first blood was simply a portent of a huge counter onslaught to come. Rangers were 3-1 up at half-time with Butcher glancing in a header, Walters scoring from the spot after Anton Rogan committed a wild foul on Drinkell in the box – more of that to come in the following season – and Ian Ferguson had the moment his career had been waiting for, when his powerful drive deflected past Bonner and he could celebrate in front of the Celtic end before making a sharp turn to the right for his own safety. The best was saved for last when Walters broke away to beautifully slot home a fourth.

---

79   David Holmes remained in place as chairman until the end of the season.

80   That Friday Souness had managed to get the Liverpool midfielder Kevin MacDonald up on loan to flesh his squad out a little. He would make three appearances, including as a substitute at Ibrox the following day.

Fresh from suspension, it was another impressive performance from Walters, this time in a more central role supporting Drinkell. So often the memory of him is mesmerised by his mercurial talent on the wing but that only serves to underplay his flexibility and finishing. Perhaps because he wasn't yet established in the English setup before he moved north or because John Barnes was such a preeminent figure for England in that area of the park, Bobby Robson was never convinced. The Rangers fans were, however, and that instant connection continued to intensify as the years went on.

Souness was furious at his side for following up such a big win with that careless defeat at Fir Park. Although in public they had dismissed talk of the title being over immediately after the new year fixture, it dominated the media and Souness fumed privately that his players had taken the noise 'as a signal to relax'. It left Celtic seven behind in fourth place and, although Aberdeen and Dundee United were closer, few writers would take their challenge seriously. But the loss at Motherwell brought gap down to just one solitary point ahead of United, as close as any club had been since September and, with the Tannadice side heading to bottom club Hamilton the following weekend – they would win 5-0 – the pressure was as acute as Rangers had felt it for some time. Their fixture that same day was back to where the first clouds had gathered that season: Pittodrie.

The 'on-again-off-again' relationship between Souness and Derek Ferguson had fortunately hit a period of bliss just when Rangers needed it. Ferguson had already popped up with a crucial goal on Hogmanay in the 1-0 win at Hamilton and would play an important part in arguably the most crucial win of the season. With Ian Ferguson in attack and Stuart Munro on the left of midfield, it was a makeshift team that produced the goods from the first whistle. As Durrant's name was belted out by the Rangers fans, the players took the best kind of revenge by going 2-0 up inside 25 minutes. Derek Ferguson and Munro may have argued about which one of them scored the first but there was no doubt about the second as Ian drew deeper into midfield to release Derek with a delightful through ball that was buried past Theo Snelders – fresh from getting his first Dutch call-up – with power and precision. Charlie Nicholas would pop up again to make life interesting before the break but the second half saw a different kind of Rangers performance, gritty and resilient, as they maintained their lead at the top, with Souness fulsome in his praise of Munro's attitude and performance afterwards.

Rangers had played 15 league games since their last trip to Aberdeen – when Souness's injury 'jinx' had started again – and only won eight of those, losing five, while still keeping their noses in front. With the return of McCoist and Woods in late January and February respectively, the foot went down in true championship fashion, that win at Pittodrie starting a 12-game unbeaten run in the league which included 11 wins. It should really have been full marks but a freak Gary Stevens own goal deep into injury time[81] at Tannadice cancelled out Munro's brilliant finish to ensure that top-of-the-table clash ended 1-1. More silverware was added – Rangers retuned to play in the Tennents' Sixes indoor

81   This match came only a matter of days after Richard Gough had headed in a 96th-minute winner for Scotland in Cyprus which caused a lot of debate around officiating injury time. Souness was more than happy to add to that debate following this dropped point.

tournament at the Scottish Exhibition Centre, led by reserve coach Jimmy Nicholl and dominated by the close control of Davie Cooper[82] – as was another signing. Mel Sterland, who played on the right of both defence and midfield at Sheffield Wednesday, arrived at Ibrox in early March for £800,000 as Souness was keen to manage his squad sensibly to the finish, with suspensions and injuries constantly obsessing his mind. Spending nearly £1m on a utility player in March just to provide another option at the same time as Souness was jetting off to Milan to discuss the potential transfer of Vasiliy Rats with Dynamo Kiev underlines the financial strength and ambition that Rangers had in comparison with any of their rivals. The same month, Celtic finally sold Frank McAvennie for just over £1m to West Ham United and spent less than half of that on his initial replacement, Tommy Coyne from Dundee. The chase for his permanent replacement would be a farce with far-reaching consequences. It was starting to become a different level.

As March headed towards April, Rangers were still on for a treble. History in the Scottish Cup – one of the other superstitious hexes that kept Souness up at night – looked to be repeating until a brilliant Ian Ferguson equaliser saved Rangers' blushes at Raith Rovers, and the replay at Ibrox was as comfortable as the next round against Stranraer. The quarter-final was tantalising when it paired the top two in the league, albeit with Rangers now enjoying a four-point lead over Dundee United. STV grabbed it – the television deal at the time was £400,000 for one live league game, one cup tie and the two finals shown live on top of the highlights – and it was due to be played on Sunday, 18 March before the Scottish weather had other ideas with the torrential, unrelenting rain leaving the Ibrox pitch unplayable.

The re-arranged game on the Tuesday evening was a classic showcase of cup football. Kevin Gallagher, whom Terry Butcher admitted he 'hated' playing against due to his frightening pace and movement, put the visitors ahead with a clever run and finish as Rangers rocked on their heels for the entire 45 minutes. The second half was a different story, however, with Drinkell and McCoist quickly putting Rangers ahead, the second goal was an absolutely brilliant piece of team play. As Rangers turned up the heat, McCoist was given plenty of opportunities for more but he spurned them and that profligacy was punished when Mixu Paatelainen equalised late on. The replay was a midweek trip in the middle of two league away games that offered up a season-defining week. McCoist was left in no doubt by his manager and team-mates that they were only having to make the journey to Tayside because of him but he assured them that he would sort it. He duly did five minutes after the break, when he was positioned perfectly to take advantage of a Walters drive that was tipped on to the bar by Billy Thompson and back out to the predator-in-chief.

It was McCoist's strike partner, Kevin Drinkell, who had scored the only goal at Easter Road the weekend before – an instinctive left-footed blast in the box – that set up the trip the Parkhead on April Fools' Day, with a four-point cushion to absorb the blow if the normal sort of result ensued. To complete the season-long Old Firm trend there was yet another early goal for the visitors, Drinkell's header putting Rangers ahead on nine minutes, but any fears of a rampaging comeback

---

82   Rangers defeated both Celtic and Motherwell 2-1 in the semi-final and final respectively.

were assuaged within half an hour. Rangers should have had a penalty when Walters terrorised Rogan but the crucial second goal was found when Ian Ferguson's drive from Wilkins' indirect free kick could only be stopped by Bonner and spun up in the air towards the goal. Goal-line technology would most probably have awarded the goal to Ferguson but McCoist didn't hang around to wait and see as he got to the ball first to make sure with a header.

Rangers were excellent for that first half, totally dominant as champions-elect. Perhaps a mixture of sitting back on what they had and Celtic's champion pride being hurt saw a change in momentum early after the restart. Andy Walker was found by Chris Morris with the penalty box to himself after only three minutes and old fears quickly reappeared. Celtic thought they had equalised through Mark McGhee but there was a clear foul in the process and John Brown nearly made sure when he went agonisingly close with a shot across goal from a Walters cross as the game stretched itself into something of a cup tie. And then, with under ten minutes to see out, Gough handled in the box before bringing down Tommy Burns as well, just to make sure, and Celtic were given that late chance of a reprieve. If there were any doubts as to whether or not this was going to be Rangers' year, then the save by Woods and clearance by Stevens would have ended them there and then. It is the kind of outcome that only seems to happen for winners.

An inexorable run to a title is only ever a formality in hindsight. Rangers still had Motherwell to come to Ibrox and a trip to St Mirren straight after the win over Celtic and neither were fixtures that had ever been kind in the Souness era. However, there was an unmistakable feeling throughout the support that a strong grip – both on and off the park – was beginning to be felt by the rest of the country. Rangers were the future, from the pre-season preparation and depth of quality on the park to the stadium, market ambition and revenue streams.

Rangers now represented modernity, however April 1989 was about to provide the footballing world with a horrific reminder of what it had hoped represented the past.

* * *

Officially, there were 47,374 spectators at Parkhead to watch Rangers toil in the spring sunshine against lower-league St Johnstone in the semi-final of the Scottish Cup. An embarrassing 0-0 draw ensued – celebrated wildly by the Saints players at the end – where the Rangers players felt that all they had to do was simply turn up. Early in the first half there were ambulance workers trackside by the traditional Celtic end, given to the Rangers support that day, treating fans who had spilled over a broken wall due to the pressure of numbers. Those complaining to the police were quickly told to be quiet and that they were just too used to the comfort of Ibrox.[83] Younger fans, sitting in the relative safety of the main stand, were confused and concerned as they watched the incident unfold to their left while at the same time listening to men with transistor radios taking about people

---

83   There was a similar report in *Follow Follow* edition three about the same attitudes from stewards at Easter Road for the 1-0 win there in October 1988.

dying. The situation at Parkhead was thankfully minor and dealt with quickly. The situation coming through the airwaves was much more serious.

So much of the Rangers modernisation story in 1988/89 ran perfectly with the pace of change happening around it. The game itself was starting to realise that the introduction of freedom of movement in employment throughout Europe after 1992 may have an impact on contracts and transfers fees and the appearance of satellite dishes on homes throughout Britain in February 1989 brought football's governing bodies to the understanding that television was something to work with rather than fear. Even the city of Glasgow itself – with the new St. Enoch Centre representing a modern retail experience at one end of Buchanan Street and the construction of the Royal Concert Hall providing a fitting auditorium for the soon-to-be European City of Culture at the other – was shaking off its hard, grimy and dangerous image.

And yet, it juxtaposed so sharply with other events. This was also a time of tragedy in Britain, a reminder of where investment was still lacking and why, despite how Francis Fukuyama would soon be misunderstood, the victory of liberal democratic history was not yet complete. The very day that Rangers resumed pre-season training the Piper Alpha disaster raged in the North Sea, eventually killing 167 people. Four days before Christmas, 270 people lost their lives when Pan Am Flight 103 was destroyed by a bomb planted on board and landed on the Dumfriesshire town of Lockerbie.[84] And then, on cup semi-final day in both Scotland and England, came Hillsborough, the tragic nadir of English football's reckless indifference which cost 97 Liverpool fans their lives and ensured that real action on reform instead of empty gestures was now unavoidable.

After a minute's silence Rangers would win that Scottish Cup replay 4-0 with a completely different attitude, the second by Gary Stevens being the stand out and carried that focus forward with a 2-0 win at Love Street which created the possibility of winning the league at home to Hearts, if Aberdeen failed to beat Celtic. It was a fitting fashion in which to settle this particular title in the end. Aberdeen drew 0-0 at home to Celtic, their 13th of 14 league draws in total, and would typify the way that the chasing pack would harm each other and allow Rangers to ease away.

'There was only going to be one result in this one,' thought Graeme Souness that morning. Nothing was going to stop Rangers as they cruised to a 4-0 win, a brace apiece for Sterland and Drinkell with the latter finishing up the club's top goalscorer for the season. 'It really summed up what we have been preaching to the players all the way through the season. If you do your own job right then no one will be able to beat you to the title. You don't rely on others – do it yourself,' wrote Souness although the latter part could have just as easily been found in the diary of the prime minister herself.

So often the destiny of the Scottish title is decided by that mini-league of six comprising of the Glasgow and Edinburgh rivals in addition to Dundee United and Aberdeen. In 1987/88 Rangers took 16 points out of 40 from those games, in contrast to 26 and 28 in 1986/87 and 1988/89 respectively. Time and again, Rangers produced a show of strength in the crunch games while routinely dealing

---

84   Rangers would play Gretna in a fundraiser in January.

with those clubs in the lower reaches. Souness was justifiably proud as he spoke to Archie Macpherson afterwards and it was no coincidence that he made mention of the injury woes and how his side had dealt with them this season in a way they hadn't before.[85] However, despite the inflatable champagne bottles and bananas being passed around the enclosures[86], these were celebrations that lacked the manic reaction that made 1987 legendary – Butcher said that it 'didn't mean nearly as much as the first one, even though this time we won it in front of our own fans' – but perhaps that told its own story. The league championship was no longer a holy grail, rather it was now becoming a routine expectation.

Later that evening, in the Parc des Princes in Paris, France played out a disappointing 0-0 draw with Yugoslavia which all but guaranteed Scotland's place at the World Cup in Italy in 1990. With a gap of five points and only three qualifying games remaining, the French manager Michel Platini was quick to wave the white flag when he said, 'We are finished. Scotland are already in Italy.' Helped perhaps by a reduction in league fixtures which allowed a free weekend to prepare before midweek internationals[87], it had been an entertaining campaign for Scotland with some fortune in Cyprus earned by some quality including a win away in Norway and a draw and win at home to Yugoslavia and France respectively. There was also a burgeoning partnership developing up front as Ally McCoist and Maurice Johnston struck up a chemistry that provided Andy Roxburgh with some reliable consistency in a crucial area of the park. Johnston's double at Hampden against France was evidence of a raw talent that had been honed and developed on the continent and McCoist was involved in both goals before both had their names on the score sheet in the 2-1 home win over Cyprus in April. Some might have imagined what this pair, good friends and international room-mates, could do in the same club team.

Such talk was fantasy at the time and even more so when, in the final week of the league season, Celtic sensationally paraded Johnston at Parkhead as their imminent £1.5m signing for the coming term. An unmistakably ambitious move by Billy McNeill, it was also a tonic for Celtic ahead of the Old Firm Scottish Cup Final. Captain Roy Aitken rubbished any talk that Johnston would receive a frosty reception after how it all ended in 1987, by promising that he would be welcomed back with open arms and that 'Celtic would be getting not just the best striker in

---

85   There was no Durrant, Brown or Ian Ferguson for the Hearts game and Ray Wilkins had to come off after 20 minutes.

86   This was a craze that was popular in English football in the late 1980s and had started at Manchester City after a bizarre story involving their striker Imre Varadi. At an away fixture there were people dressed as bananas on the pitch before kick-off. City fans started to shout 'Bananas! Bananas!', Varadi misheard, thought they were shouting his name and applauded the support. He quickly became known as 'Imre Banana' and inflatables became part of the relationship. Other English clubs adopted their own and a craze was born. Despite the other connotations, there was nothing malicious or racist about it – Varadi was English with Hungarian and Italian heritage – and was a fun addition to English football, in keeping with the growing rave scene.

87   The Premier Division reduced in size in 1988/89 from 12 to ten teams, meaning a 36-match season instead of a brutal 44-game campaign. This window of common sense would not be a long one.

Britain, but the best in Europe'. Johnston took his place at Love Street for Celtic's final league game of the season whereas his agent, Bill McMurdo, was at Ibrox to see Rangers lift the Premier Division trophy even if the party was somewhat pooped by a 3-0 Aberdeen win. Leaning by the radiator near the main doors, McMurdo was passed by Souness after the game where a throwaway comment in passing would start a nuclear reaction, 'If only we had known, Bill, we'd have been interested.'

Despite the PR exercise, Souness was told, the deal was not yet done. There was still no agreement on who would pay the tax on Johnston's share of the of the transfer fee and, even though Celtic had an agreement with Nantes and had paid £400,000 down, it was not yet concluded. For obvious reasons – not only was Johnston a Roman Catholic, he was a former Celtic player with an antagonistic past when it had come to Rangers – McMurdo hadn't considered this as an option but, by the following day, Souness was given the encouragement that the player was interested if Rangers were. He first spoke to Walter Smith, who had deep reservations. 'It was neither that I was a bigot nor someone who underestimated the player's ability,' Smith was quoted in the Glasgow Herald years later. 'I just worried about the repercussions.' The reticence was short-lived, however, and it was then a matter of convincing David Murray that evening, who needed a little longer before deciding that it was something that needed to happen for Rangers, both on and off the field. Souness was then given permission to get the ball rolling by travelling to France to meet Johnston and McMurdo to agree the major terms of the biggest transfer in the history of Scottish football, in a little cafe outside of Orly.

The manager had other issues to deal with as the cup final loomed and injuries had struck yet again, with Wilkins out and Derek Ferguson recently injuring his shoulder. Ferguson was desperate to play – he had dislocated his shoulder in Cologne and it had popped out eight times since but on this occasion it happened to the other one – however, knowing that this type of knock could be easily preyed upon by an opposition, Souness had to make the call to cut him from the final squad.[88] It was a squad that included himself on the bench instead of the fit Ian McCall and Ferguson was of the impression years later that Souness thought the match would be a breeze where he could later come on a showboat and finally end his dreadful record in the British national cup competitions. It was anything but. Rangers were flat and lethargic on a rock-hard Hampden pitch, scorched by the blazing sun and a makeshift central midfield of Munro and Ian Ferguson never quite got a hold of the game. Despite being the best player on the field, in the opinion of his manager, Gary Stevens momentarily failed with a weak pass back to Woods right before half-time and Joe Miller pounced to score the only goal. Rangers would complain that the goal came from Aitken taking a throw that was originally given to Souness's team and that referee Bob Valentine disallowed a second-half Terry Butcher header by giving an extremely soft foul on Bonner by

88   Ferguson had been involved in yet another incident, this time with Ian Durrant on crutches in a kebab shop on Paisley Road West on 4 May. Ferguson remained bitter about his exclusion, feeling that it was more this incident than the severity of his injury that was the decisive factor.

Walters, but the truth was that they didn't do enough to win a very poor game of football.

Gerry McNee, writing for the Daily Express, had pondered in the build-up to the match whether it might be best for Celtic to lose, the full impact of a Rangers treble forcing the support to properly accept and respond to the growing ineptitude of the board. Instead they were joyful at being able to take something away from the season and the impending arrival of their prodigal son. As the cracks were papered over at Hampden, 'Mo, Mo, super Mo!' echoed around the east end of the ground. 'Mo, Mo, fuck your Mo!' was the defiant response from the west enclosure, as David Murray sat in the South Stand wondering if this really was a good idea after all.

Souness, whose medal had to be rescued from the dressing room bath by kitman George Soutar, was naturally far from happy. Despite around 10,000 Rangers fans staying long after the presentation in the hope that their heroes would return to salute a fine season, the manager made it clear that his players should take this rage and use it in the future. 'Just remember this feeling. It's the worst in the world and I want you all to dredge it back up when the new season starts,' he said before adding a cryptic remark about doing something that summer that would hurt Celtic for years. Some players noticed but, tired after an exhausting season, they thought little of it. It wasn't until a few of them were back at Hampden the following Saturday that the penny should have started to drop.

* * *

England were the visitors to Hampden on Saturday, 27 May, the day after one of the most dramatic conclusions to an English league season when Arsenal grabbed the title at Anfield in the last moments of an emotionally draining campaign, and it would be the last time the two sides met for ten years, such was the associated violence.[89] At the Scotland camp at the Marine Hotel in Troon, Johnston was dropping hints to his room-mate about just how nice Souness's house was. Eventually, he had to spell it out more clearly. 'It was like being hit by a juggernaut,' wrote McCoist later. 'I actually hid my head underneath a pillow. I just couldn't believe it was happening.' The messaging in the press that week had changed from 'small snags' to 'contractual difficulties' and finished with Johnston apologising to the Celtic support that 'because of personal and contractual problems I am unable to go through with the move'. Billy McNeill, sensing that his deal was disintegrating, effectively barged his way into the camp to speak to Johnston and waited in the foyer while the player finished a call with Souness. McNeill warned him that if he messed Celtic around that he'd fight him all the way, 'I'll make sure you never fucking play again.' Johnston was sheepish and quiet. McNeill went to FIFA to plead the case that the documentation that Celtic already had in place should be enough, but it was becoming clear to most – including the Celtic board who refused to fight it legally on the principle that if the player didn't want to play, then they weren't interested in trying to force him – that Johnston was unlikely

---

89   The Rous Cup now had an international feel with an invited third party, this time Chile.

to return to Celtic. The football world would have needed a thousand guesses to predict his ultimate destination.

Even during the game itself, it was a thought that struggled to register. Terry Butcher was superb in an England defence – half of which was provided by Rangers – hell-bent on keeping a clean sheet at Hampden.[90] When he told Johnston that he was looking forward to kicking him again next season, he was told, 'No, I'll be coming back to play with you.' Butcher assumed that it was just a striker trying to get inside his head and dismissed it. Even when the pieces were all laid out in front of Rangers players and the Scottish footballing public, it was a puzzle that the collective mind couldn't possibly put together.

That summer though, Rangers fans appreciated the side they had and what they had just witnessed, regardless of the failure to make that treble happen. Decades later, this is a vastly under-rated Rangers team and no doubt the failure at Hampden that day has prevented it taking its place on the pantheon. Naturally the mythology and iconography around Graeme Souness and Rangers is so tightly bound to that first season's emotional triumph but this is a far better, more rounded and more disciplined team. It could often be powerful and direct, yes, but with Wilkins and Walters especially it was a side capable of more than a little flourish on top of the steel, and most importantly it was impactful. The necessary noise and bombast of those first two years was over – with some success ahead of schedule to enjoy – but now there had been a significant gear change. If Aberdeen had been put on the ropes with the cup final win and two clutch league victories in the middle of the season then Celtic – 5-1, 4-1 and the end of their home record – were hearing bells. The knockout blow was just about to be delivered.

---

90   England won 2-0, both goals coming from Steve Bull.

6

READ ALL ABOUT IT

'We were aiming to do something that would hopefully resemble the kind of conversations people had about football before games, covering funny stuff, theories and so on but always as fully informed about the game as fans are.'
Andy Lyons, co-founder of When Saturday Comes

'Forgive me Father for I have signed.'
Follow, Follow cover, edition eight, August 1989

It is a little ironic that on an evening that was something of a deferential farewell, we saw an introduction that was a lot more punk. On the beautiful late-summer's evening of Tuesday, 9 August 1988, thousands did what they could to get inside Ibrox Stadium to pay their tribute to a great Ranger, a final link with the club of old. Outside the stadium stood Mark Dingwall and some friends as they sold the very first edition of Follow, Follow on Edmiston Drive; a new collection of voices at Ibrox and not always complimentary. Davie Cooper's testimonial against Bordeaux was the final preparation before the 1988/89 season kicked off at Douglas Park, Hamilton, on the Saturday, where Dingwall and Co. would stand again and would do, in greater numbers, for decades to come. The one that followed was the greatest era in the club's history and an alternative account of that can be found throughout the 81 issues of the fanzine that span it. The production values changed but the move to a glossy finish from a handful of pages created by copy, paste and Xerox, didn't curb the edge in the writing, the constant complaining and the dark humour. You would't find this in the Rangers News.

That was the point. The football fanzine culture had exploded into life in 1986 with the arrival of Off The Ball in Birmingham and, two months later, When Saturday Comes. Season 1987/88 saw the one and only edition outside Ibrox of World, Shut Your Mouth. Like so many in British football in the second half of the 1980s, it didn't get to second issue and it was thought that there were something like three million British fanzines sold in one season alone, with so many being tested out and failing. Coming from the punk music scene – Dingwall's cousin John was the entertainment editor for the Daily Record for several years and had started his own music fanzine Stand And Deliver – most, if not all, were started so as to get a better picture of that particular fanbase on the record. 'I had never seen a true representation of me and my pals in the mainstream media,' said Dingwall and the same was true of Adrian Goldberg and Andy Lyons down south. This was the time of 'a slum sport for slum people' and where proclaiming your love for a football club was a precarious admission when made to potential employers or in-laws. Football fans were all thugs and hooligans and – in the case of several clubs, including Rangers – far-right, racist bigots. Up and down the country, the club fanzines that lasted demonstrated that a far greater depth, wit and intelligence existed within their support.

Race was actually the primary focus of the original issue of Follow, Follow. Mark Walters was on the cover and the first editorial was called 'Blue – The Only Colour That Matters'. It criticised the Celtic and Hearts support for their abuse the previous season but also had the awareness to castigate the few who had booed him at Ibrox – 'we're better off without such scum soiling the club' – and to admit that if a rival club had bought Walters then 'no doubt a minority would have disgraced us by their behaviour … "inspired" by the juvenile antics of racist clubs in England'. It wasn't an issue that necessarily dominated the pages over time but there was still the odd furious letter or article by people complaining about fans who sat around them giving Walters and later Dale Gordon a hard time along with racial epithets and also towards opponents, from Jean Tigana in 1998 to the Dundee United winger Jerren Nixon in 1994.

'Without thinking about it, we were confounding stereotypes.', said Dingwall. Within a couple of seasons, Follow, Follow had a variety of established writers who nicely encapsulated the broad church of the support, at least politically if not in the literal sense. Whereas Dingwall himself and contributors such as 'The Major' and 'The Govanhill Gub' came from the right of centre, a lot of the regulars were from the left. Indeed, 'Robbie the Ranger' had been a member of the Communist Party at one point and 'The Dowanhill Hack' was once the Scottish football correspondent for the Morning Star. This ensured that, from the earliest issues, the fanzine contained genuine division and debate. On some issues, such as the class divide discussed in an earlier chapter, there were surprising positions taken by some, most notably Dingwall himself, a former member of the Conservative Students Association, railing against the increasing business class at Ibrox. By Dingwall's own admission, this was perhaps more motivated by self-interest around the newly competitive demand for away tickets – where the guarantees had hitherto been the preserve of the relatively small Members Club and now threatened to explode with the growth of hospitality, leaving fewer for the average punter – than any egalitarian principle. 'We didn't realise just how much the operation was bringing into the club,' he said. 'It's now a source of pride to a lot of fans, that we were at the forefront of developing hospitality on such a scale.'

The general struggle with modernity was a constant trope, however, as it would be for hundreds of fanzines. Soaring ticket prices that prohibited younger, poorer fans from attending regularly, stadium improvements, the signing of Johnston and the introduction of security chief Alistair Hood – who it was said would happily remove you for smiling – were all blamed for the loss of one important feature: atmosphere. The Major's first column complained about the introduction of televisions in the concourses and there was one occasion in the mid-1990s where a substantial number of fans didn't reappear for the start of the second half because they were watching the conclusion of the Calcutta Cup match between Scotland and England at Twickenham. Heaven forfend! Others felt that Ibrox was becoming more like a cinema, with supporters coming to stuff their faces and sit, waiting to be entertained. According to The Hack, football – even a friendly like the match in

1994 with Manchester United which saw Eric Cantona sent off – was becoming too sanitised. The sport, he argued, should be the modern-day Christians and lions, where fans use strangers as a way of dealing with life. One cartoon in 1990 was particularly dark. Pictured from the back of the directors box, David Murray, on a seat that said 'Megabucks', asked, 'Did I hear a cheer there?' to which Hood replied, 'It's OK, boss, they must be listening to the radio in the District Bar'[91] Nothing risqué in the language but the back of Hood's chair said 'Waffen SS' and five of the six figures drawn had their legs on show, with the exception of Murray, where there was just empty space underneath the seat of his chair.

The fanzine tried to 'save' the two enclosures from modernisation – the only remaining standing sections in the stadium and the heartbeat of the hardcore support – but it was a futile campaign. A more successful response was the attempt at organising 'flag days' or 'confetti days' at Ibrox and especially trips to Parkhead. Inspired by the more visible Italian tifosi displays on show via television every weekend, some were a genuine spectacle especially in the east end of the city in 1993 and 1994. As ever, there were plenty of voices that supported the need for modernising parts of the ground and ensuring that Ibrox was more family friendly and one perceptive letter in August 1990 that warned about the dangers of nostalgia. The writer remembered with great fondness the atmosphere at the old Derry End of the ground but that, during that time, there were plenty of older voices saying that 'it wasn't the same as Hellfire Corner' which used to be the junction of the Derry and the old Centenary Stand. The past was always better because we were younger, the letter reminded us, as well as raising the very fair point that the alcohol ban that was implemented after the 1980 Scottish Cup Final riot was perhaps a greater reason than any other.

Another early debate that would run and run into the 1990s and end up a repetitive and entrenched borefest was the issue of Scotland and the Union and how Rangers fans should celebrate that dual identity. No doubt triggered by the sudden anglicisation of Rangers' identity from 1986 – and the subsequent reaction by opposition fans to it – it was an identity crisis that filled the pages of Follow, Follow for years. 'For all Rangers fans,' wrote 'The Wee Prime Minister' in April 1990, 'the Union Jack stands for something more than merely the team's colours. But rather what the club represents.' Not for all, as it would turn out, with the question raging for years as the relationship between Rangers fans and the Scotland national team deteriorated considerably.

The publication was still a place for pieces in support of Scottish nationalism, although some were titled 'Jacobite Bites Back', presumably not by the author. An article by Alan Kilpatrick in the August edition of 1993 argued, 'I'm sure I'm not alone in being both confused and disappointed with the loyal affection which many Gers fans appear to hold for our union with England … Rangers are the greatest of Scottish clubs and more than any other embody the Scottish traits of spirit and determination (The Lion Rampant on the club crest is testimony to that). I feel it's important that we don't lose or compromise our Scottishness over well-intended but confused loyalties … If the Lion Rampant or the Saltire are not the flags that fly highest at Ibrox, they should fly at least together with the Union

---

91   A pub on Paisley Road West, a short walk from the stadium.

flag but never below it.' The to-and-fro on these issues – with replies sometimes months apart due to publication dates and thus often more considered than an instant Tweet – as well as the reaction to the signing of Maurice Johnston, are evidence of a support that was nowhere near as monochrome as the nation's press had painted them.

And what of that press, both internal as well as Scotland's fourth estate? Like many such outlets, Follow, Follow naturally saw itself as a direct response to the in-house publications such as the Rangers News which they often described as a Pravdaesque uncritical read, slavish in its devotion to its owners. There was therefore a gap in the market for others to speak truth to power and it didn't take long for the schism to become public with the official club publication seemingly siding with the wider press in their initial reaction to this punk upstart's first effort. Graham Spiers, then of Scotland On Sunday, quoted the then editor of Rangers News, Stephen Halliday, as describing those behind this new 'booklet' as 'cranks'. 'These people crawl out from under stones from time to time and no doubt will crawl back again soon,' he added. It has been suggested since that Spiers presented that exact wording to Halliday for confirmation of his position but, even if there was some journalistic licence with quotations, it was not exactly a repudiation. Follow, Follow represented unwelcome criticism of the club from its own.

Before the proliferation of blogs and podcasts, it is easy to lose sight of the impact and reach that the written press once had among Scottish football fans. Columnists such as Alex 'Candid' Cameron had a massive audience to which they could preach. Even by the turn of the 21st century, the Daily Record sold more than 570,000 copies a month. By 2021 that would be under 75,000 and falling. Their voice reverberated strongly at the time of the revolution and therefore could easily get under the skin of fans who didn't need much encouragement to take umbrage. Spiers and Ian Archer were two of the many journalists whom the contributors to Follow, Follow wanted banned from Ibrox over what they had written. The latter had rarely presented himself as a lover of Rangers or the support, whom he once famously described as 'a permanent embarrassment and an occasional disgrace', and this ire was increased with a throwaway line while reporting on the appointment of Brian Dempsey to the Celtic board in 1990. Celtic, he said, 'were founded for charity, unlike Rangers, the creation of two brothers who were interested in making a few bob out of selling strips for this new game of football'. At best it was a clumsy attempt at painting a picture of a club that was overtly commercial and one romantically philanthropic, but it was a bizarre lie with which to use. Spiers' account of 'Klinsmann's a Klansman!' being sung at Ibrox – the West German and Internazionale striker had refused to shake hands with the Pope due to his strict Lutheran upbringing – was equally bizarre as it never had been. It could be argued that caricatures are the remit of humorists, not football writers, and that fans are entitled to be upset when that level of inaccuracy is left unchallenged by their club. It was being left to them to raise the wider consciousness and anger.

As with everything to do with the Old Firm, parity in reporting about the other side and their support was a necessity. When the Daily Record invited the Rev Tom Connolly – the press spokesman for the Catholic church in Scotland – for his comments on songs sung in the away dressing room at Tannadice following the title win in 1990, there were questions asked about where their outrage was when the same man of the cloth referred to children who attended nondenominational schools as 'pagans'. When pundits like Davie Provan excused the damage done to the Broomloan Road stand by Celtic fans after Old Firm games in 1993 on the fact that the seats were tightly packed together and thus damage was inevitable during celebrations or that it was a natural result of sectarian tension, fans wanted to know why the club wasn't responding by pointing out that Motherwell and Kilmarnock had enjoyed shock dramatic wins recently without any issues or that Celtic fans did the same while playing Hibs at Ibrox in a cup semi-final or indeed what that had to do with the state that the toilets were left in.

It was the same with match reports. Spiers again was the target in the December of 1995 when he reported on Celtic's 4-0 hammering of Hibs at Easter Road by saying, 'Celtic simply played lavishly here ... Theirs is an increasingly convincing cause. Someone whispered it last night: Celtic for the championship?' When Rangers defeated the same opponent 7-0 at Ibrox three weeks later, however, the tone was slightly different, 'An inspired Rangers, yes of course, but what an embarrassment for the Scottish game to have this murderous scoreline adoring its season ... some of us were cringing amid the ringing celebrations.'

Demands for accuracy and parity are one thing but sensitivity about matters of opinion are the achilles heel of all football fans, even in the modern day. Rage derived from the opinion of a writer on heroes past and present or the chances of success in a given season perhaps says more about the insecurity of one's own views rather than a sound basis on which to ban them from their place of work. Even the most acutely emotional ones such as the pieces written by Spiers on Jock Wallace, Davie Cooper and Bill Struth were still theoretically valid even when there is a reasonable suspicion of malicious or mischievous intent. He described Cooper as a 'so-called "genius"' and that Struth was 'either an idol or an idiot, depending on your point of view'. However, history should never be hagiography and the Devil's Advocate could point to Cooper's relatively low cap count or the criticism he took from Rangers fans throughout fallow periods or that Struth's own players, such as Ian McColl, said that he never gave a single tactical instruction and that his methods were very basic. The fact that these heroes and others, produced so much for Rangers should matter far more than the opinions of those not disposed to celebrate that success. When criticism came from those who were expected to enjoy Rangers' dominance then the reaction was wild. The most anodyne and seemingly obvious statements such as when Derek Johnstone said on Radio Clyde that 'it would be good for the game in Scotland if Motherwell could snatch a draw' before a match with Rangers, where the league leaders were threatening an early, unassailable lead, were treated with fury and calls for purges.[92]

Perhaps the best example of subjective opinions inducing outrage were the star match ratings for individual players. In Scotland during that era it was the Sunday Mail's marks that people reached for the day after the dust had settled on the day's

---

92   Johnstone was technically employed by the club at the time but he was not stating what *he* wanted to see happen just that a title race would be better for the rest of Scottish football, which it would.

play. At the end of each season the Mail would produce a team of the season, based on cumulative points and not, crucially, with some kind of average weight. At the conclusion of the 1992/93 season, where Rangers had won a treble and were a couple of goals away from the inaugural Champions League Final, there was not a single Rangers player in the combined XI. It demonstrated the relative depth that Smith enjoyed over his counterparts at the time and that he was able to rotate when others couldn't but the it rendered the whole concept a farce to be pitied rather than be used as fuel for offence. Where the fans had a genuine reason for grievance when it came to matters of opinion, however, is that Souness and Murray were not slow to remove those whose words stung them personally. Why not, some fans asked, defend the club in the same way?

Those who were entitled to castigate Rangers players and officials, old and new, were of course, those writing for the fanzine. Dingwall speaks of criticism he received that the writers were too easy on the club, with too many celebratory musings and not enough contributors holding the key people to account. Having read the 81 issues that go up to the end of the 1997/98 season, it is patently clear that this was not a tome characterised by positivity. Even in the middle the greatest run of success that the club had ever witnessed, Walter Smith, the players and David Murray were often in the crosshairs, especially when it became clear that European success would be a forlorn dream. Domestic success shouldn't be the standard anymore, it was said, lest complacency run through the club. 'Murray and Smith are running the club better than previous incumbents,' wrote one contributor after an evisceration by Juventus in Turin in 1995, 'but that is the same as acknowledging that Jim Baxter was better than Jim Denny.' Following a similar battering in the home tie, Dingwall resisted calling for the manager's head but said, 'There comes a time when the whole operation of a club has to be looked at. Walter is a victim of his own success – the more he wins the more we want. That's how it should be – we should never be content with what we've got.' Two months later, however, as the race for nine championships in a row was starting to reach boiling point, he turned on the press for saying much the same thing. After quoting Lenin and his call for the state-run media to sow 'discord and confusion', he said, 'In addition there is a concerted offensive to boost the morale of our opponents, whoever they may be, in order that we don't reach nine in a row. Paranoia is a condition which involves an irrational fear of persecution. My belief is founded on fact. The evidence is there for anyone to study.' The press call for Rangers to concentrate on Europe is not, in fact, a natural development of conversation but it was designed instead to make it 'easy for Walter and our heroes to slacken the pace, to settle for second best'. The pressure was getting to everyone.

As the success of the fanzine grew, so did the number of editions per season, with nearly 45 per cent of all the issues during this ten-year spell coming in the final three seasons. As such, it is a great source with which to capture the claustrophobia and nervous tension affecting the fanbase as this historic quest reached its finale. No sooner had someone waxed lyrical about the players performance on the field, smoke was rising from the pages of others bemoaning their performance off it with heavy drinking, drink driving, affairs, abortions and the general unprofessionalism that was plastered over the tabloids being a constant source of frustration and unease. What if it derailed the whole thing? What were fans prepared to put up with as long as the goals flowed? Never was this put to the test quite like the October of 1996 when news surfaced that Paul Gascoigne had been responsible for domestic abuse with his wife Sheryl.

It is important, when trying to make sense of fan reaction to this story, to remember the context in which it played out. Since his arrival in July 1995, Gascoigne was an almost daily feature in the media with pundits wanting him sold for his on-field indiscipline and feature writers doing pieces on his new home and asking, 'Would you want this man for a neighbour?' As he powered Rangers to an eighth title in a row and a double to boot, the fans' devotion was always likely to be fiercely defensive. In that context it was incredibly brave of the writers who condemned him immediately. Dingwall's editorial in the next issue held no punches, 'This latest episode is the final straw. Either he goes or Walter goes. Paying some of these clowns the money we do it's not too much to ask them to behave like human beings is it? Our beloved vice-chairman is quoted in Friday's Scotsman – "If Gascoigne plays on Saturday, scores a few goals and we win, ask the fans what they think." You can know what I'll think now Donald – I'll think he's a wife-beating bastard who is a disgrace and an embarrassment to us all.' In the following edition 'Rantin' Robert Burns' compounded that sentiment, 'Is the quest for nine or ten in a row to take precedence over all else? Will our players be allowed to do just as they please with OUR hard-earned cash, and live their lives according to the rules of the gutter? Where is the guidance? Where is the leadership? Where is the example to younger players? I'm fed up with the drink; the drink-driving; the philandering; the Rangers players on the front rather than the back pages; and its about time the men at the helm of the club got a grip and reminded the players that without the fans they are nothing, and the patience of the fans, on-field performances notwithstanding, is being sorely tested. If ten in a row is achieved at the expense of the club being reduced to a haven for sewer rats, will we be happy? … I want players I can watch, can cheer, can applaud, without thinking I'm giving a mixed message. At the Aberdeen game at Ibrox it was difficult to reconcile the pro-Gazza chanting with the events of the previous week. Were those singing "one Paul Gascoigne" not, in a way, saying that it was alright to beat your wife as long as you put the ball in the pokey on a Saturday? If so, count me out.'

Gascoigne would score a brilliant free kick at home to Aberdeen on his first game back and Ibrox shook in response. There is another chapter for another book about how we navigate the love for our sporting and artistic heroes with their human weakness, but what this perhaps did represent was that a great many fans simply let the depth and intricacies of stories wash over them. They were there to see the football and as long as results were good, they were happy. What this story showed, as with others, is that a depth of feeling, passion or interest marked the fanzine readers and contributors from the average punter, certainly in the pre-digital age where the access to such never-ending debate is available at all times. There was then perhaps a difference between being a supporter and a fan. This was especially relevant when it came to coverage of David Murray.

There is a chapter at the end of this book that looks at Murray's time in charge of the club over this period but given how scorched his reputation is in the current day, thanks to the disastrous financial mismanagement that led Rangers into ruin in 2012, the fanzine archive provides a fascinating history of the beginning of that relationship between the fans and the owner. There are genuine moments of praise and excitement – his handling of Graeme Souness's departure and his banning of the Celtic support from Ibrox in 1994 to name but two – but there are also concerns and fears from the earliest years mostly around his failure to deal with the growing overdraft at the height of the success, being too soft with the media in relation to the club and the support or his use of words being all too often something of a verbal sleight of hand. Were the support being sold a mirage in the long term? The most prominent writers all wrestled with this throughout the era, quite often shifting between a barrage of abuse to an acceptance that he was still for the best thing for the club overall, sometimes within the same article. Yes, success was seemingly never-ending but there was always a caveat that something didn't quite add up. The groans and the fears, however, were dismissed by much of the readership and certainly the wider support who took the tabloid narrative – much of whom at the time were putty in Murray's hands – as gospel.

And it is this that is perhaps the main takeaway from the fanzine era, before the all-consuming internet age. For all the colour that Follow, Follow was able to fill into the picture of the Rangers support, for all the difference and debate, the contemporaneous love letters or breakdowns over players and managers, discussion about the financial viability of the club's future and some excellent research into the past, it was only there for those who read it. The obsessives and the curious. With such a huge support the magazine was somehow able to feel both popular and niche. The written word in the red tops, the broadsheets and the in-house publication still sold more and carried more weight. The official line held firm, despite the noise coming from the streets outside. Even with the explosion of the internet message boards in the new century – where the ability and freedom was given to discuss issues and detail quickly instead of waiting weeks to read a response in a new article – there were still thousands of fans angrily un-prepared to accept the reality of the scale of mismanagement taking place.

Follow, Follow and its counterparts throughout Britain really did give fans something fresh in the late 1980s and 1990s. New voices got an airing they otherwise wouldn't have and a start was made on – in Mark Dingwall's words – creating a scaffolding around which fans could get a better understanding of their club's past, present and future. In other words, it was the foundation of activism. To the fans eventual cost – due mainly to the historical importance of the written press before the turn of the century, the hysteria which at times drowned the salient warnings and that powerful urge within us all to believe in the best – that building wasn't quite finished in time.

7

GOING, GOING

SEASON 1989/90

'Tradition means giving votes to the most obscure of all classes, our ancestors. It is the democracy of the dead.'

G.K. Chesterton, Orthodoxy

'Success will never ever replace losing a bit of the tradition of the club. But it can make the pain bearable.'

Colin McPhie, Rangers fan, July 1989

With a flash of that famous red head, it was all different. A new type of Rangers hero had arrived. Many before him had run to take their Ibrox acclaim, resplendent in royal blue, but very few had been a Roman Catholic and none had been a former Celtic favourite who had revelled in antagonising Rangers. Only a year before, Maurice Johnston had stated in his autobiography, 'Let me just spell out where I stand here. I am a Celtic man through and through, and so dislike Rangers because they are a force in Scottish football and a threat to the club I love. But more than that, I hate the religious policy which they still maintain. Why won't they sign a Roman Catholic? I hate religious bigotry, and the Rangers fans always tried to single me out in Old Firm games.' Now, thousands were saluting him around all four sides of Ibrox Stadium as he scored his first competitive goal for his new club. Their club.

But what was 'their club' anymore? Season 1989/90 was another significant chapter in the story of modernisation and the acute friction that this inevitably produces. The Johnston signing was unquestionably the standout narrative thread as it didn't just nudge the door towards a new, modern player market ajar, instead it blew it off its hinges, creating existential mayhem for fans on both sides of the divide. But while Celtic as club would suffer the same kind of angst within their support – which would prove to be debilitating for years to come – the Ibrox hierarchy resisted the noise with a laser focus. Rangers would never make a more controversial signing again and in doing so eased the path towards the modern, multi-national footballing world that the next decade would epitomise, one which would end with a treble-winning Italian captain. It was – as both Graeme Souness and David Murray have since admitted – something that simply had to be done.

But this is also the season of a lesser-known tale of modernity, one than didn't quite come to fruition but nevertheless tells us so much about the challenges that Rangers faced in trying to move forward in 1989. That first Johnston goal – securing a 1-0 win over Aberdeen in the September – neatly encapsulated something else that was going on at the time. On the face of it, it was a goal very typical of its era – a ball out wide, a cross into a crowded penalty box and a header past a helpless goalkeeper – but there was more to it than that. It was scored by one major summer signing and assisted by the other, Trevor Steven, and both players represented something of the modern themselves. They were both classy, all-round footballers, not easily pigeon-holed into stereotypical roles. Steven's cross was delightful but, without natural pace, he was not an out-and-out winger and Johnston's header was not the powerful, target man bullet, but a clever, almost sneaky goal, as he ghosted into the space between Willie Miller, Alex McLeish and Stewart McKimmie and deftly let the ball do all the work. Souness would give up on his target man approach this season and he would not seek as much width as he had previously. After a painful lesson, he would also soon come to the obvious conclusion that building a successful style in Scotland is not easily compatible with creating a successful formula on a European stage that was shedding its English influence and moving towards the skill and flexibility of Serie A. He knew that change was required and was initially willing to experiment.

Crucially, he had the freedom to do so. That Johnston goal gave Rangers their first win of the season – after four games – but incredibly, it didn't lift them from the bottom of the Scottish Premier Division. More importantly, there were only two points between bottom and top and that congestion – as the chasing pack continued to cut each other down – would provide the ideal breathing space for taking tactical risks. To what extent he made the most of that opportunity is another question. This was a season of necessary, if unpopular, change both on and off the park. If Rangers showed as much bravery and foresight with the former as they did with the latter, history might have been very different indeed.

* * *

With only 18 minutes remaining, Scotland were in full control of a World Cup Final. Two early goals – one of power and one of intelligence – had calmed the nerves of the 60,000 crowd inside Hampden and, when Gary Bollan was brought down after driving his way into the penalty box, the chance to put their name on the trophy was handed to them on a plate as the Argentinian referee pointed to the spot. All of this is true but if it reads like something from a fever dream then what happened next is somehow far more prosaic and familiar. Celtic's Brian O'Neil missed his penalty and with it the chance to put Scotland 3-1 ahead, and he would miss another later in the afternoon, the final Scottish spot-kick in the decisive shoot-out, a situation forced by a Saudi Arabia equaliser only minutes after the miss in regulation time. Of course, from a position of such strength, Scotland blew it.

The World Cup in question was FIFA's under-16 tournament in June 1989, which was hosted by Scotland. Barely 6,000 had turned up to Hampden for the opening 0-0 draw with Ghana – boasting the potential of Nii Lamptey who, despite having a fine career at clubs ranging from Coventry City to Boca Juniors didn't match the 'next Pelé' hype that surrounded him even at this stage[93] – but the tournament grew in the public's imagination as Scotland progressed, leading to a sell-out semi-final at Tynecastle against Portugal containing a young Luís Figo and then the huge attendance for the final to witness the dramatic failure against a Saudi side containing some players who looked old enough to be playing in their own testimonial.

FIFA never investigated the claims of ineligible Saudi players but, while they were in town, they were happy to get involved in the Scottish transfer story of the summer. With Celtic and Maurice Johnston in a bitter dispute over the legitimacy of the signed documents, FIFA general secretary Sepp Blatter declared that Johnston should be Celtic's player, 'We have a signed agreement, dated May 10, saying that the player would be transferred from Nantes to Celtic as from July 1. We also have an agreement signed by Maurice Johnston on May 12 stating that he would sign for Celtic on July 1. We have studied these documents and consider them to be binding for the parties involved.' So, according to the game's highest power, the transfer was on but Blatter made sure to add a caveat at the end when he said, 'Unless the parties mutually agree to rescind the existing contracts.' With the player's agent Bill McMurdo adamant that he would go through the European courts to prove that it was not a contract of employment but only 'what might be considered a letter of intent', the pressure was on Celtic to cave in and face reality. If they had paid the £700,000 remaining of the fee then it would have been a case of another club having to deal with them directly if they wanted to take an unhappy player off their hands. Billy McNeill implored his chairman, Jack McGinn, to do so in order to have that control but there was little chance that Celtic would pay over £1m for a player who didn't want to be there and with no guarantee of making that money back in a matter of weeks. By the end of that week, 30 June, while McNeill and other directors were on holiday, McGinn pulled out of the deal. The media reaction was supportive of Celtic's refusal to let it drag on. The general tabloid consensus was that it was best for both the club and for the player, who was now free to choose his next club. What they didn't know, of course, is that it had been chosen for some time.

'I wonder if he would come to us?' wrote Graeme Souness in A Manager's Diary, the book published in late 1989 that covered the period between July 1988 and July 1989. 'Now there's a thought!' It certainly was, but it was one he had before the previous season was even over, not on 1 July as the book stated. The truth about the most sensational transfer in Scottish, if not British, football history eventually came out years later but, midway through a volatile season, it was thought best to use artistic licence with the dates if not the actual narrative. Campbell Ogilvie was one of the very few to have known about the deal for weeks but, as someone who had grown up in a GP's household, he had learned to keep tight-lipped on the details that he picked up in conversation. Although the terms with Johnston and Nantes had all been signed, he still needed to be registered

---

93   The great man himself was at Hampden that day as FIFA's ambassador for the tournament. He walked around the pitch shaking hands with young fans, the author included, and charmed the world's media by assuring every journalist that their country would win the next World Cup all at the same time.

as a Rangers player. That needed more paperwork to be signed, with secrecy still the order of the day. On Friday, 7 July, Ogilvie and the Rangers CEO Alan Montgomery agreed to meet Johnston and McMurdo in the car park of the old Royal Scot Hotel in Edinburgh. 'Maurice arrived with his agent, Bill McMurdo, and our cars parked alongside one another. I was gathering the relevant paperwork and then noticed in my rear-view mirror a British Rail van with a dozen workers parked behind us, and then get out with their luminous vests on to eat sandwiches for their lunch break,' Ogilvie told the Sunday Post in 2016. 'Maurice got out of his car, with a baseball cap and sunglasses on, and climbed into my car. Bearing in my mind the transfer wasn't public knowledge, we were nervous Maurice would be spotted – but thankfully he wasn't. So he signed for Rangers in that car park in front of an unsuspecting group of workers.' And then, on Monday, 10 July 1989, a stunned Scotland attempted to comprehend the news that even some senior sports writers had earlier dismissed as nonsense. Both Johnston and McMurdo had been inside Ibrox since 5am due to Souness – with his flair for the dramatic impact – not wanting the story to leak until they announced it. As the men hid in a toilet cubicle, kitman George Soutar and a friend were chatting at the urinals. 'Who are we going to sign today?,' his mate asked. 'I don't care who we sign as long as it's not that Maurice Johnston.' Or some words to that effect.

The word 'Catholic' was never used by Graeme Souness during that press conference but it never needed to be, as he said, 'The only thing that mattered to us was that we have bought the best centre-forward in Britain and maybe even the continent. I have promised the Rangers supporters that I would try to provide the finest team possible and this is another step towards doing just that.' Perhaps more pertinently, he went on, 'We won the title in our first year but then lost it to Celtic. I don't want that to happen again and I am certain that this signing will go a long way towards achieving that ambition.' It would. Celtic would either maintain a silence or say the bare minimum in the immediate aftermath but there was little doubt that the impact on losing a player to Rangers who they had already coveted and paraded as their own would prove to be a significant psychological blow and they were not a club, at that point in time, well-placed to absorb it. They would go to the continent for their star striker – Poland's Dariusz Dziekanowski for £500,000 – but he was never likely to replace the all-round threat that Johnston would have provided them with. Even if the signing had come off, Johnston and those around him who would have been positively impacted would still have a job to do in continuing to paper over the cracks of a club whose leadership had long become stagnant.

The signing represented modern football in ways outside of religion. For Johnston to do what he did was incredibly brave when the easy option of returning 'home' was there waiting. However, he risked his own safety and that of his family, by choosing money – Rangers quickly resolved whatever financial issues that caused the original hold-up with Celtic – and the better chance to win titles. That was the modern footballing option, not the romantic one. It was one driven by naked personal ambition rather than any hoary old nonsense about community ties. He would indeed win the title whereas Celtic would finish the season in fifth place – as low a position as they had suffered since 1977/78 – and with only ten league victories, a total not seen since 1951/52. It was a colossal blow that, although it wasn't Souness's main driver, was a likely consequence of which he was well aware.

How the Rangers support processed the story will be dealt with in more detail later on but it is worth noting how public some prominent fans were prepared to show their disgust. David Miller, general secretary of the Rangers Supporters' Association and someone who was starting to make a habit of speaking to the media before he had properly thought things through, said that there would be 'a lot of people handing back their season tickets. I don't want to see a Roman Catholic at Ibrox. Rangers have always stood for one thing, and the biggest majority of fans have been brought up with a true-blue team.' Like his pronouncement that fans would reject the new season ticket prices in the summer of 1987, this prediction was rather wide of the mark.

The reaction of the true-blue voice on the street was so viscerally captured that it is sometimes easy to forget that there were true-blue voices in the Rangers dressing room too. As Souness arrived back to Il Ciocco in a helicopter with his new signing, the squad's dining room had famously been set especially for their new team-mate. As the players sat a long table, a solitary place for Johnston had been arranged in the corner, with bread and water. Jimmy Bell, a part of the backroom staff, refused to set out Johnston's kit meaning that he had to walk down from his hotel room to collect his gear each day. How much it was just a case of dressing room ribbing is contentious. Souness remarked on the protests at home in his diary by noting that the reception by the team had been supportive, writing, 'I wish the fans who have protested could have seen that. These players know that we have signed a class act. That is all that matters to them. And, really, it's all that should matter to anyone.' But years later, in his autobiography, he contradicted that memory somewhat when he stated, 'I remember some dyed-in-the-wool Rangers players in the squad would have nothing to do with him when he first arrived.'

One flashpoint was a proposed public relations photo op with Johnston and some of the English and Scottish players together. None of the English members of the squad had any problems but there was a deep reticence from those born and bred with Rangers traditions. Terry Butcher was annoyed at the apparent hypocrisy from the kind of players who had always complained that the intolerance was stronger at the other end of the city. In 1992, Ally McCoist explained that there was nothing personal towards his friend and international strike partner but that they were simply worried about the reaction at home, 'I had heard that feelings were running high back home, and I didn't want some nutter throwing a brick through my mother's window because he had thought I had said the wrong thing.' McCoist, along with Ian Ferguson and Richard Gough, have since explained the initial reaction as a tough-love kind of ice-breaker but accounts like those of Mark Walters cast doubt on that. 'I remember Ian [Ferguson] slaughtering him on a number of occasions at training,' wrote Walters in his autobiography. 'Was it banter? I would like to think so but only Ian would be able to answer that.' It was an undeniably significant impact on the dressing room to the extent that players had to park their cars inside the stadium to be checked for bombs and the training ground perimeter checked from snipers. Throughout it all, Johnston laughed it off. As Gough put it, 'Mo was the centre of attraction. He was the most talked about player in the country and that was just the way he liked it.'

On the same day that Celtic pulled out of the Johnston deal, Rangers paraded their latest big-money signing although, because Trevor Steven was out of contract and this happened before Jean-Marc Bosman changed the world, the eventual price would only later be fixed by a tribunal.[94] It was yet another statement of intent as Souness sought the best of British in every position in which he could, however in the days before large squads and regular rotation, he had given himself something of a headache. For two wide berths and two striking options, he had three players of genuine quality, not mere reserves. Although he used all three of Johnston, McCoist and Kevin Drinkell in pre-season games, with McCoist dropping deeper into midfield because of some small injuries and then appearing a trident attack against Partick Thistle, it wasn't ever likely to be a long-term option, meaning Souness would be left with a very expensive or popular substitute. With Walters being an instant hit and the new arrival of Steven, Davie Cooper was faced with the prospect of leaving his boyhood heroes to guarantee first-team football. With only ten starts in all competitions in 1988/89, his testimonial year, the writing was on the wall and he grabbed the chance of a career encore at Motherwell before the season started. With Cooper's departure went the only surviving link to the last successful Rangers side of the 1970s. It really was a season where the old was cast aside by the sheer pace of the new.

Another departure was David Holmes, the man who first started the acceleration that was now leaving him behind. With David Murray never likely to play the role of absentee owner, there was simply not going to be the space for two men who liked to exercise control. There was a degree of fanfare for the changing roles of chairman but it was mostly for Murray, who made it clear that he would not accept being simply a figurehead but wanted to take Rangers into the next big challenge of the future: conquering Europe. There should have been more for Holmes, whose role in changing Rangers remains undervalued, as he slipped quietly out of the limelight, something that he rarely enjoyed at the best of times. The contrasting styles of leadership will be explored later but there is no question that Holmes's lack of lust for the limelight hampered the chances of an appropriate send-off at the time and especially a fuller appreciation of his importance to Rangers history decades later.

Amid a pre-season that was arguably more keenly anticipated than even 1986, Johnston hit the ground running, not only scoring regularly throughout the friendlies but assisting his new team-mates too. Steven had also impressed, no more so than with his super goal in the 1-0 win over Tottenham Hotspur at Ibrox in the final match before the curtain was officially raised. He allowed Gary Stevens to do the overlap work on the right before drifting inside to unleash a perfectly executed left-footed shot into the bottom corner. It was a very balanced Rangers side – the normal back four and Woods, behind Wilkins and Ian Ferguson in the

---

94   The eventual price was £1.525m. Everton wanted somewhere around £4.5m and Souness credited the performance on the day of Alan Montgomery. It would prove to be one of the few credits he would pay Montgomery as the season unfolded.

middle, Walters and Steven on either side and Johnston and McCoist up front – and some of the football was exceptional. It was a friendly most famous for the flare-up between Ferguson and Paul Gascoigne, the latter appearing to spit in his opponent's face at one stage, inducing chants from the Ibrox crowd that would be in complete contrast to those he would receive the next time he played there. And who was first to step in to defend the true-blue, hardline Ian Ferguson? Johnston, of course. His assimilation was progressing at speed but the real tests were soon to come.

Souness opted for that same starting XI for the opening day of the season but yet again it was a flag day party that fell flat. With St Mirren offering up slightly less space than a Tottenham side that was a couple of weeks behind in preparation, Rangers were too easily frustrated and opted for the kind of crosses for which the tightly packed defence was well suited. McCoist did break free once or twice and his cut-back for Derek Ferguson in the second half should have led to a goal but was instead blocked off the line by David Winnie. By that time St Mirren were in the lead and the miss came at the cost of more than just one goal and two points dropped. Kenny McDowall's leap to beat Chris Woods to a rare cross into the box looked robust, even by the standards of the day, and it left the England goalkeeper with a broken collarbone. Ian Ferguson had recently had a great performance in goal during five-a-sides in training so Butcher told him to take his place between the sticks. In his contribution to Alistair Aird's enjoyable book on Rangers players of the 1980s, Ferguson said, 'I put the gloves on but it wasn't until the play started to resume that I thought, "What the fuck have I done?" It was a different kettle of fish playing in front of 40,000.' He needn't have worried; the visitors barely ventured over the halfway line as they held on to their precious two points. 'Once more,' Butcher wrote years later, 'we had shown no sense of occasion, losing a game we should have won.'

Rangers had made their approach for the Israeli goalkeeper Boni Ginzburg at the end of July, when the application for a work permit was first submitted. Now it was a race against time to have him in from Maccabi Tel Aviv in time for the trip to Easter Road. He actually made the move in time for the Skol Cup victory over Arbroath but his league debut was less than impressive as Rangers fell to defeat once more. If he wasn't at fault for the opening goal – getting down a little too slowly to his right to stop Keith Houchen's low drive from the edge of the area – then he was fully culpable for the second when he came rushing out to claim a deep free kick before spilling it into the path of Mickey Weir who easily made it 2-0. Rangers' play was good, their was passing crisp and plenty of chances were created but nothing stuck in the final third with both McCoist and Johnston guilty of trying too hard to get off the mark. Bottom of the league without a point or a goal, Souness refused to panic either inside the dressing room or when speaking to the outside world. 'I'm not making criticisms in any department,' he said post-match. 'Anyone who has seen our opening league matches would agree we dominated. We haven't had the breaks and that will change.'

It would have to change at Parkhead the following Saturday, where the eyes of the world were on the return of Johnston.[95] Richard Gough's injured foot,

---

95   Celtic had press pass requests from all over Europe and the USA.

which was reported to be the subject of surgery that week, was patched up as Souness opted for steel rather than aesthetics. John Brown came in for Walters and Drinkell replaced McCoist in a more direct and traditional 4-4-2. It reaped early dividends when a Steven corner was powered home yet again by Butcher's head, his celebration up the Main Stand touchline perhaps evidence of the pressure that was suddenly released. It wasn't a lead that Rangers held on to for long, however, as Celtic's fallback striker Dziekanowski scrambled in an equaliser following yet more fragility from a cross. The game followed the typical frantic pattern and, with no further goals to follow, the real narrative was around the chances missed.

Johnston's reception was predictably volatile, especially around the tunnel area and his sheepish smile during the pre-match warm-up, accompanied his recognition of the Rangers support, not all of whom were yet united behind him, but when push come to shove they showed their support for their new striker. They may have been more vociferous if he had scored two of the excellent chances that were presented to him in the first half, the second of which was golden. He snatched at both, as he done in previous games, but if Rangers were to be patient the early signs of creation and movement were surely going to be converted sooner rather than later. It was McCoist's arrival later in the game that helped open Celtic up like that, with Rangers playing more intelligently through the heart of their opponents. With the club's overdraft nearing £10m, Souness would soon have a decision to make on which striker he should cash in on and in doing so, make a statement about how he wanted his side to look.

Kevin Drinkell would start at home to Aberdeen but it would be his last. A dour game, where both sides cancelled one another out for large parts and where Butcher was bandaged up following his famous 'bloody shirt' match for England in Sweden during the week, was lit up by the moment the whole of Scottish football had been either dreading or hoping for. It was a brilliant goal by Johnston, it was the only goal in a big 1-0 win, and it wouldn't be the last time that happened during this season. Finally Rangers were off and running in the league championship but the midweek that followed would provide a harsh lesson on their place in the wider world. The club was at another crossroads.

* * *

The mood around the board meeting was downbeat. There was to be no journey to the European Cup last eight or beyond this time. In fact Rangers never even made it over the first hurdle. It was a high one, it must be said. It could have been Sliema Wanderers of Malta, Ruch Chorzów of Poland or Knattspyrnufélagið Fram of Iceland but instead Rangers had drawn West German opposition yet again and this time it was the biggest of them all: Bayern Munich. Despite a bright start from Rangers, 1-0 up in the first leg at Ibrox by virtue of a penalty from Mark Walters – pushed into a more central attacking role with Johnston due to the suspension of both McCoist and Drinkell – it was cancelled out quickly by a stunning Ludwig Kögl volley after a weak header by Scott Nisbet. An early second-half penalty by Olaf Thon and a trademark long-range screamer into the top corner by Klaus Augenthaler killed the tie stone dead. Rangers played well in the goalless return leg but it was never likely to trouble a Bayern team who would only be eliminated from the tournament in semi-final extra time by one of the greatest club sides in history: Arrigo Sacchi's AC Milan. 'Does it have to be this way?' the chairman asked his board of directors.

David Murray would be involved in two big conversations in the autumn of 1989, both of which could have altered European football history significantly. In the end only one did but it would be genuinely transformative as it was during that meeting in late September of 1989 that the ball towards the creation of the Champions League started to roll with pace. The open draw, although romantic, could cut cup runs for even the biggest clubs down to size before it started to get chilly in northern Europe. Surely there was a way to guarantee three home games at least before the real knockout fun could begin? Campbell Ogilvie was tasked with sketching out this new world and, eventually, nothing would be the same again. Once more it was Rangers, this bastion of established tradition, who were at the edge of pushing change and making progress, all in the name of footballing modernity.

Off the park, at least. Arriving in Munich for the second leg, Graeme Souness made an observation that would linger over the whole season, and ultimately for much of the new decade. 'The way the game is played back home gives us a severe handicap when it comes to having any chance of being successful at the very highest level,' he said. Because of the physical demands domestically and the need to play with non-stop pace and aggression, it was, he felt, becoming too difficult to adapt to an increasingly different game in continental competition. Critics would suggest that this was a convenient excuse for expensive failure and would point to Dundee United's journey to the UEFA Cup Final only two years before as evidence to the contrary. There is no question that the timing was deliberate but there was something in it nonetheless. Apart from the obvious riposte that Dundee United had enjoyed that UEFA Cup run without having to trouble trophy engravers for some time, the British game – or really the English game – had dominated the style of the competitions in the decade leading up to Heysel, with 12 European titles being won by British clubs[96], seven of those being the European Cup itself. There was then arguably a kind of interregnum for three seasons where sides from Romania, Belgium, Sweden, Portugal and the Soviet Union all triumphed[97], before the influence of Serie A and West Germany installed a new order, one which was increasingly different in nature from the Scottish Premier Division.

Only a few weeks after that exit from Europe, Souness was very nearly leaving Rangers. Earlier in the season the businessman Michael Knighton had agreed a deal in principle to buy control of Manchester United from Martin Edwards, but by early October he was still requiring some extra funding. That search led him to Edinburgh and a meeting with David Murray where, late into the night, an

---

96   The closest nations were West Germany who claimed five titles in that time and Spain with four.

97   This was most notable in the European Cup where Steaua Bucharest, FC Porto and PSV Eindhoven all won for the first time between 1986 and 1988.

agreement in principle was reached that allowed Knighton to get to his required target of £10m. Murray quickly changed his mind – mainly due to growing concerns about individuals having too much control in more than one club[98] – and both that deal and Knighton's were soon abandoned. Had it gone through, however, then the British footballing landscape would have changed beyond all recognition. United were 14th in the league when these discussions were taking place[99] and only a fortnight earlier they had suffered a humiliating 5-1 defeat at the home of their Manchester rivals, a fourth league loss in their opening seven games. Alex Ferguson seemed to be in trouble and would have been sacked if a Murray-backed Knighton deal had been successful where, rather sensationally, he would have been replaced by Souness, with Walter Smith being promoted at Ibrox. Although United toiled, the famous FA Cup win at the end of the season kept the Ferguson era moving forward and it would soon gather incredible pace. According to Souness in both of his autobiographies, this was a move that he welcomed, which would cast obvious doubt on the levels of commitment to Rangers expressed with not only his words but his money the previous season as well as love for Liverpool, but it perhaps was an early indicator that his patience with the game in Scotland was wearing thin.[100]

Later in the autumn he would get involved in an internal struggle with Alan Montgomery, Rangers' chief executive. It was never a relationship that was destined for harmonious success. During that season's summer camp in Italy, only four months after his arrival, Souness had to stop Walter Smith from physically intervening when Montgomery took pictures of David Murray's son in a drunken state. Souness felt that Montgomery had too much to say on the football front – his presence in Italy at all wasn't well understood as was his appearance in the dressing room on occasion – but it was most likely to do with how the money was being spent that caused the most friction. With interest rates rising, reducing the overdraft was Montgomery's primary aim but that was in natural conflict with a manager who was always on the lookout for what could be done to improve his squad in the immediate short term.[101] Souness ultimately called the shots and Murray had to move his man to media position within his growing empire on 1 November but this was set in the context of growing rumours of restlessness, to the point at which some bookmakers in Glasgow suspended betting on Kenny Dalglish coming in as manager and Souness stepping up to be chairman.[102] It wouldn't be too long before Souness's struggles with the wider game, the authorities and the media would reach a point of no return so it is understandable that a move to a job as prestigious as Manchester United would have been tempting. As

---

98   Ken Bates had interest in Chelsea and Partick Thistle and Robert Maxwell had enjoyed a stake in both Derby County and Oxford United. Tension was growing around how long that would be allowed to happen.

99   They would finish 13th.

100   Knighton has refuted the extent of these conversations a number of times since Souness's book was published.

101   The fact that Montgomery had a bigger and nicer office than Souness is not something that should be dismissed easily as trivial either.

102   You could get odds of 9/2 against Dalglish taking the job and 3/1 against Souness moving upstairs.

much as Souness believed that the deal was agreed in principle as he went to his bed that night, in reality it never had the foundations required and he would have to make do with the Scottish game for a while longer.

It was a Scottish game that Souness was changing, albeit not at the pace he required. On the day of the 1-1 draw at Parkhead in August, the Premier Division saw four goals from Englishmen and one from a Pole, a Dutchman, an Irishman, a Yugoslav and an Icelander. The rest of the country was following his lead but none were prepared or able to do it to his level and this meant that there was a condensed and competitive block forming in the league, allowing Souness room to experiment in trying to shift the style of his side to compete on all fronts in the future, comfortable in the knowledge that none would break away from that pack as, while Rangers made inevitable mistakes, their rivals continued to take points from one another. For example, a defeat at Fir Park on 4 October left Rangers in eighth after eight games but they were still only three points off the top of the table. The gap between those two positions at the same stage the previous season was ten points. Souness refused to be drawn into a heated and angry reaction to such disappointment, instead focusing on the quality of overall play and this was a consistent theme throughout that erratic first half of the season. When it came to footballing matters, on the surface it was a more relaxed Rangers manager in general, best exemplified after the 1-0 away defeat to Aberdeen in late November. A fantastic finish by Hans Gillhaus gave Aberdeen the points but Souness said immediately after the game, 'I was delighted with my players' performance, but it was one of these occasions on which it was the opposition's night.' Rangers were excellent on the ball and it was a point that Souness repeated at the end of the season: if they kept playing that way then the results would inevitably come.

It was a show of calm assurance so often missing during such inconsistency in previous seasons, especially when a month before Aberdeen had finally beaten Rangers in the League Cup Final. Two Paul Mason goals either side of a Mark Walters equaliser deservedly ended Rangers' three-year grip on the trophy in a final where the holders only looked the part sporadically. Relaxation was the key to the preparation, with some time off being given to the players the week before the final, and the sharpness that had proved vital in three knife-edge showpieces before was undoubtedly missing. If the league defeat at Aberdeen was one of the most notable performances of the season, then the defeat itself is noteworthy as it was the only loss to a side in the top half of the table that season. Rangers dropped more points on average to those sides in the lower half – back-to-back draws at home to Dundee and Dunfermline in September to add to the opening calamities and the loss at Motherwell – than they did against their closest rivals. If Souness was changing the style of the side to be more possession-based and rounded without the midfield enforcer and target man up front, then it should not be surprising that they would slip up to the more physical and rudimentary opponents in comparison to some vital, tight but controlled wins against the league's improving footballing teams.

And it was Johnston who was making that marginal difference. The only goal against Aberdeen was followed up immediately by a clinical strike to defeats Hearts 1-0 at Ibrox and the first in a 2-1 home win over Dundee United in October where his now-settled partner Ally McCoist scored an excellent winner. Souness gambled a lot on Scotland's forward line, who finally secured qualification for the 1990 World Cup in November with a 1-1 draw at home to Norway, McCoist scoring the vital goal with a brilliant lob. Kevin Drinkell was sold to Coventry City at the end of September and the only senior replacement was Davie Dodds who was brought in at the start of the campaign, with Walters able to use his flexibility when required. Rangers would only have 11 goalscorers all season, with just three in double figures – McCoist (18), Johnston (17) and Walters (12) – and the rest scoring four or fewer.[103] Given the injury paranoia that Souness regularly suffered from during his time at Ibrox – and there would be a few long-term issues in this season too – his front pairing went relatively unscathed and it was just as well, with them carrying so much of that burden. Johnston would grab a vital goal in a 1-1 at Tannadice in December to add to his tally of crucial, point-winning strikes. None, however, would come close in terms of importance than his goal at Ibrox on 3 November.

Rangers had managed to climb into fourth place by the time that league leaders Celtic visited Ibrox for the first time that season. The congestion remained a factor, with only four points separating Hibs, down in seventh, all the way up to the top. With the nine goals they conceded the previous season still fresh in Billy McNeill's mind, Celtic shook off their mythical cavalier attitude and went to blunt the champions, with the hope of nicking what they could. It was certainly a different feel to the derby than any of the four league clashes the season before, with McNeill admitting after that football was changing and saying, 'Where there will always be a place for passion in the modern game, it must be controlled.'

McNeill's cageyness nearly paid off when both Joe Miller and Tommy Coyne should have done better on a break, but Rangers were the more dominant throughout and were most deserving of the win as the match approached the end. A characteristic common among so many of Johnston's strikes for Rangers was the instant ball control and in the space of less than ten seconds, that stone-dead touch started and finished a famous move. His first touch, over by the Main Stand touchline, was greeted by jeers and whistles from both sets of supporters and one notable boo, presumably from a Rangers fan, given the proximity to the main microphones. His second touch, at the edge of the box, stopped a poor Chris Morris clearance instantly and, with three onrushing, desperate defenders coming out to close him down, gave him enough time and space to sweep the ball home into the bottom corner. There were no jeers now. No Rangers fans with their arms folded. Just sheer bedlam, as a kind of pressure unimaginable to most fans there that day – death threats and all – was released in front of the Copland Road Stand. 'Typical of Mo wasn't it?' said Tommy Burns after the match. 'You give him one sight of goal and he sticks it away, but that has always been his strength and I suppose that is why Rangers were prepared to pay £1.5m to get him.' The use of 'suppose' gave that praise a certain grudging quality but it was at least an improvement on calling him a 'wee runt' when the two first met after the transfer

---

103   There were only nine different goalscorers in the league and it would take until December for the fifth to be added, by which time Walters and Butcher had scored twice and McCoist and Johnston eight apiece.

but the reference to the fee was perhaps a subtle dig at the overall ambition of his club in comparison to their great rivals.

This wasn't some kind of momentous turning point in Scottish football – the two were not at an existential crossroads at this stage of 1989 – but it was a final blow to a staggering, stumbling football club. Like the fall of the Berlin Wall six days later, it was a famous symbolic and emotionally charged moment in history but the real story was the undercurrent of pressure that made that specific moment so resonant. Celtic were top of the league that morning but Rangers would be at the summit that evening. Of the 24 remaining league games following this defeat, Celtic would win only five, losing nine and drawing ten, and it would be six years before silverware returned to Parkhead. It was always going to be a difficult period with their cumbersome and bumbling structural issues being placed in sharp contrast to a more dynamic and ambitious rival but the psychological blow of Johnston – the initial pain being very tame in comparison to this delayed reaction – should never be underplayed.

The Pittodrie defeat on 22 November knocked Rangers off the top until just after Christmas but there had been more than enough shown in the first half of the season to warrant the bookmakers' confidence that the title would be comfortably retained. Three days after Aberdeen, Rangers hosted Dunfermline Athletic at Ibrox. A comfortable 3-0 win in the impending winter fog was notable for the first goal, scored by Johnston with an incredible first touch yet again but more for the pass by Ray Wilkins, which was both sumptuous and precise. It was his final assist in his final match for Rangers. With his contract coming to an end and the lure of returning to play in London becoming too much, Wilkins bid an emotional goodbye to a support who loved him dearly.

What happened next was a significant but vastly underrated moment in the evolution of Rangers' era of dominance. Souness could have replaced his ball-playing playmaker with another of the same mould, but he didn't. Rangers were immediately linked with John Collins of Hibs, who had been previously approached but turned down the advances due to problems arising from the religion issue, and Nigel Spackman of Queens Park Rangers, the club for whom Wilkins had just departed. Even if the issues that Collins had raised still persisted, there were other players of a similar style who Rangers could have pursued. In the end Souness replaced silk with steel. It would pay immediate dividends that season – with a powerful presence that would push the team out of the dogfight and into clear blue water – and indeed for the next two years but it jarred with his pronouncements about an incompatibility of style outside of Scotland. It was the right call in the name of expediency but arguably would have consequences long beyond the season's title celebrations.

* * *

'What good is the warmth of summer,' once asked the American novelist John Steinbeck, 'without the cold of winter to give it sweetness?' Scottish league champions are so often shaped by the season's toughest spell. In nine of the 12 campaigns during the Souness and Smith era, Rangers were significantly stronger over the autumn and winter and especially the latter. With all seasons being split into four quarters and all points adjusted to three for a win, the third quarter – covering December to February – derived the most points on average with 2.3 points per game being won between 1986 and 1998.[104] With the weather and pitches at their worst, it really is the endurance phase of the season but, with European competition either on pause or a distant memory and the League Cup taken care of, the focus can almost entirely be placed on league business and this is where Rangers thrived. Given the start to 1989/90[105] the middle two quarters of the season needed a massive response and by December, Souness's side were going into overdrive. At the start of the month, Rangers were in second place, two points behind the leaders Aberdeen but by 3 February, they were seven points clear at the top as they delivered a level of consistent pressure that the rest of the challengers couldn't deal with. Most notably, it was the key matches against the chasing pack in which they proved to be unshakeable.

On his 29th birthday, Nigel Spackman made his debut at Tynecastle against a Hearts side who were just two points behind them in third place. The home team's bright start deserved the early goal by Eamonn Bannon but once more Rangers simply played their way patiently out of trouble with Walters smashing the post before half-time and then getting some fortune with a deflected effort that brought them level. In a game with plenty of energy but few chances, Rangers' quality shone through in the end with Steven grabbing a 77th-minute winner from a Johnston assist, once more demonstrating the underlying strength that was making the difference in the top-half clashes, characterised by tight margins. It was a similar story at Tannadice two weeks later where Johnston pounced on an Alan Main error to grab a point in conditions so cold that Ally McCoist took the field in the second half wearing ski gloves.

This wider picture was further illustrated at Parkhead on the first game of 1990. Glasgow's new year celebrations had an extra significance because it was now the European City of Culture but there was little in the way of artistry and sophistication in a pretty dreadful Old Firm encounter. Chris Woods had to make an outstanding save from Paul Elliot's header in the second half but the game was settled in the 14th minute in a style that typified the expedient shift in gear that Souness had deployed. It was Spackman who started and finished it, robbing a dithering Paul McStay in midfield and powering through acres of space as Johnston and then McCoist sharply broke away to lay it back into his path seven yards from goal. It was a technically astute finish and there was no little game intelligence on show either, but it was mostly a goal of power and tenacity and it was not the kind that Wilkins was likely to provide. Souness had decided, with Steven and Walters

---

104   Quarter two brought in 2.19 points and the first and final quarter of the season, 2.02. In five seasons the first and last quarter saw Rangers drop below two points per game and that happened in three seasons for quarter two. Only twice did it occur in the winter quarter, in 1994/95 when the competition was incredibly weak and in 1997/98 when the title was thrown into disarray.

105   The first quarter produced an average of 1.33 points per game, the lowest in any season quarter throughout this era.

already established in the midfield that a deep-lying playmaker was too much and that Spackman, being 'more of a working player' in the manager's own words, provided him with more balance to deal with the challenges of the Scottish game.

Rangers were still in the hunt during the experimentation with a more ball-playing side but he evidently didn't feel that it would be enough to power through the winter and beyond. The trial-and-error flirtation with a more modern and continental style was over and, with only two points dropped in nine games throughout December and January, Souness would have felt vindicated. Not surprisingly there was more quality of fluency on show at Ibrox the following week when Aberdeen visited for a top-of-the-table clash. A young Michael Watt was in inspired form in the Aberdeen goal, making several outstanding saves, but the rearguard was eventually breached with just under 15 minutes remaining when some brilliant close control by Walters bought him space in the box to rifle a low shot into the bottom corner. McCoist popped up with a late close-range header to make sure and that goal was significant in itself as, in the tenth Rangers encounter with teams from the top half of the ten-team league that season[106], it was the first game with a margin of more than one goal. This 2-0 win would be followed up by a 3-1 home victory over Dundee United on 3 February as the margins within these crucial games were increasing at the same rate as the gap, now seven points, at the top.

Long-term injuries were not as significant a factor in this season has they had been in each of the previous three, although there were still issues to overcome with two key players. Ian Ferguson's campaign was limited by illness, a glandular problem that only improved later on when his tonsils were removed. Souness was supportive of him, despite Ferguson warning him that Rangers were a man down early in the games due to his energy levels being so low, but there was more of an edge in how the manager dealt with Richard Gough's persistent foot injury. Gough was constantly being asked to play through the pain barrier but this issue, undiagnosed for so long[107], was more severe than the usual niggles that players have to regularly ignore. Writing in 1993, Gough said that Souness was 'never one to make allowances for injury – his own or anyone else's. There was an impatience about him when it came to injuries, as if he didn't think your body should let you down.' Again, this would have been a managerial blind spot that came from his own playing career where he had never suffered a major injury and had played more than 30 games in every season since breaking through as a youngster at Middlesborough in 1973/74 until that second year at Ibrox.

That growing tension reached its climx as Gough was laid out on the treatment table following a friendly defeat to Arsenal at Ibrox jus before Christmas.[108] Souness, bitterly disappointed to lose the game because of its connotations, told Gough that he thought he was 'at it' with this persistent problem. Effectively being labelled a cheat by his manager, in front of Walter Smith and Phil Boersma, Gough

---

106   Aberdeen, Hearts, Dundee United and Celtic made up that top five.

107   It was eventually confirmed as 'Morton's Neuroma' and would need two operations to fix.

108   This was effectively an unofficial British Championship match between the Scottish and English league winners from the previous season, called the Zenith Data Systems Challenge, in an attempt to fill the European gap in the English calendar. Arsenal won 2-1.

felt that he would have to leave as taking on Souness directly would only end one way. Nothing was said the following morning but there was a festive function for the side at night, hosted by the chairman. Souness spoke at the outset and, addressing the whole squad, did something that was very much out of character. 'I have got to apologise to a certain player because of some very unfair remarks I made to him last night,' he started. 'The player knows what I'm talking about and I was really out of order with him after the game.' Gough hadn't said a word so nobody knew what their manager was talking about but after that, it was over. This was almost certainly the work of Smith and this rare public apology avoided a potentially cataclysmic departure that could have altered history significantly. 'Nothing else was said. Nothing else had to be said,' wrote Gough. 'Other than that, I didn't have a problem with Graeme.'

That, however, didn't apply to everyone. As much as Souness was keeping his cool about form and results in those opening months of the season, as he ensured that his team reverted to a battle mode on the pitch, so too did he off it. Mark Walters, for whom Tynecastle was always a difficult trip, received a late second yellow card in that 2-1 December win, the first coming from an incident with former team-mate Dave McPherson that was very soft.[109] Souness was involved in a tunnel fracas with McPherson immediately after the game as he believed that too much was made of the first booking and Lothian and Borders police were asked to compile a report for the SFA's perusal. Souness was currently still serving a year's touchline ban following his fury at the level of added time against Dundee United in February 1989 and then a breach of that ban, originally in place until the end of 1988/89, during the Scottish Cup semi-final against St Johnstone. He could technically defy the punishment by naming himself as a substitute but, with only two spaces available and his playing career in its final days, it was rarely an affordable luxury.

Hearts would again be involved the next time that Souness was hauled up to Park Gardens, then the SFA's headquarters. During a 0-0 draw with them at Ibrox on 17 February 1990, Souness was caught on STV's cameras standing inside the tunnel passing on instructions. This was found to be in breach again so he received a £5,000 fine and the ban was increased to a further two years. STV were promptly banned from Ibrox for their role in this trial by television[110]. After a relative lull in hostilities, Souness was back on the warpath with the Scottish footballing establishment and was now starting down a path from which there would be no return.

There was an impact on results too, although the players have since admitted that they relaxed after building up such a gap by the start of February. The attitude wasn't the same because it simply didn't need to be. Rangers drew four league

---

109   It was the second red card of the season (Scott Nisbet had been dismissed in a 2-2 draw with Dundee) but it was the last, as Rangers won the fair play award that season. Further evidence of a significant change in approach.

110   There was a motion to the Houses of Parliament by a Labour MP to complain about the level of competence of the SFA, the 'grossly excessive' treatment of Souness based on 'sleakit' television evidence and the nature of a penalty shoot-out to settle the Scottish Cup Final when a replay would have been better for fans. The MP was George Galloway.

games in a row – three away to Motherwell, Dundee and St Mirren and that scoreless stalemate at home to Hearts – and then were beaten at Ibrox by Hibs on 24 March, where Andy Goram was outstanding for the visitors. However, this spell illustrates exactly the reality in which Rangers found themselves. The gap at the top was seven points before that run and, with six points thrown away and five games without a win, was still as big as five points by its end. Only two points had been clawed back by a pack unable to produce a genuine chaser. Within that poor run was also the continuation of Souness's Scottish Cup curse as Rangers lost 1-0 to Celtic at Parkhead in the fourth round on 25 February. A scrambled Tommy Coyne goal just before the interval was enough as Rangers lacked energy, especially Ferguson. Terry Butcher summoned enough after the game to fully test the hinges on the Parkhead doors live on STV but it was aggression that would have been better served stopping Joe Miller's driven low cross that Coyne bundled into the net before John Brown kicked him back into it, another example of the growing frustration among the team.

Coyne's goal was described as keeping Celtic's season alive as the cup was all that they had left to play for. They would reach the final, losing to Aberdeen on penalties after a dire goalless draw, and some Rangers fans wrote in fanzines after the cup exit that the only saving grace was that it was the kind of odd result, like the previous season's final, that might keep the club and its supporters in a constant state of denial. Pressure was mounting on the Celtic board, however, and Jack McGinn was in bullish mood following the win over Rangers. 'It strikes me an awful lot of people have forgotten that with the same structure of company the club won four Premier League championships and four Scottish Cups during the 1980s,' he told the press. 'So we can't been making mistakes year in year out.' But, as soon as those words had reached the papers, they immediately seemed dated. Celtic, under their current stewardship model, were the past and Rangers, who were now being included in more and more talk of European leagues that would break off from UEFA, were the future. That would be a few more years to come though. In the meantime, Rangers had a title to secure.

* * *

For all the spotlight that was on Maurice Johnston and for all his crucial goals, it was still the reliability of his strike partner that came out on top in 1989/90. Ally McCoist was not only Rangers' leading scorer throughout the campaign but he broke two records in doing so, something that he would become accustomed to over the following three seasons. Back in December, a beautiful chip over Ally Maxwell in a 3-0 win over Motherwell at Ibrox was McCoist's 128th Premier Division goal and in doing so he broke the record that had been set by Frank McGarvey, by then winding down his career at St Mirren. On that very same Saturday afternoon, in Rome, Sophia Loren and Luciano Pavarotti were assisting Sepp Blatter in making the draw for the 1990 World Cup where Scotland were placed in Group C alongside Brazil, Sweden and Costa Rica, against whom they would open their campaign. With a relatively strong and settled squad and the most difficult match against Brazil coming last, Scotland were well-placed to finally make it to the next round for the first time. What could possibly go wrong?

What went wrong was a manager who chose to ignore that much sought-after component of a good international team: chemistry. There was a ready-made Scottish strike partnership at Ibrox and there were few better examples of that than at Ibrox with the Rangers second goal in a 3-0 hammering of Celtic on 1 April. Gough's crunching tackle on McStay was picked up by McCoist whose drive at the Celtic defence ended with a beautifully clipped ball across to Johnston who, typically, controlled with grace and finished with power. The celebrations, although not as wild as in November, were still enjoyed with great relish, with a 'get it up you' gesture aimed at the Celtic board and kisses to the Rangers fans. Rangers were already 1-0 up through a Walters penalty, the result of a moment of pure footballing comedy when Anton Rogan slam-dunked a Terry Butcher cross clean off the head of the onrushing Gough. The ridiculous nature of the handball was matched only by the incredulity on his face, somehow shocked that he should be cautioned for such an obscure law of the game. The third goal, another penalty after a reckless push by Peter Grant on Johnston, presented McCoist with the opportunity to break another scoring record, this time Derek Johnstone's postwar league tally of 131 goals for Rangers. It was emphatic, as was his response after going nearly two months without a goal. Rangers ended their slump in a definitive manner and, with only five games left, were in pole position to retain their title.

The intended audience for that game was over 600,000 but it didn't quite reach that mark in the end. British Satellite Broadcasting had paid the SFA and SFL over £12m for wider broadcasting rights but, due to problems in manufacturing their 'squarial' – a satellite dish that wasn't a circular bowl but a flat, edged surface – they only officially launched on 25 March 1990, the week before the Old Firm game. The nascent production was scrappy in places – the team line-ups failed to appear on the graphic prior to kick-off – but the chemistry in the commentary box was immediate as, for the first time on a Sunday afternoon by virtue of space technology, Martin Tyler and Andy Gray narrated the drama of British football into the homes of an increasingly interested audience. Before long they would give a voice to the new era that was becoming increasingly visible on the horizon. STV broadcast the following Sunday's match as Rangers got the point they wanted at Pittodrie in a pretty dreadful 0-0 draw that once again had Souness bemoaning the physicality of the league now that he was buying more players that needed protection. Johnston and Steven combined at Ibrox against Motherwell, with the striker setting up the midfielder to equalise after Nick Cusack had headed the visitors in front early in the second, before Johnston pounced yet again late on to secure the win. Only a big swing in goal difference could now prevent a third Rangers title in four years as they headed to Tannadice on 21 April to finish off the job properly.

It was a fitting way in which to do it. A 1-0 win away from home against a rival side was so typical of how this team targeted their prize. The creator of the winning goal, from his right foot of all things, was Stuart Munro who, alongside Johnston, was ever-present in competitive games that season and it wasn't Johnston for once but the other big signing of the summer, Trevor Steven, too often overlooked, who was on the end of a cross instead of delivering one, as he guided a brilliant header past Main to start the party off. 'The way to win league championships is, first and foremost, to see off your major rivals,' Steven said later, and it was this killer streak that ensured, even after such a nightmare start, such a comfortable campaign.

The trophy was presented at Ibrox the following week after a 2-0 win over Dunfermline but arguably the biggest cheer was a for a late Rangers substitute. Not wishing to end his glittering playing career as a losing cup finalist, Graeme Souness took his final bow with his one and only appearance of the season. It was the first trophy of a new decade, one which would produce 18 in total, including nine league championships, in stark contrast to the 1980s where the League Cup provided much of the scarce solace to the supporters. To retain the championship with such ease and being able to look forward with such uncapped optimism was simply unthinkable four years earlier and that was why, despite the tension surrounding his choices and the new courses that he was mapping out, Souness's ovation was so loud. Even if he was no longer loved by the entire support, it was still a heartfelt 'thank you'. Most inside Ibrox that afternoon would have expected to be back celebrating the same thing at the same time the next year. None could have imagined that they would be doing it without Souness, the father of the revolution.

'The fans have backed me, the manager has backed and most importantly, the players have backed me,' said Johnston after winning what he came back to Scotland to win. With a glare on him throughout the season that even Souness may not have received in his first year, Johnston never missed a beat, always prepared, always giving his all and making so many crucial contributions towards success. Mark Walters may have had reason to doubt the sincerity of Ian Ferguson's teasing when Johnston first arrived but there was no question of his assessment years later. 'That was my second Championship and if it is remembered as Mo Johnston's year then I, for one, would not argue with that tag.'

* * *

The noise of the Rangers fans who were still celebrating around the streets of Dundee was still audible as Archie Macpherson started his post-match interview with Graeme Souness. The title had been won less than an hour before but, as his interlocutor raised the subject of Europe, Souness bristled before going on yet another monologue about a subject that was clearly dominating his mind. Understandable for a man hungry for the next challenge which, after retaining the title for the first time, combining that success with European respectability clearly was. After making the fair point that Rangers had never been eliminated by a bad side in the four attempts – three West German teams and the champions of Europe from two years before – he picked up the thread which he started back in September, 'Our football doesn't lend itself to doing well in European competitions. Either the amount of games you play or the style of football that's played. It doesn't lend itself for you to change your system, change your players to, all of a sudden, go and do well in European football. Our football demands a certain type of player. It's a Catch-22 for us. I was fortunate when I played for Liverpool that we had the right balance. Where we had the grit that's required for the British game and we had enough flair to go and compete against the best of the Italians, the best of the French and the best of the West Germans. We managed to cross that bridge. Now that is something that we [Rangers] must do. I would say that the Premier League is a harder league to win than the English First Division. The four times that you play each other does not help. It does not help if you're looking further ahead, i.e. to do well in European competitions.'

Souness had correctly identified a problem but he seemed less sure about committing to the obvious solution in practice. When the league title is the number one priority, 'Catch-22' was the perfect way to sum up his predicament and his summer activity in 1990 would suggest that he hoped to bridge both worlds simply by personnel alone. He would get his target man in Mark Hateley, another midfield enforcer in Terry Hurlock, more out-and-out width in Pieter Huistra and then he would try to balance that with the continental class of Oleg Kusnetsov from Dynamo Kiev. However, the issue was not so much the individual players but the way in which they were used. As his career on the continent would show, Hateley had more to his game than being an out ball but, when the domestic style and tempo demands it, then it should be no surprise that Rangers would use him in that way and hence, become a more direct team as a result. Switching back to the patient and compact unit that Souness tried to develop during this season – 1989/90 saw both the lowest average goals for and goals against during this period – was far easier said than done.

If the extent of this strain became apparent in 1990, it has remained a dilemma for both Rangers and Celtic well into the 21st century as the 'project managers' who tried to quickly modernise the playing style were given short shrift when domestic superiority was threatened. Three of the four seasons of relative Old Firm European success – 1992/93 and 2007/08 for Rangers and 2002/03 for Celtic – all derived as much from a sense of dogged team spirit and uncompromising anti-style as they did to adapting to and then bettering the prevailing dogma. Arguably though, when Rangers found themselves so far in front, this year was the time to commit to a more rounded, technical, passing side and push ahead until it became so comfortable that the approach on a Wednesday night under the European lights didn't need such an overhaul from Saturday's instructions. The direction of European football was not heading towards a direct style based around a giant centre-forward, wingers and no composed ball-players in the middle of the park, indeed it was decidedly moving away from it. Only Tomáš Skuhravý, who would shine at the World Cup for Czechoslovakia and then move to Genoa, comes close, but then he had classy midfielders around him in both sides, as did Julio Salinas at Barcelona and Spain. There was unquestionably a move towards power and, especially with Arrigo Sacchi's Milan side, an exceptional work ethic off the ball, but the style was still based around good all-round technique and clear tactical planning. Souness was not a man who dithered but his reticence over the next 12 months to use the class of Trevor Steven in the middle of the park perfectly exemplified his reluctance to consistently deploy a ready-made solution to a problem that he had already identified.

So much of the contemporaneous viewpoint of the Rangers support in 1990 – much of it discussed in other chapters of this book – is redolent of Philip Larkin's brilliant poem about the gradual decline of England, Going, Going. The penultimate stanza reads:

And that will be England gone,
The shadows, the meadows, the lanes,
The guildhalls, the carved choirs.
There'll be books; it will linger on
In galleries; but all that remains
For us will be concrete and tyres.

What made it once great has been thrown away in the name of modernity and progress. Season 1989/90 was one of modernist change in so many ways with the obvious signing of Maurice Johnston, the rest of the league's willingness to look beyond their own shores in the search for players, the Taylor Report's early recommendations on all-seater stadia, the serious discussion of European super leagues and the development of satellite broadcasting of live football in exchange for proper money into the game. But it was on the pitch, during a position of relative strength, that Rangers didn't drive on and break new ground, instead being held captive by ties to tradition and accepted wisdom. Souness saw the future clearly yet blinked and in doing so, he set in place a stylistic template that wouldn't be broken until it was too late.

8

GIVING UP THE GHOST

'This is a quantum change in Scottish football and possibly in Scottish society.'
Brian Wilson MP

'Tradition is not the worship of ashes, but the preservation of fire.'
Gustav Mahler, composer

Sensationalist hysteria is just everyday language for tabloid newspapers and football fans but on 10 July 1989, everyone could be forgiven for indulging in hyperbole. Some of the scarf-burning, season ticket-destroying and wreath-laying for the demise of Rangers Football Club outside Ibrox that week was a media stunt but there is no question that the impact of the signing was deeply felt, initially at least, by a support who had been lapping up the new success while also being wary of Graeme Souness's declaration from the outset that he would sign a Roman Catholic if the right player became available. Jock Wallace had said similar, one fan remarked to a television crew outside Kilbowie Stadium before the first game of Walter Smith's temporary charge against Clydebank, but nothing had ever come of that. Most would have known that Souness was unlikely to pay such lip service to the matter in reality but none could have imagined who that first player would be. It was the man in question who really set fire to that Scottish summer.

Many fans vowed never to return, as the Rangers that they knew – deeply bound by tradition – was over. One was filmed for BBC Scotland's Reporting Scotland in a Rangers pub that day with his replica top on, which he said was his 'last act of defiance because I'll certainly not be wearing it any more'. Another was in such a hurry to rush to Ibrox from his workplace to confirm that the rumours were true that he hadn't removed his hard hat, his welder's goggles still resting on them. He told STV that he would have to think about whether or not he would be back and when pushed, admitted that the reason was because of Maurice Johnston's religion. Others told reporters such as The Scotsman's Neil Drysdale that 'hell would freeze over' before they would return to Ibrox and 'put money into that wee Fenian bastard's back pocket'.

Most fans dealt pragmatically with the reality facing Rangers – especially with the increasing need to find the best Scottish talent available regardless of background – and concluded that if they were going to have to sign one, then it might as well be one of the best. The fact that Celtic were left shattered by the signing, once play got under way again, softened the reaction considerably. Sporting oneupmanship counted for more than religion in the end.

There was a time when it genuinely wouldn't have. The story of the Old Firm origins and their sectarian connections is the subject for an entire book, some of which out there are sharp and engaging and others wildly overblown, as if 1930s Glasgow was like living under the Third Reich. It is not the purpose of this chapter to plot the full history of this infamous tale but there are several things that need to be highlighted, so as to best understand the impact on this era and beyond. The most important of which is that, for large parts of the 20th century, Rangers and Celtic were a genuine cultural expression of a genuine religious identity.

Identity is at the heart of it all. How people saw themselves, and how they wanted the world to see them, mattered a great deal. After the dust had settled on the Glorious Revolution, the Act of Union, the Jacobite rebellions and the Highland clearances, late-18th century Scottish identity was firmly wrapped in the Calvinist Kirk. 'To be Scottish was to be Protestant,' it was said. According to Sandy Jamieson, fewer than 100 Catholics were thought to have lived in Glasgow in 1790. By 1850, following waves of immigration from the west, a quarter of the city's population was Irish Catholic. Like any relatively sudden shift in demographic, it wasn't smooth sailing. Theological differences were hotly debated and folk tales of burning ancestors were shared with a passionate zeal, but in a practical sense the consequences were acute. The Protestant fear and mistrust manifested itself mainly in employment discrimination, as unions sought to protect the Protestant working class in skilled trades and professions and the Catholic insecurity was characterised by a kind of ghettoisation with communities closed off by separate education – state funded since 1918 – and a decree on mixed marriage in 1907 that, if it had to happen at all, that any children produced must be raised within the church of Rome. Religion mattered. One of the biggest sectarian riots of all was not at Ibrox, Parkhead, Hampden or even in Glasgow, but in Edinburgh in 1935 when 20,000 supporters of the Protestant Action Society stoned and jeered 10,000 catholic attendees at a Eucharist Congress. Ireland's role in the First World War and the introduction of the Protestant-dominated Belfast firm Harland and Wolff to Clydeside only intensified the temperature by adding questions of political and national identity to the religious one.

So often sport acts a substitute for war for those not involved in the real thing or when words and articles of faith don't do the trick, and it was no different in Glasgow. The explosion in mass popular appeal for football with the introduction of the half day of work on a Saturday and its combative and combustible style made it the perfect vehicle on to which communities could project their identity and have their heroes win their battles for them on a Saturday afternoon. There has been some academic debate about whether Celtic, formed in 1887 by a Marist priest called Brother Walfrid, were started for sectarian or pious reasons, with all seemingly missing the obvious point that the two are rarely mutually exclusive. It is both possible and probable that there were strong motivations to provide the Catholic poor of the East End a sporting focal point and belonging as well as being driven by a concern about them mixing with Protestant men in soup kitchens and being converted to the reformed faith. The fear of apostasy is never far from Christian charity. Of less debate is what happened next. The initial startling success of the 'Irishmen' led a Protestant call around the country for their own contenders. By the 1920s, it was clear that Bill Struth's successful Rangers – with their strong Protestant Clydeside roots, ingrained work ethic and

Presbyterian rigour – would be the ideal candidate. All over Scotland, Rangers became the natural team of thousands and so started a trend – still in place to this day – where buses would leave all parts of the country to head for Ibrox. Religion and politics were now firmly made manifest in sport.

It was there that Rangers' signing policy – or what should really be called a practice – began in earnest whereby they would not knowingly employ a Roman Catholic so as to ensure that this identity grew even stronger. Catholic players Laurie Blyth and Don Kichenbrand were signed in 1950 and 1955 respectively but their religion was not known at the time and their Ibrox careers were shortened soon after it became apparent. Even association with popery by marriage caused players problems such was the case with Alex Ferguson and Graham Fyfe. Sometimes a Catholic-sounding name was enough which explains why Rangers passed on Danny McGrain, much to Celtic's benefit. Any attempts at overtly preserving a Catholic line-up at Parkhead were dismissed by the Celtic board in 1895 and the club have made capital on that ecumenical stance ever since. The pragmatic truth is that Celtic could ill afford to limit their selection pool to such a small section of Scottish society. That same openness struggled to make it to the levels of senior management and the stewardship of the club, however, with Jock Stein – a Protestant from a staunch Rangers family but who had played for Celtic with distinction – leaving his reserve coach post in tears after being told that his religion would likely prevent him getting the top job. Eventually it didn't – only after he had shown exceptional promise as manager of Dunfermline – but there was never to be a post-managerial reward as a director. The best that the greatest figure in the club's history could be offered was the chance to run the Celtic Pools. By the time Maurice Johnston signed for Rangers, Celtic were yet to have a Protestant on their board.

As the 20th century developed at pace, Rangers' stance looked increasingly indefensible both legally and morally. It was a discriminatory position for an employer to take but, perhaps uniquely in employment or equality law, the critics were not the ones queuing up demanding to be given a job. The pragmatic approach that Rangers took – on the rare occasion anyone spoke candidly in public on the matter – was that it was effectively an abstract argument. Of course it was possible to sign a Catholic, but who would want to do it and what would Rangers really gain from it? Signing and playing are two different things and playing well, with commitment, is an entirely different ball game altogether. Would a Scottish player from an Irish Catholic background really give everything for the cause? Would they bleed blue when the going got tough? For a club and a support who historically eulogise hard workers who had run about a great deal but always had a caveat ready for those with a degree of flair and who could find a team-mate with an accurate pass, it was a fair question.

Or at least, it used to be. In the eras of Struth, Symon and Wallace – where commitment and effort was venerated above all else – scepticism about what a player who had grown up supporting Celtic would give them came from a reasonable place. As the 1990s approached, however, the Johnston signing demonstrated that this was now a bygone era and with it, a huge myth was blown away. This particular taboo, like mixed marriage generations before, was an imaginary construct; something that couldn't possibly happen until it does and then everyone eventually shrugs and gets on with their lives. Technically Graeme Souness made good on his promise within two months of arriving. John Spencer was actually the first Catholic he signed, Rangers' first – knowingly – since the First World War. He had signed schoolboy forms in 1982, leading to some members of his family refusing to speak to him again, and he became a professional in the summer of 1986. John Greig had said in a television interview in the same year that this was probably the best way for Rangers to break the barrier, with some young Catholic players easing their way in. For some reason the signing of Spencer wasn't deemed worthy by the outside world. It had to be a big one.

Maurice Johnston was perfect casting. The product of a mixed marriage – his father a Protestant Rangers fan but who followed his mother's faith and went to a Catholic school – he revelled in playing for his boyhood heroes before he got professionally restless and then rejected their advances for the more difficult but rewarding option. What is more – and this is the most important part of this whole saga – is that he gave his all for Rangers in the two full seasons that he was at the club. This was what professional footballers now did and that is what generations of supporters struggled to comprehend. Fans see themselves in every player signed because we see them as living our dreams, not theirs. It was the Rangers support's inability to conceive of giving their all for Celtic that distorted their perspective.

It is also important to note that the religious tag Johnston carried was nominal. He practised no religion at all in reality and in that respect, he personified modern Scotland. At one stroke the Johnston signing made football fans realise that religion no longer mattered when it came to scoring goals but also gave rise to a renewed academic interest in the subject, where extreme conclusions generated the greater research funding. Scottish academia had finally discovered the hot topic of sectarianism just as secularisation was taking hold and as a result, would fan new, phantom flames just as the real ones had been slowly dying out without the same kind of attention. Perhaps making up for lost time, a fresh Catholic persecution complex with little basis was given far more credence in universities and the media than a firmly justified one decades earlier ever did. One lesson was clear from the Johnston fallout: whether supported by evidence or not, sectarianism sells.

On the day of the signing, Labour MP and Celtic author Brian Wilson did the rounds of television news stations. After starting with criticism towards Johnston for the way the Celtic deal had collapsed – the relevance of which on this particular story was not entirely clear – he was positive about the implications of the move for Scottish society. Could MoJo wearing blue really heal Scotland's deep religious division? Cooler heads may have argued that, by 1989, it didn't need to. The religious divide was dissolving and it had been since the 1960s with greater secularisation, mixed marriage and equality in employment all taking effect. Only 17 per cent of Scots regularly attended church in 1984 and by 2016 that was down to 7.2 per cent, just under half of whom were over 65 years old. Even the number of people who would bother to nominally refer to themselves as religious had dropped in every census taken over the last 40 years. By its very definition, religious hatred cannot be expressed with a shrug. Religious bigotry requires religious zealots. And yet, despite the increasing apathy towards the supernatural, an imaginary theological hatred and fervour would be held responsible for a great many of modern Scotland's ills in the 1990s, from political nepotism to violence, on and off the football field. In 1995, following his imaginary playing of a flute in a pre-season friendly – the result of a dressing room practical joke – The Guardian genuinely feared that it might derail the Northern Ireland peace process[111] and perhaps the apotheosis came in 2011 when a story about two football managers arguing on the touchline[112] was found to be just cause for commencing a summit on sectarianism in the Scottish Parliament.

It was something of a nonsense. For there to be religious hatred – such a passionate term – religion has to play a significant role at the centre of life. It once did and, as such, Scotland was a deeply sectarian country for the latter half of the 19th and the first half of the 20th centuries. Manifestations of that religious identity – politics, sport and culture – could therefore be fairly tarred with that particular brush. The population did see them as emblematic of a genuine tear in the fabric of society. Once that root motivation disappears, however, those arguments become hollow. Sir Tom Devine, one of the leading academics on the subject, has argued for some time now that the experiences of the major religious groups in terms of discrimination and hate crimes, are 'exceptionally similar'. But still, the old folk mythology is so hard for so many to give up completely.

A large part of that is down to the very visible pantomime that football so readily provides us with. Attend any Old Firm game now or over the last 30 years and you would be forgiven for thinking that the Kirk and the Chapel still dominated thousands of lives with some of the songs and iconography on show. But it is dress-up. A sort of postmodern community signing. A way for people to feel a part of something bigger, even just for an afternoon. A nod to the history that made the fixture what it is, when practically all that is left in the modern world is just the football. Almost all. It is fair to say that the other development of this deep historical religious identity – political and national identity – is still alive and well and it remains strongly represented by the two fanbases. As the theological disputes waned in the late 1960s, they were replaced by the increasingly violent politics of Ulster. Songs became more political and xenophobic than overtly religious but, even to this day, there is still an element of paramilitary cosplay about the whole performance. The Troubles didn't make their way to Scotland, despite genuine fears at the time, but unionism and republicanism, with some Scottish nationalism thrown into the mix for good measure, are still a valid touchstone for a signifiant proportion of supporters. These are issues that still divide us. These are, at least, real.

But, although their roots are in religious conflict, can we really say with a straight face that, in an overwhelmingly secular country, these displays are evidence of a

---

111   He would do something similar at Parkhead in January 1998 and ex-Celtic midfielder and now pundit Davie Provan would again raise fears that it could destabilise the good work that was being done in constitutional negotiations. It did not.

112   By this point Ally McCoist and Neil Lennon were in charge of Rangers and Celtic but it is hard to think of another case whereby a fairly common occurrence on the sports field would lead to a parliamentary inquest into theological tensions.

religious hatred? Of course not. Certainly not now and arguably not even when Johnston sat down in that Blue Room for the first time. For much of the century there would have been a riot at Ibrox after such a signing. A boycott by fans would have stuck. As always, people's actions are more indicative than their words. When it came down to it, the true-blue loyal Rangers support didn't really care about his religion at all. Which should be unsurprising when religion was a significant part of life for so few of them. You simply cannot have a problem with religious hatred when so few care about religion in the first place.

More accurately there was, and arguably still is, an issue with political sectarianism and xenophobia, one where the future of Scotland and the Union and the potential unification of Ireland still matters to many. But to define the situation more appropriately would bring others into the conversation outside of the Old Firm. Fans of other Scottish clubs react to the perceived positions of both Glasgow clubs on constitutional affairs and with plenty of passion, vitriol and abusive language to boot. The appetite for widening the net of blame appears to be very light as would characterising Barcelona v Real Madrid, Boca Juniors v River Plate or Galatasaray v Fenerbahçe – all of which have a political division at the heart their story – in exactly the same way. Instead, they simply represent the colour and passion of the beautiful game, something that Rangers and Celtic are rarely allowed to do. Despite hooliganism and violence scarring the game in cities all over the world, criminality surrounding the Old Firm is almost always reported as being faith-based and not because far too many people place far too much emotional fortune at the feet of strangers and that the resulting tension, when mixed with drink and drugs, becomes too much.

The most vociferous reaction to the Johnston move was from Celtic fans – Mo's father was attacked on the weekend of his first appearance for Rangers – but, if it was any other two clubs involved, this would be rationally explained without the need to reference excommunication and transubstantiation. The following summer, the Johnston affair was made to look very small-time when Florence burned after Roberto Baggio was sold to Juventus. The Fiorentina support hate Juventus – the establishment club of Italy – and this deal was treated like treason. In reality the Celtic rage was fuelled more by a sense of footballing disloyalty and justified fear about what that could now mean on the park. Football rivalries exist the world over – many with an old grudge as their origin story – and this beautiful irrationality is sold as part of the charm. Looking too closely at that – at what makes calm, professional people lose their minds in crowds of 60,000 or 6,000, at the top level or the bottom tier – is understandably resisted because it would likely include the inquisitor themselves. Far easier, then, to blame the pantomime villains.

The footballing benefits were obvious but what did the signing of Maurice Johnston do to Scottish society? Rather than an event that changed attitudes because it happened, it was more an event that could only happen because attitudes had already changed. It was symbolic of what was possible in 1989 but would have been almost impossible in 1959. What came after the signing – the effort, the desire and the success – was a necessary encore to the main event. Gustav Mahler almost certainly did not come up with that tradition aphorism himself, it would have been one that he rephrased, but his intentions were positive. The composer who bridged the romantic and modern eras of classical music warned against worshipping the past for its own sake. Such action is lazy and safe. Instead we should hold on to the creative spirit that has been passed down to us and change the form if necessary.

The Johnston signing perhaps exemplified that observation perfectly. Those fans who worshipped the faded and hollow practices of the past because they were shared by their own imagined communities were only fooling themselves when they defiantly predicted that a 'true-blue' team would still be able to succeed in modern football. Instead, this important chapter of Rangers' modernisation was evidence of the management preserving the fire of the original founders story and the best qualities of those who kept it burning for 120 years, by ensuring that sporting excellence was all that mattered.

Outside of football, however, in universities and editorial rooms throughout Scotland, a new industry was born from the sensationalism of the Johnston transfer that sought to relight the fires of the past, instead of stamping on their ashes. Those new flames may have been theatrical special effects, but – for those who came into contact with them – they could still burn.

9

UNDER PRESSURE

SEASON 1990/91

'No pressure, no diamonds.'
Thomas Carlyle, historian and philosopher

'They came, sat down and never got behind the team. They were more intent on the silly little chants about who they feel should and shouldn't be in the team … Don't come to sit on your hands and criticise.'
Graeme Souness, 12 January 1991

Mark Walters had scored penalties before for Rangers. Seven of them in fact, and some big ones too, in crucial moments in cup finals, Old Firm games and against Europe's elite. None felt as important as this one. It was a bright and warm Saturday afternoon on the first May bank holiday weekend but few would have been feeling the heat as intensely as Walters. Usually so calm and decisive from the spot, his body shape this time was wayward and off-balance to the left as he chipped the ball high and wide to the right and another chance to equalise went begging. Nothing was happening for Rangers in front of goal in the second half as the Motherwell goalkeeper Ally Maxwell made saves from point-blank range as well as seeing his crossbar shudder from a Scott Nisbet header. Ironically the 1-0 deficit still left Rangers with the overall advantage in the title race. Even a Motherwell second wouldn't alter that. A third would have changed the game entirely but, with only five minutes left, that was unthinkable.

'There's a distinct championship feeling here at Fir Park,' said Gerry McNee on commentary as the match kicked off. Thousands of supporters had squeezed in for the penultimate game of the season perhaps more in hope than in expectation of a title party, something that required both a Rangers win and for Aberdeen to slip up at home to St Johnstone. The most likely scenario was two narrow wins by the odd goal, which would still leave the challengers having to come to Ibrox on the final day of the season and win by five goals. No, a Rangers win in Lanarkshire would be enough, as long as Aberdeen didn't go goal crazy at Pittodrie, for them to secure a third championship in a row for the first time since 1935. It was starting to feel like a normal service but there was nothing normal about the situation Rangers faced that day. This new era of regular success had been engineered by Graeme Souness and was driven on by Terry Butcher but by then, neither manager nor captain were employed at Ibrox. Even the new skipper, Richard Gough, was in a hospital bed listening on the radio as the squad became more threadbare the closer the finish line approached. The pressure was becoming intolerable.

But then, pressure was the theme of the whole season as Souness's war footing with the governing bodies expanded to encompass the media, Perthshire tea ladies, the Rangers support and two of their greatest heroes, serving only to create more strain for all concerned. The same abrasive personality that had transformed the Scottish game had now created a monster from which Souness himself had to escape. His players, however, couldn't escape it and the real story of 1990/91 was their ability to respond to this tension, both external and internal. It was a season where individual players showed the strength of character to emerge as new leaders or to simply survive and where, collectively, during some of its darkest hours, they responded with trophy-winning performances. As Ian Durrant later described them, those were days that 'summed up the true Rangers'.

There was no day that summed up true Rangers more so than the league season's denouement at Ibrox that was a drama which had been scripted by Rangers the week before. Walter Smith, in only his third game in charge, and beside his new assistant Archie Knox for the first time, was still encouraging the team to push forward for an equaliser at Fir Park that would have likely changed very little unless they could follow it up with a quick winner. With Aberdeen winning 2-1 late into the day, as things stood a draw in the final-day showdown would be enough. It was still enough when Motherwell sprung a counter and Dougie Arnott scored a brilliant goal to make it two. It was then, with only four minutes remaining, that Rangers should have cut their losses and moved on, holding on to that slender goal-difference advantage over Aberdeen, but still they charged, leaving wide-open spaces aching to be exposed. Inevitably that naivety was punished again when, with only one minute remaining, Arnott and Motherwell repeated the same trick. What could have been a league-winning day finished up feeling like a catastrophe. For 23 weeks Rangers had been top of the table and now, with only a week remaining, they were second. With 23 points from the last 24 and with 26 goals scored in those 12 games, Aberdeen were heading to Ibrox in red hot form, with Rangers scrambling around to find even half-fit players. For that week in May, the whole era that is now synonymous with Rangers dominance hung by a single thread.

* * *

Where Italy had provided Rangers with regeneration in the summer of 1988 and the space for integration and adjustment in 1989, this time it provided only a portent of the tempest that was about to hit throughout the coming season. Italy, of course, was the centre of the footballing world in the summer of 1990. The World Cup lacked the sufficient degree of technical assurance for the purists but there was no shortage of drama for the increasingly large casual audience, the operatic soundtrack of Puccini and Pavarotti being in perfect harmony with the sporting glory and tragedy unfolding in their living rooms on a daily basis. The latter would eventually have more of an impact on Rangers than the former.

Scotland were based in Genoa as they prepared for their opening group game against the Central American minnows, Costa Rica. Ally McCoist and Maurice Johnston, who between them had scored eight of the 12 Scotland goals in qualification and 35 for Rangers the previous season, were initially expected to lead the charge in the Stadio Luigi Ferraris right up until the tournament kicked off on Friday, 8 June. With Scotland playing on the Monday, head coach Andy Roxburgh was already giving broad hints to the press on the Saturday that Bayern Munich's Alan McInally – whom he believed was feared in Costa Rica and was regarded as the 'Scottish Marco van Basten' – would start in the opening game, especially as he had said the day before that McCoist was struggling with fitness. 'Ally has a hamstring problem that he didn't tell us about. He was carried away by his enthusiasm and desire to be involved in the World Cup and decided to keep it quiet,' Roxburgh said. 'We will have to assess his fitness over the weekend.' McCoist's account, in his 1992 autobiography, was that he was fully fit and that Roxburgh had started to tell him that he looked 'a bit jaded' in training, despite Scotland defenders telling him that he was on fire.

The story of his non-selection is one that McCoist has told many times as he picked up Roxburgh incorrectly on the morning of the game when he said, 'Mo and Nally' instead of 'Mo and Ally' but, whether the hamstring problem was a fiction by the manager to cover his general doubt around McCoist, his sense of stunned surprise on matchday is very much at odds with the fact that the media had expected the front two that Roxburgh chose. Nor does his account of his Sweden exclusion fully correspond with reality. In a game that Scotland now desperately needed to win following an embarrassing 1-0 defeat to Costa Rica – who looked very comfortable indeed with the more direct approach that Scotland adopted – Roxburgh opted for both Robert Fleck and Gordon Durie to play alongside Johnston. McCoist was now the fifth-choice striker after entering the competition as a stick-on starter and feared that there was a leak in the camp as, when he told his father the news, he didn't seem surprised, acknowledging, 'He told me that all the papers back home had been speculating on a Johnston-Fleck striking duo, and, surprise, surprise, it turned out that they were right.' That doesn't quite ring true, however, with the Evening Times for one expecting Durie to play alongside the Rangers pair as late as the day before. McCoist would start in the final game against Brazil but rarely featured in a drab 1-0 loss that all but confirmed another early exit[113] and he blamed it on the psychological blow of the early demotions. It was the start of a difficult year for McCoist but one that would make him considerably stronger at the other end.

The experience wasn't that much more enjoyable for the other Rangers players in the Scotland squad. Johnston had scored what turned out to be the winner against Sweden, who were seen off 2-1, but should have done better when he was denied from close range by Taffarel with the game against Brazil tantalisingly poised at 0-0, whereas Richard Gough lasted only for 45 minutes of the opener before having to be replaced and then sent home due to the recurring foot injury that had dogged his season. Six other members were either former or future Rangers but the Scottish champions only provided three players to the 22-man

---

113   Such is the nature of 24-team tournaments that Scotland could have progressed depending on later results. They didn't.

squad in 1990.[114] They provided more to England, four players being the most from any club to that squad in fact, and they had a decidedly different summer. Chris Woods didn't see a minute of play, although arguably should have seen all of it ahead of an ageing Peter Shilton; Gary Stevens was dropped after the first game and only returned for the third-fourth place play-off, Trevor Steven played in the final two games and Terry Butcher said his farewell to international football. He played in five of England's seven matches – missing one for tactical experimentation and one through injury – but it was a struggle. He needed a small knee operation immediately after the tournament and by his own admission, at that top level, 'I have to say I was hanging on in Italy.'

It would be a future Rangers star who would be the man most associated with England's renaissance story in Italy. Paul Gascoigne's fearless displays and raw human vulnerability started the rebirth of English football both at home and abroad. Even during the group stage, with trouble flaring on a nightly basis on England's special outpost of Sardinia, the official UEFA line was that they didn't expect English clubs to return to European competition in 1990/91. Within days of the festivities ending, it was announced that Manchester United and Aston Villa would compete in the Cup Winners' Cup and UEFA Cup respectively while Liverpool – the First Division champions – sat out for an extra year. At a stroke, the carrot that Rangers were able to dangle to top English talent was taken away and, in time, the marketability of the domestic game down south would create a competition with which Scotland could not compete. The days of Rangers being Britain's biggest club were suddenly numbered.

On the same day that Scotland defeated Sweden, Graeme Souness finally got his man. Mark Hateley had been the number one striking target since the Rangers revolution got under way and now, after a nightmare 18-month spell following an ankle injury, he decided that it was time to leave the principality of Monaco and come back to British football for £1m.[115] The Rangers manager's delight was obvious but he must have known that, with this signing, would come inevitable tactical and man-management issues, the latter of which was almost instant. McCoist told of what he perceived as Souness's 'nastiness' when his boss bumped into a mutual friend during the World Cup. When Souness was asked how disappointed he thought McCoist would be at not playing in those opening games, his response was, 'He'll be even more disappointed when he finds out who I've just signed.' Knowing that it would get back to McCoist quickly, during a difficult time, it was felt to be more than a little offside but an early indication of the kind of conflict that Souness was actively starting to court.

When his Rangers squad returned to Italy for pre-season training at Il Ciocco, their first free night with licence to drink led to those simmering tensions being released in a less-than-productive manner. Johnston, angry with the management team for threatening the partnership that he and McCoist had cultivated, had an argument with Hateley in the hotel bar. Johnston threw drinks around and Hateley responded with some physical restraint, which required his new team-mates to

---

114   Jim Bett and Robert Fleck were former players, Andy Goram, Stuart McCall and Gordon Durie would follow in time and Dave McPherson would eventually fall into both camps.

115   £500,000 was paid up front and the rest based on how many games Hateley would play.

loosen. Johnston was sent home in disgrace, his face all cut, not – according to McCoist – because of that alteration but because he attempted to jump on Scott Nisbet's bed during the night, only to find the mattress had been removed thus leaving him face down on the supporting springs. Either way, it wasn't a good look for Rangers in more ways than one, with constant speculation – not exactly extinguished by either Murray or Souness – that Johnston would be on his way. By the time the team returned, he apologised to Souness, made his peace and was one of the players chosen to model the new Admiral kit for the new season.

Tactically, Hateley was left in no doubt what Souness's plans were, even though they ran slightly contrary to the footballing observations he had made the year before. In his 1993 autobiography, Hateley had no qualms about describing himself as a physical target man, even though the role didn't fully capture the whole range of his ability. That was, according to him, what his European suitors had in mind, especially the AC Milan side of the mid-1980s – before Arrigo Sacchi and the three Dutchmen – 'a big powerful British striker was what they wanted'. As has been dealt with earlier, it wasn't what European sides were necessarily looking for now – something that Souness seemed to accept at one level – and thus, this was evidence of a certain degree of inconsistency. Accommodating all three was always going to be a problem – none of them was a back-up reserve – and it was a headache he compounded, in theory, with his other major signing of the summer. Oleg Kuznetsov's move from Dynamo Kiev was protracted – he wouldn't arrive until the October, after the Soviet season concluded – but, with Gough and Butcher an established pairing in the centre of defence, Souness was left with another puzzle to solve in order to have all his best players involved at the same time. His solution, one that he assured the press had long been in his thinking, was to play a three-man defence, incorporating Kuznetsov as a sweeper. 'It's the way to play the game,' he said, and it was indeed something of the zeitgeist due to its successful use at the World Cup. 'To do it properly, of course, you need to have the right players. When Oleg Kuznetsov arrives I believe we will have them.' He wouldn't wait that long.

The word 'scattergun' would be too harsh a term to use for the Rangers management's thinking in the summer of 1990 and the early season itself, but there is enough in their decision-making that doesn't necessarily flow logically. What was logical was the singing of the young Dutch winger Pieter Huistra from FC Twente[116], as there was a danger of being too reliant on Mark Walters on the left, as was, much later on in the season, the youthful defensive backup of Brian Reid from Morton.

After spending so much of the previous season on loan at Dundee, Rangers were never going to turn down £750,000 from Hearts for Derek Ferguson. He should have been a star that lit up this era instead of fizzling out under dark clouds and, although his initial reaction was to stay and fight for his place, Souness

---

116   Huistra, along with Kuznetsov, was something of a departure in that Souness was finally prepared to spend money on non-UK players, something that other Scottish clubs had taken the plunge on. Until then his focus since 1986 had been the best of English that he could buy. Jan Bartram was an inexpensive gamble, Avi Cohen he knew well from Liverpool and Boni Ginzburg was an emergency.

made it clear that he would be left in the reserves like others with whom he had no intention of using. With Derek gone and namesake Ian still struggling with illness and injury, the centre of midfield was still in need of reinforcement and it is here that Rangers appeared to lack cohesive thought. Jan Mølby was the main target all summer and both player and club were in agreement, however Liverpool held an option for one more year which they used and so the deal was dead. Similarly, a move for Jim Bett to return from Aberdeen also fell through and a late enquiry about John Collins failed too. That was one Celtic transfer that Souness couldn't hijack and he went to Parkhead instead. All three were ball-playing, cultured midfielders, so the signing of Millwall's Terry Hurlock in that role came as something of a surprise. Souness, and some of his players, have been keen to stress that Hurlock was a far better footballer than he got credit for and that is undoubtedly true but, when his reputation for being a bone-crusher was so dominant, being able to make a ten-yard pass seemed like a minor miracle. It was also another physical influence that didn't correlate with Souness's concerns about shaping his team for Europe.

Although the prevailing narrative around this season was that it was always a matter of Hateley and Johnston starting as a partnership – and they did to great effect in a 3-1 opening-day win at home Dunfermline, with the new boy opening the scoring – those early bigger games in the season, away to Hearts, at home to Celtic and away to Dundee United, saw Souness adopt a very different shape indeed. The opening day saw the usual 4-4-2 but for those three games Rangers played more of a 3-4-3 with McCoist being shoe-horned into something of a trident attack[117]. This meant that Rangers played with Richard Gough (a right-footed right-back at previous clubs) on the left-hand side of a back three and Gary Stevens playing in such a defensive line for the first time.

Presumably Souness saw Stevens moving to more of a wing-back role when Kuznetsov arrived even though, when England switched from a 4-4-2 to a 3-5-2 in the summer, he had to make way for Paul Parker due to Bobby Robson's doubts around his ability to perform the function. In those three games, Souness effectively had no full-backs but instead had Huistra and Trevor Steven covering the flanks, the latter lacking pace but possessing an overwhelming tendency to drift into the middle. It was an outlook that had mixed success. Rangers were excellent at Tynecastle in a 3-1 win with some encouraging interplay and movement between the front three and were unlucky to only to draw 1-1 at home to Celtic where Pat Bonner had to be at his best to stop a very comfortable victory. Pleasingly, both matches saw both Huistra and Hurlock get their first Rangers goals, the latter a crucial low drive to level up against Celtic, ensuring a cult status for the Londoner that endures to the present day. The final experiment came at Tannadice on 22 September and, after a bright start that saw Johnston put Rangers into the lead, it ended in a 2-1 defeat. The match was tied at 1-1 when Alan Main launched a long kick downfield. Terry Butcher was caught slightly out of position, running backwards and with a striker close to him, but attempted the header back to Chris

---

117   Accepted wisdom and BBC Scotland graphics suggest that he was part of a midfield five
       – McCoist had played in the middle of the park earlier in his Rangers career – but the
       patterns of play do not support this.

Woods in any case, even though Gough – now on his left – was covering if he had let it bounce behind him. It left Woods, who had come off his line to try and deal with the threat, helpless as the ball looped over him and into the net. It hadn't touched the ground from one box to the other. Earlier in the month Butcher scored another own goal at home to Raith Rovers in the League Cup but made amends soon after with a rocket into the top corner in a 6-2 win. The one against United 'was my last and best own goal', Butcher joked years later.

It would be his last of any kind at Rangers. Butcher would never play for the club again.

* * *

On the morning of League Cup semi-final against Aberdeen at Hampden, Souness pulled Butcher aside for a chat. Although the weekend's costly error was still fresh in the mind, this was a decision that was based on an early, but unavoidable, pattern of form. The captain, the man whose absence derailed an entire season not too long ago, was going to be dropped. 'I was distraught, in tears,' Butcher wrote later. According to McCoist, 'It was like a slap in the face to see that colossus crying.' Butcher had asked specifically to be left out of the match entirely, so has his downbeat presence didn't affect the team as a whole, but given that it was common for the the scarce two substitute spaces to be reserved for more progressive options, it may have been a redundant request. Amid the inevitable media storm, Souness ditched the three-man defence for the standard 4-4-2, this time with McCoist and Johnston spearheading the attack, John Brown coming in to replace Butcher, Stuart Munro returning at left-back and Trevor Steven and Nigel Spackman taking shifts in covering the right of midfield while in reality both were happy for Gary Stevens to do the real leg work down that side. Rangers were excellent on the night, showing an ability to respond to adversity that would prove crucial over the campaign. A 1-0 scoreline flattered Aberdeen as the Gers dominated throughout, the only goal coming from a Steven burst through the middle of the park – a role he was desperate to make his own – and it was enough to ensure a fifth final appearance in a row.

The initial concern about Butcher's absence, with little being said publicly about his future, was assuaged by the eventual arrival of Kuznetsov in October. His debut – in a 5-0 home win over St Mirren – was sensational. Coming out of defence so comfortably with the ball, starting moves and, on one occasion, smashing the bottom of the post with a long-range drive,; he was showing everything that fans had hoped that they would get from him after seeing him close up when Dynamo Kiev strolled past Rangers at Ibrox in a pre-season friendly in August. In this signing, Souness had a player who fitted his European profile down to the ground with experience, class and intelligence in abundance. And then, within 20 minutes of his second game for Rangers, away to St Johnstone, Kuznetsov broke down after an innocuous challenge. His cruciate ligaments were torn after his studs caught in the turf and Souness, after the bureaucratic struggle to bring him to Ibrox, would never be able to select him again. Rumours grew throughout the decade that this knee injury was in the post, the result of a botched operation a few years previously in East Germany.

There is perhaps a post-hoc colouring of that story given how poor Rangers would later be in the 1990s when it came to due diligence with new signings. Kuznetsov played between 25 and 40 games every season for Kiev during the six years before his move to Ibrox and was an almost ever-present for the USSR at the 1986 and 1990 World Cups and the 1988 European Championship, the final of which being the only game he missed – and that was due to suspension. If there was a deep inherent risk then it was well covered by consistent and excellent performance levels and, even for a manager who seemed to be struck with a serious injury to a key player every season, this was desperately bad luck for both Souness and Kuznetsov and was yet another sliding door which closed off a route towards a more technical evolution of his team.

'We're fucked,' Walter Smith has long been rumoured to have reported back to Souness following his scouting mission for the second round of the European Cup. Following the 10-0 aggregate hammering of Valletta of Malta – with Chris Woods showing a slight lack of respect by taking, and missing, a penalty at Ibrox in torrential rain – Rangers were handed an infinitely more difficult challenge with a trip to Belgrade's 80,000 strong Marakana, to face Red Star. Smith's assessment was on the money as Rangers were ripped apart by a classier and technically superior outfit who could cause problems just as serious through the middle as they could on the flanks, as was proved by Duško Radinović's punishing run and low cross in the eighth minute that John Brown could only deflect into his own net. Fortunate to be only one goal behind at half-time, Rangers continued to hang on past the hour. Previous trips in Europe had taught them that a 1-0 defeat was not terminal. Others, however, had fallen apart as the end drew near and this would be one more of those.

One Rangers fan tells a story where he popped into a Belgrade cafe that morning for some beer. Upon serving the Bear, the cafe owner pointed to a man at the other end of the bar sipping a coffee and drawing on a cigarette, saying, 'He'll be playing you today.' It was Robert Prosinečki and he would do more than just play as he pulled the Rangers midfielders around as if they were attached to his hands with strings before sailing a brilliant free kick beyond Woods to make it 2-0. Like Steaua Bucharest and Köln, Rangers succumbed late in the game and a Darko Pančev goal, when Richard Gough appeared to just stop moving with him, put the tie to bed before the Ibrox leg had even entered the equation. Souness's observations from the previous season were once again given credence. Red Star's ability to keep possession and rotate it quickly was too often in stark contrast to the natural Rangers inclination to knock it longer into the wider channels to Huistra and Walters, especially when the lone striker was Johnston who was chosen ahead of Hateley, the more natural target man.

It was a bizarre selection on paper but evidence of the tightening effect that the UEFA constraints were starting to have. Woods and Walters were naturalised and Stevens and Steven were dead certs to start, meaning only two more foreigners could be used. The strength and experience of Spackman was always likely to be utilised alongside Ian Ferguson in the middle of the park but if Souness was wedded to the five across midfield that he had used away from home in Europe before, then his only other option was to play Nisbet alongside them, push Steven out wide and use Hateley up top. Souness, understandably, preferred to have Steven in the middle against such a technical opponent but it meant having a completely isolated Johnston unable to utilise the genuine pace and width around him without support. A 4-4-2 would have been possible, with Huistra sacrificed for Steven, but with the obvious risk of being completely overrun. It was a straitjacket that was only going to become more suffocating as the years progressed.

The opposition were truly world-class, as they would go on to prove, but Souness was, by then, showing little sign that he was able to counteract the challenges faced at this level by way of coaching or new ideas. The early examples of nous in those first two or three years were not followed up thereafter as getting close to Bayern or Red Star proved a lot more difficult than altering the dimensions of the playing surface and packing numbers into midfield.

As the chairman's European ambitions seemed to be driving on with limitless energy, the team's appeared to be going backwards. There had been disappointments before but the gulf in class that night was as big as any Rangers performance since 1986. In an ideal world – one without any limits on foreign imports – this result may have marked a positive change in the direction of the revolution. History may well have noted it for bringing about the end of the 'First Revolution' – that domestic journey from jesters to undisputed kings which was nearing its completion by then – and the beginning of the second. Where Rangers had once plundered the British Isles for the best of its talent, those players would now head to the continent and get the level of technique and tactical awareness that Britain was not providing. That pursuit would have almost certainly required a foreign manager too. For the first time there was a sense that Souness was now tactically out of his depth, something that the Glasgow Herald's Jim Traynor suggested in his final Red Star report following the 1-1 draw at a wet and half-empty Ibrox. Upon attending the next press conference, Traynor was promptly banned and dismissed is a 'little socialist' because he was jealous of footballers earning ten times what he earned. A year on from calmly managing some bad results with a fixed, positive outlook and justified optimism, Souness – with his newly acquired beard – was turning into Lear. It was the pressure.

With the Ukrainian injury at Perth on the Saturday and the Slavic evisceration on the Wednesday, an Old Firm cup final lay in wait at the end of one of the worst weeks of the Souness regime. It was about to get a whole lot worse. Terry Butcher had felt his exclusion unwarranted due to him being rushed back from injury and not being able to train fully with the squad because of his own individual sessions. However, he committed himself to working his way back into the side by playing a couple of reserve games in the interim. He played an hour of a match on the day prior to the final, after which Souness informed him that John Brown was a doubt and would he play against Celtic. Butcher refused. Because Rangers had accepted a bid from Leeds United earlier that week, he felt that he couldn't join back with the squad, 'I told him I was not the same player any more because I knew he wanted me to go.'

Later on, the following week, Butcher was stopped outside Ibrox by Jim

Delahunt of STV – who were still banned by Souness – to get an update on his future. Seeing the interview taking place from his office window, Souness went berserk and called a press conference of his own to explain exactly why Butcher was out of the team and why he would be leaving. 'He was shaking with emotion, anger or both as he faced the cameras,' wrote Butcher. 'Normally he is very relaxed in front of the media.' There was no normal any more. Butcher would reject the Leeds offer in the end, instead opting for his own entry into management at Coventry City. Years later Butcher expressed a tone of regret, 'In hindsight, I was wrong not to play in the League Cup Final. I was still employed by Rangers, I was reasonably fit, and I had been asked by the manager.' But his approach to the game was all very emotional and he felt that had been ripped out, 'Maybe deep down I just thought I couldn't do it.' Although in deep conflict with one another at the time, perhaps both men – the two architects of such great success – were facing the same internal dilemma.

And yet, despite the storm, Rangers won the cup. It was not the greatest final that Hampden has ever witnessed, in appalling conditions that matched the mood. Rangers were denied the most blatant of penalties early on[118] when Bonner upended McCoist – playing up front with Hateley due to an injury to Johnston – but Celtic took more and more control as the game wore on and deservedly took the lead with a clever low Paul Elliot header in the second half. With their backs to the wall, it was back to basics for Rangers. Twice they went long from deep inside their own half with Hateley the target, and to great effect. Hateley won the first ball cleanly, McCoist controlled the knockdown and Walters poked the ball low into the bottom corner to take the game into extra time and, after Dziekanowski shot tamely at Woods from a golden position, a new Rangers leader emerged. Hateley and Elliot challenged for Spackman's long free kick but neither got much on it and, as it bounced in between Peter Grant and Bonner, in sneaked Richard Gough, the new skipper, to stab the ball into the net and win a trophy at his first attempt. Souness was understandably delighted as he danced across the pitch with a lightness he hadn't shown in some time. It would be the seventh and final time that he paraded silverware around as Rangers manager but the manner in which his side won – against form and the prevailing mood – would outlast him by some years.

With the exception of a hiccup at home to Dundee United at Ibrox on 10 November[119], the form that proceeded that difficult week in late October was excellent and once more, it was in spite of an internal strife that Souness seemed to stoke rather than dampen, this time centring on his deteriorating relationship with Ally McCoist. He came on as a substitute to score the winner in a 2-1 success at Parkhead on 25 November and yet Souness reserved his praise for Johnston, who had scored a fabulous lob to put Rangers into the lead while suffering from flu. A month later at Ibrox, he once more came off the bench to score two brilliant second-half goals with his weaker left foot that put Rangers into a 2-0 lead against

---

118   Referee Jim McCluskey had been the target of a private investigator, hired by the Celtic Supporters' Association, who feared bias.

119   A 2-1 defeat thanks to a Darren Jackson double. McCoist had missed an early penalty and scored an equaliser.

Aberdeen, with whom they were jostling at the top of the league.[120] The first was one of the best of his career, the chest control taking him away from Brian Irvine and the spin and finish leaving Michael Watt helpless.[121] 'The Judge' – so-called because he was spending so much time on the bench – seemed to have secured maximum points from a pretty lacklustre display. Rangers, however, would have to make do with a share of them as two late Jim Bett goals saved a draw. Despite the spectacular nature of McCoist's goals, Souness reportedly never moved a muscle. When the team gathered back at Ibrox on the Monday, Christmas Eve, Souness was not full of seasonal cheer. 'You were all dreadful against Aberdeen – a shocking display,' he said, and then he looked at McCoist, telling him, 'Even when you scored that goal, I couldn't force myself to cheer, I was so down at the way the team were playing.' 'What did I have to do to please the man?,' pondered McCoist years later. It is not unheard of for managers to betray their emotions in the stands or on the bench or indeed, for them to be more concerned with the overall team performance than one individual's, but it was unquestionably a relationship heading towards the rocks despite the fact that McCoist would deliver so often when required.

The collective response to that internal pressure was a show of tough resilience, with three wins around new year that Aberdeen must have gambled against. At Tannadice on 29 December, Rangers were 1-0 down to a side who had beaten them twice already that season. Johnston responded quickly and then, with five minutes to go before half-time, Mark Walters came up with one of his finest career goals, when he chipped Alan Main from the edge of the box. 'Souey said my goal had been worth the admission money alone!' wrote Walters. 'We all like to receive a little praise now and again, not to fuel the ego but because it can make you feel good about yourself if for some reason you're feeling down.' Clearly then, Souness was able to offer it up to some, if not all, of his players. If that Walters goal was sublime, his effort in the new year clash with Celtic was ridiculous, his corner going straight over Bonner and directly into the net. Hateley would grab his first Old Firm goal to wrap up the points late on and ensure that Rangers remained unbeaten in league clashes against their great rivals for over two years but it was a game remembered most of all for the shameful behaviour of the Celtic support in the Broomloan Road Stand during the minute's silence on the 20th anniversary of the Ibrox disaster.

Three days later it looked as if Rangers would drop a point at Tynecastle as the match wore into injury time, still goalless. This time there was no fluke, no defensive error or direct assault. It was a long patient, passing move that ended up engineering a simple tap-in for Hateley to keep the five-point gap at the top. Despite the weather – both literal and figurative – Rangers were matching results with some brilliant football, some of it the best of the era.

It wasn't fully satisfying Souness, however. Little was by this stage. An 11-match unbeaten run was extended at home to Dunfermline – it would eventually go

---

120   Rangers were three points ahead.

121   Aberdeen's number one, Theo Snelders, had been given an 11-week layoff thanks to a broken cheekbone suffered in an accidental collision with McCoist on a soaking day at Pittdodrie at the start of October.

further to 17 – and yet Souness found the need to criticise the fans for their lack of fervour and their consistent need to gripe at the selection of Hateley and not McCoist, despite the clear reality that, given the penchant for a hitman, it was Johnston keeping out Super Ally and not the new signing. That is the nature of football fandom though, with its irrationality and outright devotion to heroes. It was beneath Souness to react like that and it was perhaps telling of the mounting pressure that was building inside. Some kind of release was required but little did anyone know that a potential solution was just around the corner.

On the morning of Friday, 22 February, with his side three points clear at the top of the English First Division, Kenny Dalglish resigned as manager of Liverpool.

* * *

For such a quiet town, Perth continued to be the source of so much trouble for Graeme Souness. On his drive home on the night of Wednesday, 26 February 1991, he told his friend Ian Blyth, 'I've had enough of this … It is becoming unbearable.' Back in the October visit to McDiarmid Park, Souness had followed his new, expensive and injured defender back into the dressing room to sit with him. He asked the St Johnstone tea lady, Aggie Moffat, to fetch him a cuppa, which she duly refused. After the next trip in February, another frustrating draw, Souness asked his players to place the mud off their boots into piles so it was easier to clean up. Moffat was not impressed – she also complained about the general state of the dressing room and a smashed jug of orange juice – and said she would go directly to the chairman, Geoff Brown. Souness then duly followed her into the corridor shouting and swearing about what she expected the floor to look like after a game of football. Brown assured Moffat that he would look into it, to which Souness replied, 'I am here, look into it now.' When Brown made a move to take hold of Souness's arm, the temperature increased dramatically as threats were made if he didn't remove his grip.

It was an embarrassing farce that was starting to become part of the script. By this stage Liverpool had made contact, but had been quickly rejected. As Souness admitted in his 1999 book, however, 'A seed had been planted and it was only human nature to wonder privately what it would be like to go back … Many of the people I knew during my time as a player were still at the club so perhaps it was only natural to daydream about what it might be like to go back.' After the drive home, that breezy reverie turned into a more concrete desire.

As with Souness's arrival at Ibrox, the accounts of his departure are rather inconsistent. According to Walter Smith in 1994, Souness first raised the question when they were enjoying a sauna at a hotel health club near the stadium. He just wanted to sound Smith out about the idea which, after some time, he duly gave his assessment which was along the lines that this would be a difficult job. He couldn't light a fire under Liverpool in the same way he had at Ibrox as Rangers had gone so long without a title whereas the Reds, although they would need a lot of work, were still the reigning champions of England. In order to do the job he needed to do he would have to 'tread on a lot of toes'. Souness rejected the offer and assured fans in Rangers News in the week after the St Johnstone game that he was going nowhere but then, a few weeks later in March, the subject came up again when the two were on a flight down to London to watch a match. This time Souness wasn't looking for an opinion. He was taking the job. Would Smith go with him as his assistant? Smith wrote that he didn't want to leave Ibrox, a place that he had worked so long to get to and even then, he felt that he would not fit into the famous Liverpool boot room, having never graduated from it himself.

Souness's account in 1999 was slightly different, although the scenery remained the same. He had accepted the job by the time he sat down in that Bellahouston health club sauna and was asking both Smith and Phil Boersma to go with him. Boersma was immediately delighted, 'Walter was also very keen which was important to me because I was prepared to turn the job down unless Phil and Walter were joining me.' The flight to London, according to Souness, was to meet with Noel White and Peter Robinson from Liverpool at the Heathrow Holiday Inn. It was then that Smith's cold feet became a problem, especially over the issue of getting in the way of the existing backroom staff, specifically Ronnie Moran and Roy Evans. He wasn't going to make the move but, by that time, Souness's mind was firmly made up.

'Graeme must have been under considerable personal pressure,' wrote Smith. 'There must have been tremendous inner turmoil, and yet he hid that from everyone. Not a single player suspected anything. It was amazing how he was able to concentrate his mind the way he did. I admired that immensely.' Although Smith was surely correct to appreciate the pressures around his manager at the time, praise for the control is overplayed. Until the day that he was told by a bag handler at Heathrow, on his way home from seeing his children, that Dalglish had left Anfield, Souness had enjoyed the longest unbeaten run in his entire spell at Rangers.[122] It was extended that night in Perth, the first game after the news broke, but it was ended at Pittodrie at the weekend – a 1-0 defeat that cut the gap at the top to four points and where both McCoist and Johnston were wasteful in front of goal – and worse was to come with league and cup double-header at Parkhead on 17 and 24 March. Rangers lost 2-0 in the Scottish Cup quarter-final and, because of the three red cards to add to the growing injury list[123], fielded a nonsense of a side in the following league game where Celtic added a goal to their previous tally and Rangers limited the dismissals to just the one.[124] They had seen four red cards in over two years before receiving the same amount in just two games. Injuries were starting to bite – although there were still nine regular starters at Aberdeen – and of course, this slump had happened at a similar stage the previous season, but the dramatic nature of it cannot be extricated from the manager's own situation, especially as his handling of McCoist took an even more bizarre turn.

---

122   Fifteen league games and two in the Scottish Cup, with the only the one draw at home to Aberdeen.

123   Hateley, Walters and Hurlock all saw red.

124   Just Scott Nisbet this time in a starting XI that included four strikers – Johnston, McCoist, Davie Dodds and John Spencer – with midfielders Pieter Huistra and Sandy Robertson on the bench. Dodds played at the back but the general set-up made little sense.

Before the cup tie, the players were given some time off to relax. McCoist took the opportunity to head down to Cheltenham for the National Hunt Festival. Unlike golf, it wasn't a banned activity and he ensured a late flight got him back home in time for the squad meeting up again. Souness asked him that morning if he had been to the races, as he often enjoyed doing, and smiled when McCoist confirmed. On the Sunday of the Scottish Cup tie, McCoist had to be stopped from leaving the ground by former Celtic player Bobby Lennox, such was his rage at not even making the bench. Rangers were awful and Celtic, even though they had Peter Grant sent off first, deserved their win. In addition to the three suspensions, Trevor Steven suffered a bad knee injury which ruled him out for the rest of the season, so the mood around Ibrox was getting more bleak by the week. Souness's response was to use McCoist as a scapegoat by forcing him to attend a press conference and apologise for going to the races, which he was keen to caveat by starting off with, 'In the manager's opinion there has been a brach of discipline.'

However, there had been no breach of discipline and there was no fine, which would have been standard practice. This was purely another episode in a personal battle of egos that McCoist was always convinced was rooted in the fact that he was one of the few original players, along with Stuart Munro and Ian Durrant, still around. He was also incredibly popular, more so than Souness as had been made clear all season, and it was yet another stressor to add to the manager's list. McCoist would play the following week due to Hateley's suspension but excused his performance in his autobiography, a little like the appearance for Scotland against Brazil, by saying that the damage had already been done and that he was carrying a knock in any case. McCoist couldn't have it both ways but there weren't many fans prepared to hear any more. This was a deliberate humiliation of their hero and, even among some of the most conservative opinions, it was evidence of a deep-rooted malaise which was now threatening the title bid. In an edition of the Rangers Historian on 15 April, Robert McElroy wrote that Souness had contributed to this apparent collapse and that 'should the dream of a third successive league title for the first time since the war finally crumble, then surely the time will have have come for a reappraisal by the Rangers board of the current management situation at Ibrox'. Little did he, or most fans, know that it was something that had already been carried out.

Even by the end of March, David Murray had no idea that his manager was planning his exit. On Sunday, 1 April, Souness took his first trip to see his prospective side at their game with Southampton, chosen specifically because, with his estranged wife and children living in Guilford, he could easily pass it off as taking in a game while visiting. It was at half-time of this match that he told his father, who had accompanied him to The Dell, that he was moving. He understood and took the news well but this wasn't the reaction his son was most concerned about. During their usual dinner date in early April, Murray had picked up on some unease and, while driving Souness back to his flat, said, 'You're going to Liverpool aren't you?' According to Souness, the two sat out on a wall on a nice spring evening weighing up what needed to happen as Murray offered him whatever he wanted and even suggested taking some time out for a year while remaining on the board. Like a married couple talking about how to manage an affair, Souness told him that he wanted to leave once the league had been won but Murray responded that it would be best if he went now. Like many a jilted spouse has correctly predicted, Souness was told that he was making a big mistake.

Once Murray was in the loop, around the second week of April, he wasn't in the mood to mess around. Souness had recommended promoting Smith both on grounds of ability and a better profile compared to the pressure that he had attracted. Murray immediately wanted a big name but Smith's proactive questioning about what would happen next and assurance that he wanted to stay were crucial in those early days. Murray asked, what Smith called the 'unnecessary question'. Of course Smith would take the job if offered but Murray needed more time. Richard Gough was approached for his opinion and his response was short and certain: give it to Smith. So much of the work being done on the training ground was his anyway and it made sense in order to get this title – now only a matter of two points – over the line. The name of Ray Wilkins was also suggested as a possible alternative but Murray's mind was now set. As he and Smith walked down the tunnel before the game with St Johnstone on Saturday, 13 April, Murray said, 'That's it. If you want the job then you can have it.'

There was a certain poignancy about Souness's final game in charge. The previous week had seen yet more title jitters as Rangers drew 0-0 with Hibs at Ibrox but the one ray of light was the return of a hero as 28 months since that sickening day in Aberdeen, Ian Durrant finally made his comeback. A player in whom his manager believed before – and most crucially after – his injury helped ease the nerves by scoring the first goal in the 3-0 win over St Johnstone. Ibrox, despite the noticeable empty spaces, saluted one of their own while having no idea that they would never get the chance to do the same for the man who developed him into one.

Three days later, Graeme Souness left Rangers.

* * *

Around midday on Tuesday, 16 April, Richard Gough bumped into his now former manager on the famous marble staircase at the main entrance to Ibrox Stadium's famous Main Stand. 'All the best,' Souness said to him on his way out. 'Make sure and win the title.' Gough noted the visible emotion that was underwriting those words, 'He was almost crying. This tough, often ruthless man, was close to tears. It was a very emotional moment for him.' There are obvious similarities with Souness's political hero Margaret Thatcher, too, who with moistness of eye and almost 20 weeks to the day had left a post that she had made her own with an abrasive single-minded approach, a little sooner than she wished but having unquestionably changed the surrounding environment forever.

The brief press conference that had preceded that meeting was tense as Murray explained why no man was bigger than Rangers Football Club and why the move had to be done at that point, before Souness interjected to say, 'I would like to state that I wanted to to say until the end of the season but it has been decided by the board that they feel that its in the best interests of the football club if I go now and I have to accept that.' The chairman looked irritable as he took a sip of water, never really speaking as smoothly as he had with the media before or would again, and at one stage Souness went to hold the back of Murray's chair as he spoke. 'I feel I've gone as far as I'll be allowed to go to try to achieve success at this football club,' said Souness, with particular emphasis on the word 'allowed', as if there was no agency at all on his part. Contemporaneous commentary likened it to a scolded schoolboy in the headmasters's office but there is far more parity of status than that. It was like the final session of couple's counselling, with both parties trying valiantly to deal with the end.

The reaction from the Rangers support towards Souness was mixed, with natural anger being tempered by a wide acceptance that his life in Scotland was not sustainable, separated from his family and having the prospect of a lifetime touchline ban from the SFA hanging over him as that interminable war continued. 'He's been forced out by the SFA' was the leading line from those interviewed on the day, a footballing nation that never really forgave him for turning their game upside down. The same tension between pain and appreciation is evident in the next published issue of Follow, Follow in early May. The front page offered up the star prize of an Austin Metro for anyone who shot Souness and there was anger at the perceived 'lies' he told when he initially turned down the Liverpool job in February, but nearly every letter of complaint was prefaced by some variation of 'he was by far and away, the best thing to ever happen to Rangers'. One letter, by Professor Graham Walker but under the pseudonym 'MacDougall', was the most balanced and interesting of all. At times it read like an immediate detached analysis or one from a fan some years down the line, 'The guy could be brutal, dangerously temperamental and cynically ruthless; he created as many problems as were visited, often unjustly, on him. Nonetheless he gave us – and restored to us – a true sense of greatness and made us believe that anything was possible and achievable.' Later on, it was more like a melancholic love letter about a departed partner, 'He was no fly-by-night: he stayed five years, although it now seems like five weeks. Already I feel something wonderful has gone, although there is no reason why something as great cannot be achieved in the future … Unfortunately, the squalidness of the way the affair has been handled and the parting shots and innuendoes encouraged the feelings of betrayal. I don't think all this should be allowed to tarnish some treasured memories: Dynamo Kiev at Ibrox, the 5-1 game, Pittodrie '87 … none of us deep down would have missed the last five years for anything … So from the heart thanks, you piss-elegant arrogant bastard – if we ever win the European Cup I, for one, will toast you.'

The reaction towards the chairman was much more straightforward, as Murray was showered with praise for his decisive action and leadership. 'At times he's seemed very distant from us,' wrote Mark Dingwall. 'Yet he has more than redeemed himself by booting Souness out as soon as he heard of the move. If he didn't want to stay forever, he wouldn't stay at all.' Very quickly the conversation was about who was next, the entire country unaware that Walter Smith had already agreed to take over. Dalglish was an early front-runner as was George

Graham, who was by then well on his way to winning the title with Arsenal. Ray Wilkins, whom Smith would approach first to be his assistant, was quoted alongside Franz Beckenbauer who, less than a year after winning the World Cup with West Germany, was not enjoying life in Marseille. Some Rangers players and their friends were set to make a tidy sum at the bookies that week as hints were given by Smith that he'd be there for a while yet. On Friday, 19 April, Murray was in the same room at Ibrox to announce that Smith would be the next manager of Rangers Football Club. Some of those wanting to collect their winnings had to wait a while as some bookmakers refused to pay out for a matter of months as they felt that Smith might just be a caretaker. A hint then that it was an appointment that made sense to ensure continuity for the remaining four games of the season but jarred slightly with the overall sense of ambition that Rangers had enjoyed projecting. For now, however, the bigger picture could wait. There was an extremely close title race coming to its conclusion.

Smith's first two games in charge were nervy affairs but increasingly makeshift Rangers sides had managed to come away with two 1-0 wins. At Love Street on 20 April, with Aberdeen already 3-0 up at home to Motherwell elsewhere, the pressure was intensifying with each passing minute against St Mirren. Interestingly, Smith opted for a three-man central defence, the first time Rangers had used such since Butcher's departure, but with Nigel Spackman dropping deeper to support John Brown and Scott Nisbet due to Richard Gough's suspension and even after seeing out a jittery opening spell, it was still something of a toil as the game reached it's final quarter. In an era where youth development would be heavily sidelined by expensive expediency, it was somewhat ironic that such a crucial and brilliant goal would be scored by a 19-year-old home grown talent. Sandy Robertson, who had set up Mark Hateley for his first Old Firm goal back in January, controlled a low cross by Gary Stevens with maturity beyond his years and followed up with a hooked, left-footed volley into the top corner that was pure youthful exuberance. Gough returned for the midweek home tie with Dundee United, along with Johnston and Walters, which saw a touch more attacking fluency but just the one goal, this time a low Ian Ferguson header in the first half.

Smith had navigated those early tests well but realised that he needed someone to do his old job. With Wilkins unwilling to leave London, he turned to Archie Knox, someone with whom he spoke constantly but who was then preparing for a European Cup Winners' Cup Final as Alex Ferguson's assistant at Old Trafford. Incredibly, much to Ferguson's outrage, once the two men met in Carlisle to talk the plans over, Knox left immediately. Ferguson refused to speak to Smith for a short period but would win that final without Knox in any event. Knox's first match on the Rangers bench would be at Fir Park and with the potential of some immediate silverware.

Scotland had been in San Marino for a European Championship qualifier the week before, when Gough was sent home, feeling very unwell. After a couple of days in his own bed he was taken to hospital where hepatitis from food poisoning was the diagnosis. With so many of the squad, such as Kuznetsov, Munro and

Steven injured for the long term[125] and players with niggles or lacking match fitness like Brown, Durrant and McCoist, the management duo did not need to see their captain laid up in a hospital bed where he would follow the rest of the season via the radio. But Rangers still held the advantage and a win that matched Aberdeen's in terms of margins would have meant that the final-day meeting would have required the Dons dishing out an unlikely hammering at Ibrox. A win was certainly possible but 5-0 would have been pushing the boundaries of reality.

Motherwell, inspired by Rangers old boy Davie Cooper, were preparing for the upcoming Scottish Cup Final – which they would win in a classic encounter with Dundee United – and this verve was evident throughout the opening stages as once again there was more than a hint of stage fright for a Rangers side that felt as if it was hanging on. As Ian Ferguson later said, it was 'one of the worst performances I can remember the team giving when the chips were down'. John Philliben, who had scored more than one own goal in previous Rangers visits to Fir Park, blasted one into the correct top corner from a Cooper dead ball, despite Ferguson's attempts to save it on the line with his hands. There was better from Rangers in the second half but Maxwell was in inspired form – something that he would famously extend to the cup final – and, with Walters' penalty miss from such a soft decision from Andrew Waddell, the same referee who had been so card happy in that Parkhead quarter-final, it felt very much like one of those days. With Aberdeen just 2-1 ahead the smart move, as the game ticked past 85 minutes, would have been to ensure nothing careless happened but pressure so often forces the hand. As Rangers pushed and pushed, a defence without a natural leader was left wide open and the second Motherwell goal, scored by Dougie Arnott, was a classic piece of swift counterattacking football. Rangers' advantage was now just one solitary goal and, with a matter of minutes remaining, the shop should have been closed. With a mixture of naivety and panic, Rangers continued to flood forward and a replica goal was produced at the very end as Arnott delicately clipped the ball over the despairing Woods. It was a goal that many fans and pundits believed had changed the destination of the championship with Aberdeen, now ahead by virtue of goals scored, were in the driving seat right at the very last turn. In a way, they were absolutely right.

There was a burst of celebration in the Aberdeen dressing room when they heard that Motherwell had gone 3-0 up. With Rangers' injury list and their stuttering form, the title would surely only go one way. But that is where the pressure changes the dynamics. Rangers had been creaking for weeks with internal strife and trying to hold on to a position of strength and now, suddenly, it was all off. Aberdeen's form – 11 wins and one draw – had come from an exciting, positive 4-3-3 setup added to having no burden of expectation. Now there was and the manager Alex Smith, in agreement with his senior players, decided to change back to a more robust 4-4-2 and try to ensure they got the solitary point that they needed. It was a negative thought that grew as the week went on. Changing in portacabins

---

125   Stuart Munro had been rushed into playing in that Old Firm cup match in March despite struggling to walk but such was the pressure with injuries. Souness admitted to Munro that he was wrong to select him but had become desperate which was just further evidence of such muddled thinking that had become endemic.

in the bowels of the Main Stand – due to renovation on the new upper tier – some Aberdeen players, such as the imminent Rangers signing David Robertson, started to show fear. Robertson later recalled, 'I remember looking to Paul Mason, because we could hear the Rangers supporters thumping and singing upstairs, and we just looked at each other as if to say "this is going to be pretty difficult here".' The league leaders only had one injury issue: goalkeeper Theo Snelders was replaced by young Michael Watt, who had performed well at Ibrox during his last two visits but he couldn't repeat that on 11 May. It was the pressure.

The week at Ibrox had been very different. Once the disappointment and frustration from Fir Park had been worked out, the mood had changed. 'I'm normally looking at the downside,' wrote Ian Ferguson in his autobiography, 'but not that day. I can remember sitting upstairs having a bite to eat with Coisty and saying to him, "We're going to win today, we're really going to do it," and totally believing it myself because the whole atmosphere just felt right.' Walters remembered a similar feeling, 'We were deflated after that [Motherwell] game and desperately wanted to play Aberdeen the following day. So I honestly couldn't see past us winning. I had never seen a bunch of guys so fired up for a game in my entire career. I had been playing for ten years and had never witnessed desire and hunger like it.'

It was fitting that the hero of the day would be Mark Hateley. It wasn't him keeping McCoist out of the team and he had already scored a not insignificant 13 goals by the morning of the final day. He should have been a player who was shown instant respect but instead had suffered a season-long endurance test in gaining it. That test would be over by 5pm. One major reason why Hateley had made the move from Monaco, with such small crowds even when they won the league, was atmosphere. 'I wanted big games,' he wrote in 1994. 'I wanted games where you could feel the tension sweep down from the terraces and stands.'

Few matches would fit that description better than this one as Ibrox, shorn of the tension associated with holding on to something by their fingertips, was vibrant and positive as they backed their battered boys into battle. A battle it was, with some of the early challenges ferocious but none more significant than one between Hateley and Watt for an early high ball. 'I remember walking down the tunnel and I saw this young man and thought he was a mascot or something!' Hateley told Heart and Hand – The Rangers Podcast. 'I thought "here's an opportunity", so I turned to Gary Stevens when we got out on the field and asked him to hang one up in the first ten minutes, not to fire one across, but one where the goalkeeper could come for it. Sure enough he did, the young boy came out and I caught him with a real sore one and the moment he hit the floor the two centre-halves, who would normally be all over me, didn't want to know. They left him on the floor and from that moment I thought, "We cannot lose this game."'

Aberdeen's Dutchmen, Hans Gillhaus and Peter van de Ven, both missed early chances that would have been buried the week before. The leaders had much of the ball as Rangers tried to hold some early shape, not helped by Tom Cowan breaking his leg and having to be replaced by Ian Durrant, left-back not being a position for which he was ever famous. As the interval approached, Aberdeen still held all the cards. 'I remember big Alex [McLeish] saying to me, "Come on, we are nearly halfway there,'" Robertson told me. 'Two minutes later big Hateley scored and we were never getting back into the game just because of the support and determination that the Rangers players had.' It was an absolutely crushing header from a perfect Walters cross – the last of many that he had provided for Rangers forwards – and it pushed Ibrox into new levels of noise and fervour.

Watt had no chance with that one but the second goal came from a spill from a fairly tame Johnston shot as he saw Hateley rampaging towards him, from where he made no such mistake. Alex Smith changed back to the 4-3-3 and Aberdeen looked back to their fluid best but, even with yet another Rangers injury – John Brown's achilles going as he was told it would before the game – they couldn't make a dent. Rangers – with a rookie manager, a squad down to the bare bones, a team playing positional musical chairs and with no great form going into the biggest league match in generations – were champions again. There is a very convincing argument that, without that third Motherwell goal, the nervy grip that Rangers had on the title would have been loosened by an Aberdeen side with a strong wind behind them and with nothing at all to lose and that Ibrox, too, would have been too tense to get fully behind the side with the freedom and fervour that they were able to show that day.

It was the pressure.

* * *

There would be more cohesive, more consistent and more claustrophobic seasons to come for Rangers throughout the 1990s, but none with pressure quite so acute as this finale and one where internal obstacles were just as challenging as any brought by an outside contender. A pressurised environment is the perfect way to test greatness, the 19th-century Scottish philosopher Thomas Carlyle believed, and a diamond was beginning to form at Ibrox under the strain of 1990/91. It may have finally been all too much for the man with the biggest bravado in the country but it was evident throughout the season that he had, by then, created a sense of collective character that could now stand many of those tests with or without him. Winning an Old Firm cup final from behind after a week from Hell, stringing together the most consistent run of results in his era despite him creating dressing-room havoc and grabbing the number one prize, during a backdrop of traumatic upheaval, and with players willing to put their bodies on the line for the cause; it was a season of trials that would reap even greater rewards in the years to come.

Saturday, 11 May 1991 was another major turning point in the direction of the revolution and it was an inherently inward one in that it would be the last serious domestic challenge that Rangers would face for five years. There would be more new pretenders but pretence their challenge most certainly would be. Aberdeen, shattered by that final-day capitulation, would never be that close again and Celtic, teetering on the brink as a club, were left far behind in the distance. It was a great victory that also kept a successive run of titles intact, something that would shape the focus and identity of the club in the years to come.

'The history of the world is but the biography of great men,' wrote Carlyle, and that theory is so often applied to the explanation of sporting achievement, with its insatiable need for heroes. There have been few more dominant personalities at Rangers than Terry Butcher and arguably none more so than Graeme Souness but the decline and departure of that overpowering presence allowed for the emergence of quieter leaders in Walter Smith and Richard Gough, who would ultimately become more successful. The mental strength and inner character of Ally McCoist and Mark Hateley was tested to the limits but it is hard to argue that one of the most explosive striking partnerships in the club's history would have been forged quite as tightly without it.

In the longer view of this season, however, the power and influence of those great Rangers men is diminished as the footballing landscape began a transformation well outside the range of their agency. English football's time as the sick man of Europe was over. Manchester United's win over Barcelona in the final of the European Cup Winners' Cup was something of a false dawn in terms of a renewed dominance of continental competition, but it was a stark reminder to any big English talent that not only did they have access back to the biggest stage but they could actually compete. Despite all the promise, Rangers didn't get close to maximising their opportunity as the biggest British contender in those years of exile and the humiliation in Belgrade only served to underline that. It was the dramatic night for England in Turin the previous summer, however, that had kickstarted the real change and was the genesis of a marketing idea that would leave Rangers, and Scottish football in its slipstream. The summer of 1991 saw the first formal proposal for the new FA Premier League and British football would never look the same again.

This significant challenge from across the border was further compounded by the increasing realisation around the impact of UEFA's 1988 decision on foreign players. One other problem with the law was that it was wholly and entirely illegal, being, as it was, in direct contravention of European law on the free movement of labour. It would take until the Bosman case of 1995 for this to be recognised but the window in between its implementation and withdrawal could not have come at a worse time for Rangers. It immediately placed caps on any further ambition to tackle Europe by bringing in the best talent they could afford in order to play a style that could be consistently competitive. By the time it was lifted, football was almost a different sport. The same external opportunities and decision-makers that created conditions for the revolution to take root were now shutting it down at the key moment of its development. Although few would agree at the time, the revolution was slowing down towards its natural end.

Ironic then, that almost immediately after the Souness era came to a close – one where he tried to mould and bend Rangers into something less Scottish – Rangers were forced to become more Scottish than ever before.

10

THE MEN WHO FILLED
THE BLAZER

'History will have to decide whether I was good for Glasgow Rangers but certainly Glasgow Rangers were good for me.'
Graeme Souness

''Hey Smith, do we have to watch this rubbish all season?' I looked at my watch. We had been playing for 17 minutes.'
Walter Smith

'Maradona is vastly overrated.'

It was classic Graeme Souness then and remains so now. The excessive language loaded for effect, and the unmistakable masculinity that was to follow. 'I don't doubt his skills for a moment but sometimes I think he should be in a circus. What I mean is that he hasn't won too many medals has he?' He soon would. Souness was speaking from Scotland camp in Mexico the day before the second 1986 World Cup group game against West Germany by which point Diego Maradona had already scored against the holders Italy, on his way to staking his claim as the greatest player of all time. Technically the new Rangers manager was correct – the boy wonder had not yet matched his hype with silverware – but the lack of appreciation for individual talent in a team sport was underlined by that most reductive and machismo piece of football verbiage: show us your medals.

It is so typically Souness that it is almost impossible to imagine it coming from anyone else in the game. It certainly wouldn't have come from Walter Smith. On the face of it, the men who changed Rangers were very different people. Souness loud and verbose; Smith more studious and careful with his words. The outspoken Thatcherite and the dignified Labour man. One who wouldn't shirk confrontation if it reared its head, the other who seemed to need it with his morning coffee. In the words of Sue Mott in a Sunday Times piece from 1992, 'To Smith, the former apprentice electrician, Gucci is something you say to babies when tickling them under the chin. To Souness, it was lifestyle.' Together they were a dream, amassing precious metal at a rapid rate but, in the end, it was Souness's apprentice who let his work do the talking, more than doubling his record of managerial achievement with 21 major successes to his mentor's ten. Despite their different characters, both demonstrated that one had to have it in abundance if they were to be successful at Ibrox, a job more akin to being prime minster than head coach. 'Tracksuit managers' had failed before and have done so since, suggesting that a real Rangers manager needs to own the office. They need to fill the blazer.

Both Souness and Smith did but their spells in the job were not without difficulty. One challenge in trying to compare the two managers is the extent to which the game had changed during their reign. The dynamics of football in 1986 were almost unrecognisable by 1998 thanks in part to the player power and market reform that they had both helped to unleash. In 1986/87, reigning English champions Liverpool spent just over £1.5m and Tottenham Hotspur a million more whereas Manchester United wouldn't commit the funds to get Terry Butcher. In 1998, however, English Premier League clubs spent over £335m in total, with Dwight Yorke's move from Aston Villa to Old Trafford being the most expensive at just over £17m. Compared to the challenges that Smith had in navigating the limitations of foreign players, the impact of the Bosman ruling and the growing influence of agents, the world that Souness worked in during his spell as Rangers manager was a far simpler one.

He thrived in it. Given his success at Ibrox with transfers, it is remarkable that, after his managerial career ended, Souness the market trader was thought of as more Derek Trotter than George Soros. His Liverpool career was beset by bad dealings, trying too hard to clear out the ageing legends too quickly. Peter Beardsley had a few good years left in him when he was replaced by Dean Saunders, the sale of Steve Staunton was something he could have done without and Neil 'Razor' Ruddock and Julian Dicks were redolent of an older era of English football. His nadir came at Southampton in 1996 when he was duped into believing that Ali Dia was the cousin of the then FIFA World Player of the Year, George Weah. Dia came on as a substitute before being taken off and never seen again. It was the ultimate embarrassment. In his first managerial job, however, Souness rarely put a foot wrong.

It was easy to buy your way to success, the Scottish footballing public would often tell Souness, but as has been discussed previously, sporting history is full of expensive failure. The players need to be right for the job and the money used wisely. Although he wasn't around when all of his signings were eventually sold on, Rangers made a profit of over £1m on the men Souness brought in as well as the £2.5m he generated from the players he inherited. If signings didn't work then he moved them on quickly, a ruthlessness that perhaps Smith would go on to lack. Even the medium success stories did their job and departed – for good money – when something better raised its head. But the big calls were the best of all. Only Oleg Kusnetzov and Colin West, because of injury, could be regarded as flops. On the vast majority of occasions where Souness stuck his neck out for a player they delivered, in some cases long after he was gone. In fact a best XI of Souness signings – Chris Woods, Gary Stevens, Richard Gough, Terry Butcher, John Brown, Mark Walters, Ray Wilkins, Ian Ferguson, Trevor Steven, Maurice Johnston and Mark Hateley (with Graham Roberts, Pieter Huistra and Kevin Drinkell on the bench) – might be hard for any other Rangers manager to beat in terms of what they gave the club, for as long and relative to the standards of the time.

The standards of his successor's time changed sharply and often. Where Souness had the carrot of European football, the draw of a modern stadium and the willingness of a board to spend what rivals couldn't, Smith needed to keep meeting rising expectations of a support demanding bigger and better prizes in a footballing world that was exploding. He was backed, however, in a way that Souness could only dream of. Between 1991 and 1997 Smith spent over £59m on transfers, recouping beyond £26.5m in that time. Ostensibly it was an outlay required to conquer Europe. In reality, it was all to stay ahead of a Celtic side who had spend less than half of that during the same period and who lacked the head start that Rangers had created for themselves, both on and off the field. Whether his market activity was as much value for money as his predecessor is questionable but Smith wouldn't have had the success that he did, without identifying the right men.

In the next chapter we shall see how well Smith dealt with new boundaries by snatching the best Scottish talent available. Across each summer between 1994 and 1997, he signed a genuine Rangers legend in Brian Laudrup, Paul Gascoigne, Jörg Albertz and Lorenzo Amoruso. In David Robertson, Gordan Petrić, Alan McLaren, Joachim Björklund, Alec Cleland and Sergio Porrini he was always able to build a rearguard but failed to find a suitable replacement for Ally McCoist, with Oleg Salenko, Sebastián Rozental and Marco Negri failing for different reasons. Smith enjoyed bringing in a winter gift with which to energise his squad for the final push with Dale Gordon, Gordon Durie and Erik Bo Andersen being used to great effect when there were required in the middle of a campaign. After 1992, Smith's biggest market failing were marquee signings that did not solve the problems that he had. Breaking the British transfer record for Duncan Ferguson in 1993 when Rangers – in Mark Hateley - had one of the best target men in Britain already in place, and then having to play Ferguson out on the left wing on occasion, created problems just as it did when he brought in the dominant right-sided centre-half Basile Boli, when his captain already played in that position. Rozental's injury weeks after arriving from Chile in December 1996 was unfortunate but the salary given to Jönas Thern in 1997 when it was known that he was literally on his last legs was an act of reckless hubris.

Smith's two most famous signings spoke to his main strength as a manager but arguably helped to create his biggest weakness when assessing his first spell at Ibrox. Nobody needed expert scouting to discover Brian Laudrup and Paul Gascoigne in the mid-1990s but it took a special man-manager to whisper them back into the groove following a difficult spell for both players in Italy. As a result, it arguably changed Smith's mid-1990s side into a more individualistic one. In a book about change, when it comes to tactics, neither Souness or Smith were particularly revolutionary, although the patient build-up introduced in 1986 was certainly a big adjustment for the Ibrox faithful to deal with. The two dominant ideas of the time between 1986 and 1992 were Arrigo Sacchi's muscular version of 'Total Football' at Milan and the West German 3-5-2 sweeper system. According to Alistair Bain of the excellent tactics website retrofootballanalysis.com, the Souness era, of which Smith played a huge part on the training ground, was originally more in line with the former, with an immediate appetite to dominate a game through to the experimentation with ball-playing centre midfielders, twin strikers instead of a target man and the key ability to use width on both sides with Trevor Steven and Gary Stevens, instead of mainly through Walters on the left. His attempted transition to the increasingly en vogue 3-5-2 needed more, and better, foreign players and when it was clear that this was an impossibility, the end was nigh.

Bain's analysis of the incredible 1992/93 Champions League run makes the case that – perhaps because what came after was so disappointing – Smith's early tactical success has been forgotten or dismissed. Smith built a cohesive 4-4-2 unit that could squeeze the space domestically in the knowledge that pace at full-back would often provide cover but against better opposition in the 1992/93 European campaign, they were happy to concede possession and the best chances and instead tried to exploit specific weaknesses that he had identified in their opponents' setup. It was smart and secure and so nearly pulled off the greatest result of all time. As the heroes of that effort suffered physically in the years afterwards, there was an increasing reliance on new individual brilliance. What worked well enough at home was easily isolated in Europe. Any confidence in a systemic reliability was soon non-existent and a decade of tactical sophistication throughout the continent further sharpened the disappointment and sense of regression at the time.

Regardless of system and ability, every club needs players who are fit and tuned to execute their plans and it is here that both managers struggled to change the culture completely. Earlier chapters have documented Souness's endeavour to revolutionise the dietary and social habits of his players and, although there were some definite improvements in cultural attitudes, there were always limits as to what he could ultimately do. By 1992, Smith appeared to have relaxed the stance. A profile piece for the short-lived monthly magazine Scottish Football followed Smith and his squad as they prepared for a league match at Tynecastle and then the visit of Marseille to Ibrox for the first Champions League encounter. An Italian TV crew were also following them and watched in stunned disbelief as Smith and his players walked out the front door of Ibrox, up along Paisley Road West to a cafe outside Bellahouston Park where they enjoyed bacon rolls and cups of tea. Later in the afternoon – before the trip to Edinburgh for an overnight stay – training at a local cricket club consisted of knocking the ball around for 20 minutes before heading back to the minibus. 'We don't really train,' said Smith. 'You can't. There are so many games and so many injuries to contend with that you just keep the players going. The hard work is done in pre-season, when the players build up their basic fitness. After that? It's just a question of them ticking over.' It wouldn't have been out of place in many British setups – Arsène Wenger's more successful dietary revolution was still four years away – but it wouldn't have happened in Milan or Marseille.

There were no complaints that season because the European run had generated so much pride. When it soon provided humiliation, the questions started, especially when the players themselves spoke out. In an infamous interview with L'Équipe in September 1994, Basile Boli was candid in his criticism of Smith's failure to guide his side past AEK Athens and into the 1994/95 Champions League. He described the tactics as 'crazy' (Boli was played at right-back and both Mark Hateley and Duncan Ferguson were selected alongside one another) and the attitude was 'all wrong' in the build-up.[126] Some years before, Ally McCoist had made a revealing statement when he ruled out the prospect of him becoming a manager in the future, 'It's not for me. I couldn't wield the big stick. I'd only be fining my players if they hadn't been out the night before.' When Rangers players were on the front pages more often than the back because of drink-driving, domestic abuse and affairs, the criticism intensified. As did questions about why Rangers were picking up so many muscle injuries or buying players who were immediately out for sustained periods of time. Souness's blind spot for a proper medical staff wasn't corrected by Smith. The physical strain of success would eventually show and any advances in professionalism that were made since 1986 seemed to regress. In Smith's final season of this era, 1997/98, the year that the domestic juggernaut finally stopped, France Football would describe Rangers as the 'stupidest club on the continent'.

That was all in the future of course, after Smith had got his hands on 13 trophies in six years. It wasn't simply a case of buying big to stay ahead of weakened opposition; there were crucial moments when his team had to show character and he, more than anyone else, infused his side with that in spades. From the baptism of fire that was the conclusion to that 1990/91 season, through to his final match as a manager in 2011, there were plenty of footballers who were willing to run through fire for Smith. 'The team that drinks together, wins together' was an oft-repeated phrase during the 1990s but, although it created limitations in more rarefied environments, domestically there was truth in it. Spirits helped to produce spirit and Smith was an expert at building a culture where his players felt ten feet tall. 'You do less coaching and more man-management,' Smith said in a Sunday Times interview from 1992. 'There was no way a Walter Smith or Graeme Souness was going to tell Terry Butcher how to play football. All you do is give them an enjoyable environment to play in.'

There is a sharp contrast in that statement with the way that football management was heading. The age of the auteur was beginning, with Saachi, Wenger and José Mourinho – none of them players of great note – more than willing to tell world-class talent what to do and how they wanted them to play. It was about the players fitting into their particular vision, not the other way around. Smith's only vision was silverware and empowering his players to execute what they could do under pressure was the quickest way he saw to achieving that. Brian Laudrup would call Rangers the best move he ever made and that was, without question, because of the freedom that Smith allowed him on the field. He, like Terry Venables, was the father figure that Paul Gascoigne needed in order to feel secure enough to express himself properly. And, as the next chapter will show, there was the handling of Ally McCoist, who was managed in a very different way to his predecessor. Smith could easily have got that wrong, or failed to get over the line in front of Aberdeen, ensuring that the history of Rangers would have looked very different indeed. He instinctively knew however, how to press the correct buttons and had observed how Souness would often misjudge it badly, 'I don't think I'm particularly confrontational as a person. These five years have made me

---

126   The interview would famously be described as 'lost in translation'. The first of many similar accounts of European footballers struggling with the British culture in the mid-1990s.

a wee bit wary of situations like that. I've learnt, you might say, how to avoid bold headlines.'

It would be a mistake to paint Smith as a soft touch. He too could leave players trembling in the dressing room – Gascoigne's need for new underwear after a particular tirade was evidence of that – and he could be just as caustic with the media as Souness had been.[127] It just wasn't as incessant as his predecessor, where it felt as if there was a battle to be had every week, outside or in. Smith seemed to know when to use it for maximum impact. He had a very limited career as a player and understood the realities of a struggling professional footballer. Souness was not the first or last superstar player-turned-manager whose boiling frustration with the mere mortals at his disposal never seemed to cool for long enough. It is impossible to think of Smith's insecurity leading to him treating a player in the way Souness did McCoist but likewise, Smith rarely – if ever – displayed the kind of ruthlessness with big names on the way down in their career as Souness had done with Butcher.

We should be cautious of broad brush strokes. Both men were as contradictory as the rest of us. Smith, a reserved man of overwhelming class and dignity, could still be terrifying with colleagues and he would be arrested for a touchline fight. A man who could pinpoint weaknesses in the best in Europe and consistently deliver Old Firm success but who saw no real value in coaching the players he bought and once said in a newspaper interview, 'What is a tactic anyway?' Souness, the wolf in an empty room, who somehow still managed to inspire a togetherness in title-winning teams, even under the most intense moments of pressure. Fearless in the tackle, literal and metaphorical, but who shirked the further modernisation of his Rangers side.

Nevertheless, the supporters saw in both what they needed to. The man who was a revolutionary agent of change and the man who had a reliable grip on power. The man who gave them swagger and the man who gave them assurance. For a younger generation, Souness had provided the hope of an exciting future. For an older one, Smith had slain the ghosts of their domestic past. Consistent with this whole story, they were just the right characters for the circumstances of their time. Souness would never have lasted much longer at that speed; Rangers needed more control at the time he left. Smith could never have created the Big Bang that started it all; Rangers needed a figurehead much larger than life.

Despite the bumps and bruises, their failures and shortcomings, both men were of course incredibly successful and part of their legacy is that they created the two templates of the modern Rangers manager. The arrogant fire when the whole place needed shaken up like Dick Advocaat and Steven Gerrard and the cooler reserve when an even keel was required, like Alex McLeish and Giovanni van Bronckhorst. When Rangers found themselves in a mess in 2007, it was Smith who got the call to return and steady the ship as only he could. Even post retirement in 2011, fans still called for another temporary return during the darkest of times in the lower leagues. His unrelenting success is an unforgiving benchmark.

Fans have rarely craved Souness back in that seat since his departure but

---

127   Ask Chick Young, whose reprimand from Smith – and Archie Knox – in the Ibrox tunnel is
        now the stuff of YouTube legend.

interestingly, throughout the years between the plunge to the Third Division in 2012 and Gerrard's arrival in 2018, his image adorned a thousand avatars on social media. Whether it was the aftermath of a heavy tackle, a raised fist in celebration or him looking down the barrel of a shotgun, he became a go-to icon for a support who badly needed leadership and strength. Something bigger and more ethereal than getting the next signing right, choosing who to play up front or even winning cups. He was symbolic of a lost sense of identity. His contagious sense of self-belief is the gold standard.

Graeme Souness and Walter Smith still bestride the modern history that they themselves created. Whether it be the diligent collection of trophies or the force of personality required to embody the club, they are still the men against whom every future Rangers manager is compared. It could be generations before we see their likes again.

11

ALCHEMY

SEASON 1991/92

'Walter knows a lot about football, but he also knows an awful lot about what makes human beings tick.'

Ally McCoist

'You are an alchemist; make gold of that.'

William Shakespeare, Timon of Athens

By 1991, the BBC's A Question of Sport had long been established as a national favourite, providing living rooms around the country with genuine light entertainment and enjoyable challenge by way of a cast of sporting stars from the past and present. Bill Beaumont was the team captain who enjoyed the more recognisable guests for the episode which aired on the evening of Tuesday, 28 October. Up against Ian Botham's team of the British Open Squash champion Lisa Opie and the IBF world flyweight champion Dave McAuley, Beaumont was joined by the England Test cricket bowler – and future show captain himself – Phil Tufnell and the Leeds United and Scotland captain Gordon Strachan. By then, Strachan was already cultivating a reputation for a sharp and quick wit, at least by footballing standards, and so he would prove that evening. 'Which Scottish football international,' asked the host, David Coleman, 'took two wickets in the NatWest Trophy?' 'Andy Goram took the two wickets,' Strachan replied. 'But he didn't make any catches.'

The majority of those in the studio would have found it funny as a generic gag about a goalkeeping colleague – a Scottish one no less – but anyone watching with a passing interest in Scottish football would have known that it was more pointed than that. Goram was having a torrid start to his time at Rangers. After telling Hibernian that he wanted to move that summer in order to win trophies, he had already been held directly responsible for Rangers' eliminations from two different cup competitions. The following night Rangers would lose 3-2 to a young Dundee United side at Tannadice, with Goram responsible for the late winner, spilling a Darren Jackson shot straight to the feet of Duncan Ferguson and presenting him with a simple opportunity to give United both points. Goram had always assumed that crises of confidence happened to others, not him, and yet there he was, in a maelstrom of doubt, desperately hoping that the ball would come nowhere near him during games and with his international captain making him a punchline on national television.

Pressure on Goram inevitably meant pressure on Walter Smith. The ideal consistency candidate for a caretaker role in the aftermath of Graeme Souness's departure was now being questioned as the man to take Rangers on to the next level in the longer term. Smith had overseen yet another early European exit but, in the shape of Sparta Prague, he could not at the time point to undisputed quality in the way that Souness had been able to do with Bayern Munich and Red Star Belgrade. Even the League Cup, where a Rangers appearance in the final felt as if it was part of the sponsor Skol's contract, had been given up at the semi-final stage. Smith's big turnover of players in the summer had led to predictable early difficulties in squad cohesion and he had yet to find a solution to the three-striker issue that had dogged the previous season, opting to start with Souness's preferred combination of Mark Hateley and Maurice Johnston before chopping and changing every week throughout October. The culmination of this frustration was a touchline clash with the St Johnstone manager Alex Totten, whom he had replaced as assistant manager at Ibrox five years earlier, which saw both men charged with a breach of the peace. Never having had this overall responsibility, he was being constantly questioned about his signings and his ability to manage them. 'I learned that management is a difficult game,' wrote Smith three years later, 'and there was a brief period where I questioned my own credentials.'

By the end of the season, however, a national joke was on his way to becoming the greatest ever Rangers goalkeeper, the club's greatest strike partnership had been firmly established and a band of brothers had been created that would go on to shape the greatest season in Ibrox history. From a position of deep doubt and great uncertainty, Smith had created alchemy.

* * *

Only the summers that bookend the Souness and Smith era – 1986 and 1998 – saw more transfer activity than Smith's first one in overall charge at Ibrox. With five players in and five out, it is comfortably the highest turnover in the close-season of any of those that made up the nine successive titles. Smith had very little choice. Despite UEFA's imposed maximum of four 'foreigners' in European competitions in 1991/92 being known for three years, Smith found himself with a sudden need to change the make-up of his squad. It was back in March 1988 that UEFA first began an imposition of limitation – starting in 1988/89 – however they provided clubs with a grace period of three seasons whereby their existing foreign players would not be counted as part of the four. Until 1991/92, therefore, Rangers were allowed to field the likes of Chris Woods, Terry Butcher, Ray Wilkins and Mark Walters – all of whom were signed before the summer of 1988 – as effective Scots. Domestic pressures perhaps pushed this need for forward planning to the back of the collective mind but there was no room for manoeuvre now.

'If it wasn't for that UEFA rule, the truth is that Andy Goram would never have played for Rangers. I was the only option at that time. There was no other Scottish goalkeeper with the right experience and the correct credentials. That's footballing fate at work,' So wrote Goram in his autobiography. As a young goalkeeper he had initially been 'stunned' by the signing of Woods, to which he credits David Murray's 'financial muscle' – evidence in a ghostwritten memoir years later, of the historically deficient blur between the Marlborough and Murray eras – but now he would be replacing him as Rangers' number one, something he described as a 'daunting task'. Goram had been on Rangers' radar for some time and Souness had tried to sign him before. He would have done so had it not been for a caper around the streets of Edinburgh.

Souness and Goram had met by chance one night and had talked about the possibility of moving. The Hibernian keeper had said that he would love to move but, according to Souness in his autobiography, 'He needed £30,000 in a hurry. He had a reputation as a gambler but I did not want to know what was going on in his private life. As this was a rather delicate situation I decided not to inform the chairman about the player's request and agreed to make him a personal loan without involving the club.' There was an agreement to meet at Tynecastle, which was very close to where Souness lived, where the money would be handed over but the manager felt that he was being followed by a man on a motorbike, 'As I drove away I noticed the same motorbike with the distinctive number plate at the end of my road. It was parked alongside a car and there was somebody sitting in the driver's seat. I was beginning to get suspicious and as I turned into the main road I was keeping an eye on my rear mirror. Sure enough the motorbike was behind me and 200 yards ahead was a set of traffic lights. I went through them on amber. I knew if he did not stop that I was being followed. He ignored the red light and stayed on my trail so I decided to take him on a bit of a wild goose chase. Instead of heading for Tynecastle, I drove towards the area where I used to live. I know those streets like the back of my hand and I was on familiar territory.'

Souness assumed that either the motorcyclist was sent to ensure that the deal went ahead or was there to hijack it. He called his brother who was in place by the time he drove back to his apartment. The bike drove away, never to be seen again, but Souness lost interest immediately, 'I did not want anything more to do with the player after that. To this day I have never asked him [Goram] what it was all about but I would be curious to hear his side of it.' By the following summer, Rangers had to take that gamble and went through more traditional means to land Goram for £1m while Woods – the last remaining player of the four who came north and changed everything – left for Sheffield Wednesday for £200,000 more than that outlay. It was a change that the supporters understood but still struggled to adjust to initially. Goram was rated highly in Scotland but he didn't possess the stature of Woods. For many this felt, for the first time in five years, like a backwards step.

There was a similar reaction to the eventual sale of Trevor Steven. Big names had left Ibrox after the revolution but almost always at the club's desire. This was the first where a bigger fish had flexed their own financial muscle as Marseille agreed to pay £5.5m for the midfielder. Souness was indirectly responsible when, after his inflexibility over the sale of the French champions' original target, John Barnes, he suggested to Marseille president Bernard Tapie that Steven might be a player who fitted their bill. Rangers could not turn down that kind of money and, even if there was a discomfort associated with the reality check that the transfer provided fans with, there was general praise for the hardball manner in which Murray was able to drive such a big fee.

There was no Anglo-Scottish swap this time as Smith replaced Steven with more continental class in the shape of the Ukrainian Alexei Mikhailichenko, who signed from Sampdoria for £2m. Having already impressed at Dynamo Kiev and for the USSR, this was considered a brilliant bit of business. Mikhailichenko wasn't a Steven replacement on the pitch, however, as he would more often take up the role vacated by another crowd favourite, Mark Walters. A consistent creator and goalscorer, Walters was an instant hit at Ibrox and a player who was taken close to the heart of the support. He followed Souness to Anfield in a move that he would later regret. At the time though, it was felt that it was his only hope of playing for England as Graham Taylor seemed less inclined to honour service north of the border now that English football was retreating from its exile. Talent aside, the emotional loss of Woods, Walters and Steven that summer should never be underestimated. All three were inextricably linked to the success story that Rangers fans had been living.

Another cult hero on the way home was Terry Hurlock but in this case, his Scottish replacement was generally seen as an upgrade. Stuart McCall had scored for Scotland in the 1990 World Cup and notched two in the 1989 FA Cup Final for Everton, both to no avail, but was known more and respected for his battling midfield qualities. It was a late deal – Rangers had played two league games before it was sealed – and was dependent on the Steven sale going through. With too many midfielders at Goodison Park and needing the money for other deals, Everton boss Howard Kendall was willing to part with McCall. Rangers' engine room was given even more energy and, along with the very promising talent of Aberdeen's left-back David Robertson – a deal that was arranged while Souness was still manager – there was a lot made of the Gers re-establishing their Scottish identity. That tension between that native heart and continental wit would soon become the narrative of the decade.

Besides rebuilding half a team, Smith's main problem when taking over was what to do with the attacking triumvirate that had caused so much stress for his predecessor. Ally McCoist had high hopes that there would be a fresh start for him now that Souness had left but those looked forlorn by the time that the season kicked off. McCoist had suffered a troublesome pre-season through injury and, when a hernia was finally diagnosed and treated, he was a few weeks behind his team-mates. Despite that, he wrote that he was due to start the opening game of the season, at home to St Johnstone, but pulled a thigh muscle in training. Whatever the reasoning, Smith started the new season with Mark Hateley and Maurice Johnston up front, just as Souness had done for much of the previous campaign with McCoist reprising the role of 'The Judge' for the whole of August. He had to approach Smith. 'I was coming up for 29, and I couldn't afford another season like the previous one,' McCoist wrote. 'I had to have first-team football for the sake of my career, and although I didn't want to leave Rangers, I would have to start thinking about it seriously. I told him, too, that despite all the problems I had never said that to his predecessor.'

McCoist's big issue was that he could hardly argue that Smith was getting it wrong up front. In the five league games and two League Cup ties Rangers had scored 24 goals, 13 of which had come from Johnston and Hateley, with McCoist grabbing the fourth from the bench in a 4-0 win over Dunfermline, his emotion obvious to all. Five of Johnston's eight goals had come in the cup – four against Queen's Park in a 6-0 romp and one in a 2-0 victory over Partick Thistle – but it was Hateley's all-round game that looked most impressive. He took to the pitch on that opening day as if the title-winning epic against Aberdeen had been played only the Saturday before. With a full season under his belt and now fully accepted by the Ibrox faithful, he seemed to own the opposition box with a rampaging hat-trick against St Johnstone and a double at Parkhead in the first Old Firm encounter of 1991/92, the latter being so indicative of things to come. Liam Brady was now in charge at Celtic and hopes were high for the new era if he could possibly hold on to 'The Maestro' Paul McStay, whom the media were sure would be the subject of multimillion-pound bids the following summer. Allied with John Collins, Celtic did have ball-playing capacity in the middle of the park, however the fading light of Charlie Nicholas could not be re-ignited and the big summer signing of Tony Cascarino from Aston Villa – effectively their answer to Hateley – was a disaster. With only four goals that season he was eventually exchanged for Chelsea's Tom Boyd in February. On the final day of August, there was no question as to who the real deal was.

Hateley's first goal, just before the break, is a piece of film that could sum up the Old Firm battle for the 1990s. Tommy Coyne was easily dispossessed by Richard Gough who fed the ball to Stuart McCall in acres of space in the middle of the park. A brilliant through pass caught out Celtic's other summer signing, Gary Gillespie, leading a scandalously high line, and Hateley was suddenly in the clear in front of the chasing Derek Whyte. The sheer power of the acceleration took him away from the pursuit and the coolness of mind on a roasting-hot afternoon allowed him to round Pat Bonner and roll the ball into the net where Whyte also eventually ended up, in a tangled mess. His celebratory run up the Parkhead touchline towards the Rangers dugout was another show of powerful aggression. Not for the last time, this was his stage. The second, just after half-time, was more rudimentary in its approach, coming from a long Goram kick, but it highlighted the relationship that Hateley had with Johnston as they worked the space with two simple headers before the strength and accuracy of the former Monaco man's left foot buried the ball in Bonner's left-hand corner.

It was no wonder that McCoist approached Smith that week to get clarity on his future, later admitting, 'Walter was just superb – there is no other word for it. He said he understood my frustrations perfectly, but that he didn't want me to leave the club. He appreciated, however, my service to Rangers, and in return he wouldn't stand in my way if I really wanted to go. But he stressed again that I would get my chance, and not to do anything hasty for a couple of weeks. We agreed to sit and think things over for a spell. Walter was as good as his word, and my opportunity came soon afterwards, that night at Tynecastle.'

McCoist's season would change on the midweek cup trip to Gorgie on 4 September but this was the second journey that Rangers had made there already and the first match, the third league game of the season on 17 August, had proved to be a nightmare at the other end of the pitch. 'Scott Crabbe drifted one over my head at Tynecastle,' wrote Andy Goram. 'The ball started out three yards wide, and I didn't move my feet quickly enough. I was sure it was going past. It's such a horrible noise for a keeper to then hear that brush of leather on the net as it settles behind you.' It was a freak early goal that Rangers never recovered from, suffering their first defeat of the season so quickly. Stuart McCall had only signed the day before and his debut was something of a sharp education, 'I found out at half-time about the levels Walter would demand. He let us know that the standards the club had set must be maintained and we had to carry on being successful. In no uncertain terms he told the defenders and captain Richard Gough in particular that he was not happy with them. They were playing it around at the back and not hurting Hearts. He wanted them to get it forward quicker for Mo Johnston and Mark Hateley. It came as a shock to me. If we had played like that at Everton we would have felt it was something to build on. At Rangers you were expected to win every week, home or away, to be classed as successful.'

Although Rangers recovered immediately and ended the month only a point behind Hearts and Aberdeen, that blunder was a sign that Smith's new signings, especially his goalkeeper, were going to take some time to adjust. 'The abuse was raining down on me,' said Goram. '"What a waste of money!" That was Rangers fans singing, not Hearts fans singing – it can wreck you.'

Things were about to get a lot worse.

* * *

Jock Brown could be forgiven for making a mistake with the Rangers goalscorer on commentary. Not only did McCall and Johnston share that distinctive ginger hair but McCall's finish – the wait, the position and the acrobatic execution – was almost trademark Mo. Extra time had not long started before that goal finally put Rangers in control of their European Cup first round tie. McCall had grabbed the first of the night too – a scrappier effort just after the break which put Rangers on parity after that disappointing 1-0 defeat in Prague two weeks earlier. Sparta were considered awkward at best and most of the previews in the media and in fanzines were laden with expectation of a smooth progression. Compared to the two previous seasons, such relative relaxation was understandable but they would shock more than just Rangers that campaign as they knocked out the most recent beaten finalists, Marseille, in the second round before running the eventual winners Barcelona close, including a home victory, in the new-look group stage of the European Cup. This, of course, was a Rangers idea which was getting its trial run before being marketed in its own right the following season. The disappointment that Rangers wouldn't be present in the new format would have palpable enough in any case but the way in which it happened made it all the more bitter.

The upper hand, forced by McCall's volley, lasted for only five minutes as Sparta immediately probed the five-man Rangers defence with Oleg Kuznetsov making only his second start of the season as a sweeper behind John Brown and Scott Nisbet in the centre of defence, a formation that hadn't been used at any point that season. Lumír Mistr's cross was not stopped by David Robertson and Nisbet did all that he could to stop Horst Siegl from being able to control and get a shot away. There was simply nothing difficult about what Goram had to do next: an easy stop as the ball bounced back to him. 'Through my hands and in it went, and we were out of Europe,' he recalled.

Goram had made two good saves in the first leg, as he did in other matches, but they were barely remembered when the clangers were so loud. He was blamed for Jirí Němec's freak looping winner in Prague, he would also cost Rangers a draw at home to Falkirk in late October as well as both points at Tannadice a few days later. For Goram, the most painful mistake came against his old side at Hampden in the League Cup semi-final on 25 September. It was a flat Rangers performance overall – with Gough injured and Kuznetsov and Mikhailichenko both playing in a 2-2 draw with Hungary for the USSR – and Hibs were worthy of their win yet the only goal of the game still contained a sense of the ridiculous. A hooked Pat McGinlay punt found Mark McGraw who occupied a reasonable amount of space left by Brown, in between the retreating Robertson and Nisbet. The pace of Robertson ensured that he would have been close enough to put pressure on McGraw by the time he controlled the bouncing ball but it was made academic by Goram's decision to run to the edge of his penalty area and punch it out to Mickey Weir who had time to place his delivery right on the head of Keith Wright, unmarked between the stranded Goram and Nisbet and Stevens on the goal line. Both were helpless as he carefully cushioned his header home from four yards. Spooked by that early setback, it was a judgment by Goram that was clouded by doubt and pressure. His old team would go on and defeat Dunfermline in the final – only the second League Cup Final without Rangers in 11 years – and Goram tried to make light of it in the dressing room the following day. He wrote, '"Just think, if I was still at Hibs, I would have a League Cup medal in my pocket." Quick as a flash, McCoist turned to me and said, "Listen you, if you were still at Hibs, then we would all have League Cup medals in our pockets!" The banter was brutal, but behind the smiles I was so low.' Team-mates like Ian Ferguson noticed the impact too. 'He [Goram] felt that he had let the team down and he was miserable,' Ferguson wrote. As with any team, a shaky goalkeeper can send tremors through the rest of the squad. It was the first major problem for Smith to address as a man-manager.

Goram wrote, 'I'll never forget the way the gaffer managed the situation. It summed him up. He took me into his office and sat me down. This was no bollocking. This was a job description. He said, "Look, son, this is what we need from you: consistency. How do I help you get there?" He didn't understand the position, and he didn't pretend to. Instead, he sent for Alan Hodgkinson. The irony is that earlier in my career I didn't understand the man or his methods. Then it clicked, and he became the mentor who made me the goalkeeper I was. So I needed Hodgy in those dark times at Rangers, and Walter made it happen."

Smith was shrewd enough not to try and fix every problem with his own hands but knew when to bring in someone more suitable on to the staff to work with talented players who were just struggling to adapt to life at Ibrox, a situation different to any other club that they had been at before. 'People don't realise how lonely Ibrox can be when the place is against you,' Goram would later reflect.

'Your first hurdle at Rangers is to prove to the players you are good enough to be there, but if you fail to win over the fans, it can become miserable. However, if I'd had an easy time at the beginning, I don't think I would have become the goalie I did. I can only name two players who I saw truly hit the ground running at Rangers, guys who were at their peak from day one: Paul Gascoigne and Brian Laudrup. They cruised it because they were geniuses.'

Smith's attention to the human being, so often lacking at Ibrox in the recent past, would soon pay off. Celtic visited Ibrox the weekend following the defeat at Tannadice and, although there was a bad error to allow a Celtic equaliser from the normally ultra-reliable Nigel Spackman, Goram was excellent and confidence began to grow again. It was McCoist who had given Rangers the lead with a clever run and low diving header on the hour. Where an Old Firm goal seemed unlikely at the end of August, it felt inevitable by the start of the November as this was his tenth strike in seven games. The prevailing narrative around the McCoist renaissance under Smith – started by the man himself in his 1992 autobiography – was that, soon after the chat with the manager, he was given the start against Hearts in that League Cup quarter-final on 4 September, scored a fantastic goal in the dying summer's light from a Hateley knock-down, was never out of the team from that moment on and a phenomenal partnership ensued.

The reality is slightly different. On that night Smith chose, as Souness did at Tynecastle a year prior, to go with all three in attack. It was a brilliant finish by McCoist, wearing the number-11 shirt, but he had that yard of space because the Hearts defence was being pulled about in all directions. Graeme Hogg had to come out towards Hateley and Craig Levein was occupied with Johnston, which left John Millar out of position and left helpless to block McCoist's low, dipping shot. Two weeks later, McCoist was stretchered off with a groin injury in Prague, after missing a great chance to give Rangers an invaluable away goal. He would miss the 2-1 win at Love Street and was on the bench as Hateley and Johnston started both the semi-final defeat to Hibernian and the 2-0 loss at home to Aberdeen on the Saturday before coming back into the starting XI to face Sparta at Ibrox due to an injury to Hateley. Johnston too would suffer a small knock as Smith rotated throughout October – even using young John Spencer in attack – as he tried to finally settle on the winning formula.

From Sparta onwards, however, McCoist was an ever-present as the goals started to flow. Perhaps the pick of the bunch was an indirect free kick into the top corner in a revenge 4-2 victory over Hibs at Ibrox, as McCoist celebrated with a joyous Archie Knox down on the touchline – a world away from the scenes ten months before, when Graeme Souness barely moved a muscle after that stunning strike against Aberdeen. The cup exits and dropped points were more a result of Goram's issues and the defensive frailty exacerbated by Gough's intermittent injury throughout the early autumn than by any bluntness in attack. Rangers scored 16 league goals in October and some of the football was staring look very impressive, due in no small part to Mikhailichenko's increasing prominence. Even in the defeat by Aberdeen, he was a standout performer. Contrary perhaps to their own personal demeanours, there was early evidence that Smith was prepared to be more adventurous than Souness. In 1988/89 and 1990/91 Rangers averaged 1.72

goals per league game, falling to 1.33 in 1989/90. By the end of November 1991 that average was already at 2.48 with 50 goals in 21 league games.

It was only by the end of October that Smith had settled on his best front pairing. Although McCoist retained his place, Smith alternated his partner five games in a row. Johnston started the home match with Falkirk on 26 October and rescued a late point to save more Goram blushes but it would be the last goal that he scored for Rangers. He was dropped for the trip to Tannadice, where McCoist scored two in that 3-2 defeat, and would remain on the bench for the next few weeks. While McCoist was willing to endure that pain and frustration because of a deep-rooted love for the club, Johnston was absolutely not. A restless professional by nature, he made it known that if he wasn't going to start for Rangers then he would prefer to start for someone else. It was actually Stuart McCall who helped him make the choice between Leeds United and Everton. If he wanted a more enjoyable approach to work-life balance, then Howard Kendall would be a better bet than Howard Wilkinson.[128] Johnston performed fairly well for Everton during the rest of that season, scoring once every three games in a three-man attack with Tony Cottee and Peter Beardsley, but his prolific touch was already on the wane by the time he arrived at Ibrox, becoming a more all-round forward and scorer of important goals rather than lots of goals, and his career fizzled out from 1992/93 onwards. One could argue that he missed out on another league medal by not joining Leeds but it is doubtful that he would have made the kind of difference that their eventual loan signing in the following January would: Eric Cantona. Either way, it was a quiet and subdued exit for the man who arrived with such sensational noise. Another major Souness signing had departed and with it, one selection headache for Smith. It was McCoist and Hateley now.

Rangers kept in touch with the surprise leaders Hearts throughout November. Apart from a freak 1-0 defeat at home to St Mirren on 23 November, there was far more consistency and continuity in both performance and result. The air had cleared. Smith's only visible frustration was a touchline bust-up at St Johnstone on 12 September, where he and Alex Totten were both charged with breach of the peace. The match finished 3-2 with a late Nisbet winner snatching the points but by November those margins were becoming a lot more comfortable.

It is easy and appealing to draw a straight line from the Johnston departure settling the forward dilemma but that simplicity would ignore the impact of the signing of Dale Gordon from Norwich City for £1.2m. This, Smith felt, was more of a replacement for Trevor Steven on the right and his two goals and general display in his debut away to Dunfermline were very impressive in a 5-0 win. McCoist and Hateley would build their understanding but it is redundant without service. Gordon added to the creativity of Huistra[129] and Mikhailichenko, on which the pair would thrive. It was also something that Smith would use time and again as the years progressed if he felt that his team needed something extra to fuel their winter push. From Gordon to Erik Bo Andersen, Rangers were able reach out for quality reinforcements in ways which few others really were. As

---

128   Rangers sold Johnston for over £1.5m so ensured a profit to keep every party happy.
129   Huistra received his first Netherlands call-up in November, well-deserved after an excellent
        start to the season.

much as the transformation from Souness to Smith would develop, some things remained the same. As had been the case before, as soon as Christmas came into view, Rangers would go into overdrive.

* * *

Although Rangers had some work left to do in order to create a gap on the field – after the St Mirren shock they were three points behind the leaders Hearts – off the field it was beginning to look like a chasm. Four days before Christmas, the new Club Deck, a third tier on the Main Stand that seated 6,700 more fans at a cost of nearly £20m, was formally opened at the 2-0 defeat of Dundee United. There were initial complaints from the new debenture holders, who had paid between £1,000 and £1,500 to guarantee their seat, about the lung-busting climb up the stairs and some of the restricted views, but it was an undeniably impressive and modern addition to the antiquated beauty of the Main Stand's facade. By 1991 the issue of stadia had been forced to the fore of most conversations in Scottish football after an agreement to accept the Taylor Report's recommendations for all-seated grounds by August 1994. There would be some nostalgic resistance to any plans to seat the two enclosures – the only parts of Ibrox without seating – but, for a stadium of that size, few would argue that Rangers had the best in Britain. Their city neighbours meanwhile, were in a very different position, although that was something that the Celtic chief executive was not quite prepared to admit.

Terry Cassidy had caused a bit of consternation with the Rangers board when he said publicly that Ibrox was 'not a particularly good stadium' and that the problems with being landlocked were not ones that he would wish to have. Cassidy instead proclaimed that not only would Celtic have a stadium that met the new criteria by 1994 but that it would be the 'best in Europe'. At a 'Save Our Celts' rally on 1 December, this was mocked by Professor Tom Carbery, a lecturer at Strathclyde Business School who had recently sat on football's sub-committee on the Royal Commission on Gambling. 'I have no faith. I do not believe they will do it by 1994,' Prof Carbery said to an agitated crowd before going even further when comparing the club to their great rivals. He praised the last three Rangers chairmen, including Murray, for their foresight on this issue and said that Rangers were 'almost round the Ludo board while Celtic has still to throw a double six. Mr Cassidy's message is that it is going to be all right on the night. I don't think it will.' Cassidy was forced to admit that raising the venture capital required was perhaps 'insurmountable' but it wasn't 'for the want of trying'. When pressed by Celtic fans to evidence any kind of investment in an increasingly dilapidated ground he referenced the £130,000 spent on new toilets in the 'Jungle'. When this did nothing to assuage the grumbling, he countered with, 'What? Do you prefer to use other people's back pockets?' The contrast between the two operations was further sharpened when, during the same week, it was announced that Rangers were entering into a new £11m kit deal with Adidas. The club was pulling away far into the distance.

In some respects, it did try to drag the rest with them. It was Rangers, through Campbell Ogilvie, who tried to bring an early end to the incessant, repetitive grind of a 44-game season where teams met at least four times every campaign.[130] With the support of Aberdeen, a new structure was proposed that would include a winter break and with the Premier Division splitting off after 22 games to try and ensure a more relevant and competitive conclusion. A state of navel-gazing was almost permanent throughout Scottish football during this period but it was especially so around the time of these league proposals. The overall quality was felt to be getting worse, with Davie Cooper describing a recent Lanarkshire derby for Motherwell against Airdrie as war and not football, 'It was embarrassing to be involved in. It was the kind of game that shows why we never do anything at international level. I don't think I managed to get more than a couple of touches during whole of the first half, because the ball seemed to be up in the air all the time.' Cooper had enjoyed those moans for years, it must be said, but opinion pieces on the subject were becoming more and more frequent. It was to no avail. Too many clubs wanted – some would argue that they needed – their regular Old Firm fix and so the proposals were rejected 'across the board' in January 1992; the monotony continued.

If any team was rising above the increasingly dreary and direct football, then it was Rangers. From 30 November to 14 March Smith's side went on a 19-match unbeaten run in the league and Scottish Cup, scoring 42 goals in the process, 23 of those coming from McCoist and Hateley.[131] There would be plenty of comfortable routine wins, some that were ground out, and two 0-0 draws including a surprising blank at home to Airdrie in January. However, three performances were most significant in shaping not only this season's title race but many more to come.

Throughout this story, the 150-mile trip to Aberdeen has so often been the most precarious yet memorable. It was where the pain was ended in May 1987 and where it was suffered in October 1988. It was where the fuse was lit on the previous season's dramatic finale leading all the way to the return fixture on the very last day. Even as Aberdeen's stock waned over the decade, it was still a journey that few truly relished. Wins were tough to find up there and it had been 24 years since Rangers had even scored more than twice at Pittodrie. On 4 December, however, Aberdeen were in some trouble. Despite having beaten Rangers at Ibrox at the end of September and being joint-top of the league with Hearts at the start of November, they were in freefall. Jocky Scott, one of the official 'co-managers' alongside Alex Smith, had left to take outright responsibility of Dunfermline in September and ignominious defeats to Airdrie in the League Cup and BK Copenhagen in the UEFA Cup precipitated a collapse in league form. One win in six league games in November, a 1-0 victory over St Mirren courtesy of an own goal, left Alex Smith's side languishing in fifth place, just as Walter's men were getting into their stride.

Before November 1991, McCoist and Hateley had only ever been on the same score sheet three times for Rangers: once in a 2-0 league win over Motherwell in February 1991 and in cup drubbings against Valletta and Cowdenbeath during the same season. Now they had enjoyed three in succession, the most notable

---

130 It had been introduced in 1991/92 and it would take until 1994/95 for a return to a 36-game season.

131 Only six of those matches saw a score sheet without the name of McCoist or Hateley on it.

being the three second-half goals they scored at Easter Road to settle a 3-0 win over Hibs on 19 November. There was something different about this night, however. This was the first time they had both fired in a 'big' match and they did it in a style that would become so familiar over the course of the next 18 months.

Rangers were ahead within five minutes. Ironically, it was McCoist who won the header from Goram's kick and Hateley who was alert to the second ball, showing great control and patience as he waited for his partner to get into position at the edge of the box, where he enjoyed a neat piece of interplay with Dale Gordon before the new recruit fired a low shot to Theo Snelders' left. The Dutch international made a great stop but Hateley was there to pounce, rifling the ball into the back of the on the up-step. It was a difficult chance to take, at that speed, but evidence of the new kind of confidence flowing through Hateley by this point. Rangers were pulled back when Theo ten Caat followed up a Hans Gillhaus penalty which hit the post but that parity wouldn't last for long. Again it was McCoist who came deep – midway inside his own half – to take a ball from Gary Stevens with his back to goal but an excellent show of strength of control eased him away from Peter van de Ven where he found his new strike mate who instantly flicked it into midfield where the counter attack could really get into full flow. Just like at Parkhead in August, it was Stuart McCall who received the ball and threaded a pass through the two centre-halves – this time Brian Irvine and David Winnie – where Hateley turned on the afterburners and bore down on Snelders with a frightening aura. Pace, power and precision. Hateley was now an established presence in a Rangers shirt – that had been unthinkable just 12 months before.

It was McCoist who made it three just after an hour and it was arguably the pick of the bunch. Hateley's knock-down found its target but there was still work to be done as the ball bobbled around McCoist and the retreating Alex McLeish. Any effort was made to look easy as the number nine scooped his shot over Snelders in one move to put Rangers 3-1 ahead. A dangerous game was looking very comfortable indeed. Perhaps too comfortable as five minutes later, Hateley gifted Aberdeen a lifeline with a careless back-pass that Brian Irvine, despite Goram's efforts, was able to capitalise on. All this did was set the stage for another individual display of excellence for the final 30 minutes. Goram had made some crucial saves at Fir Park the Saturday before, with the game finely poised, before Gordon and Stevens made sure of the points, so his recovery was well on the way. There were three saves in the latter stages at Pittodrie that were top-class, especially the second one, where he had to reach far to his left to stop a beautifully dipping Ian Cameron shot which looked destined for the top corner. In both boxes Rangers were starting to look as if they had struck gold. Hateley was denied a hat-trick when he moved a little too soon for the offside trap but it wasn't to matter. Regardless of the Aberdeen form, this was a statement win and performance. Hateley was asked by Jock Brown afterwards about his new relationship with Ally McCoist. 'It's going to score goals,' he answered.

There was a similar story at Parkhead on New Year's Day in a match that arguably saw the debut of the 'Walter Smith Parkhead Playbook'. On a foul afternoon, Rangers were more than happy to allow Celtic the ball in the knowledge that there would be mistakes and that they could break with devastating pace. McCoist and Hateley missed three good chances between them in the first half before the trap was successfully sprung right on half-time. It was Peter Grant this time who lost possession to Nigel Spackman, who in turn set Gordon on his merry way to drive into the exposed Celtic backline. His pass across the pitch towards Hateley was kicked down into the turf where it span up nicely for McCoist to bundle home. As the two walked slowly back to their own half, still locked in a warm embrace, it was as if they had been playing up front together for five years.

Tony Mowbray, whom Celtic had brought in from Middlesborough in November, bulleted an equaliser from a corner, but Rangers weathered the following storm well, aided by Celtic's lack of knowledge around the new FIFA directives on blood and open cuts, as Paul McStay comically was presented back to the touchline on a couple of occasions before finally being allowed back on to the field. Rangers had found their way back into the game by then and the substitute John Brown was starting to make his presence felt. Celtic goalkeeper Gordon Marshall had made a brilliant reflex save from Huistra minutes before clumsily bundling McCoist down in the box from a piercing Brown through ball. Hateley had been moved on to penalty duty and cooly but powerfully drilled the ball into the corner. Celtic tried to respond but they faced a very focused and determined rearguard. One nice moment of play ended up with a brilliant McStay shot from just outside the box, only for Goram to rise high and tip it over the bar. Goram's restoration was completed that day and his legend in Old Firm games, especially in Celtic's own backyard, was born.

Tired legs on a heavy pitch allowed for one more special individual moment. Rangers were really just keeping possession as the clock ticked down when Brown found himself with the ball and plenty of defenders backing off him to cover McCoist and Huistra up ahead. Once he was within range, he wound up his left foot and drilled one home off the inside of the post before hurdling the advertising boards to take his acclaim. As Brown's childhood dreams came to fruition, Rangers were now only one point behind Hearts and ten ahead of Celtic.

Despite Rangers being restricted to a surprise stalemate at Ibrox to an increasingly awkward Airdrie, Hearts couldn't deal with the heat that the team in blue were producing. The Edinburgh side's 15-match unbeaten run was sensationally ended at Tynecastle with a 4-0 defeat by Aberdeen on 11 January, by then in the final throes of Alex Smith's reign, and he would be replaced by club legend Willie Miller in the February. This was followed up by a 2-1 defeat at Airdrie before the visit of Rangers on 1 February. With Rangers now two points clear at the top, it was Britain's match of the day. The prevailing narrative, even on ITV's Saint and Greavsie, was that a Hearts win would be the best thing for Scottish football. Evidence perhaps, with the increasing likelihood of a fourth title in a row and the growing off-field power, that there was now a genuine concern among anyone not associated with Rangers about the prospect of such a long period of dominance. Rangers travelled to the east coast slightly understrength as Hateley was still not passed fit after a short spell out but Smith had already spent £500,000 on a replacement when he signed Paul Rideout from Notts County, then in England's top flight. No other club was doing that just to replenish their reserves for a tricky few weeks.

Needing the win, Joe Jordan's side started the brightest in a pretty tense and often bad-tempered affair but the champions grew in stature as the game went on, with Rideout forcing Henry Smith into an excellent low save and Mikhailichenko hitting the bar with an audacious volley from 25 yards. Following a bit of scrappy play in the box, former Rangers player Derek Ferguson was unlucky not to open the scoring with a powerful strike that deflected over off the head of Stevens. When a similar pattern of play took place in the same box in the second half, his old team-mate McCoist made no mistake as he blasted the ball high into the roof of the Hearts net. A delirious McCoist ran to the jubilant terracing, literally pulling a face as he did so. It was his 26th goal of the season and it was only the start of February. All that frustration and self-doubt were now a distant memory. He had played the long game and was now propelling his side towards another title.

It was an ugly 1-0 victory but it wouldn't be the last time a Walter Smith team would deliver maximum points in such a way, should the situation demand it. Smith had suffered bad results at the start of that season and would of course do so again over the years that followed, but in terms of crucial league games – against rivals at a stage of the season where the outcome is genuinely impactful – it would take until January 1998 before he suffered defeat in one. The structural advantages are undeniable but plenty of rich clubs have lost their grip on power. Key matches are still decided within the margins and that day was one of many where Smith was able to motivate and organise his resources so as to ensure there was no scope to give others hope.

The lead over Hearts would be seven points by the middle of March as Rangers eased through the gears towards the finish, but that procession was halted in the most painful way when Celtic visited Ibrox for the final Old Firm league match of the season. After the new year defeat, and with a ten-point gap rendering any title challenge realistically over, Liam Brady had managed to salvage something of his debut season as his side put together a 12-match unbeaten run with only one league draw included. Celtic won 2-0 thanks to goals from Charlie Nicholas and Gerry Crainey, and it could have easily been more. Rangers were insipid and complacent and couldn't shift the levels up when they were caught cold. Also, the reactive cat-and-mouse plan that had worked so well at Parkhead didn't fit so well at home when 35,000 people were passionately advising that the players should be more on the front foot and the triumphant Celtic team were quick to comment publicly as to just how easy they found life at Ibrox.

Such talk was ill-advised. Ten days later the pair would meet again, this time at Hampden in the Scottish Cup semi-final, where Celtic would find a very different Rangers side. With both the elements and fortune against them, Smith's men had their back very much against the wall. Which, it would turn out, was exactly what they needed.

* * *

Not for the first time, Rangers were having a problem with the Scottish Cup.

It wasn't quite at the levels of the great Bill Struth side who, despite sweeping all before them so often in the championship, had to wait 25 years to win the cup again but it had been 11 years since their last victory and that was too long for a club so far in the ascendancy in Scottish football. The emotional resonance created by the sheer drama of the semi-final is understandable but it perhaps unfairly overshadows the rest of the run itself. Any hopes that 1992 would finally be the year were dampened when the third-round draw – the stage at which the Premier Division teams enter the competition – sent Rangers to Pittodrie to face Aberdeen. There was an element of farce about the tie from the outset. Sky had earmarked it to show live on the Wednesday night before the traditional third-round weekend, the last one in January. An unnecessary midweek trip north did not go down well with supporters who would normally travel but did find favour with those able to watch from the comfort of their own homes. In the end, all supporters were left frustrated as an objection from the Irish FA about a live broadcast hampering attendance at one of their fixtures that evening meant that instead of being shown live, the whole tie was broadcast after the final whistle. All of that umbrage would have been forgotten about by the time fans finally got to bed; Rangers won 1-0 thanks to an early McCoist strike and a very late Goram save. Alex Smith was teetering on the brink by that stage but Rangers had their issues too as Hateley – who had suffered a knock in the New Year's Day clash at Parkhead – was still confined to the sidelines. Missing a player who was starting to become the scourge of Aberdeen and being unable to play his replacement, Rideout, because the late switch in scheduling meant that he was not registered in time could have fed the hoodoo complex. This was starting to feel like a different Rangers, however.

McCoist's wish for a home draw in the next round was granted but it would be no bye to the quarter-finals. The holders, Motherwell, travelled to Ibrox where they always, despite the craft of Cooper and some emerging talent, dragged a game down to its basic elements. Rangers struggled to find their rhythm and passing fluency that afternoon and Motherwell were deservedly ahead through a well-worked Phil O'Donnell goal; they could have doubled that lead but for Goram. Smith swapped Dale Gordon for the youth and pace of Gary McSwegan and, although it wasn't completely transformative, there was at least greater urgency. 'That was Alexei Mikhailichenko's day,' wrote McCoist later, and it surely was as the Ukrainian's two composed finishes turned the tie on its head. The consistent heroics at either end of the pitch during this season created a lot of underrated performances but in any other year, 12 goals from 31 games and many more assists from a new signing on the left of midfield would get a lot more praise and attention. Perhaps it was his languid, laid-back style that often struggles to land well with the Scottish footballing public who far too readily romanticise effort over the ability to actually pass the ball. Archie Knox described it perfectly in his autobiography when he said, 'Chenks was a terrific player but let's just say he wasn't the most active at times. When we warmed up with little games in the dressing room, he'd just sit at his seat and not even move. One day I encouraged him to warm up but yet again he declined my advice and said, "I'm OK thanks." I repeated my encouragement so he stood up, walked over to the hair dryer in the corner of the dressing room and blew hot air up and down his body. He said, "There – I'm warmed up now, Archie." Regardless, Rangers were toiling in this match and their mercurial ace saved the day and kept the cup quest on course.

St Johnstone away was the quarter-final prize. Rarely were trips to McDermid Park comfortable ones – only in October was there a need for a late Scott Nisbet winner in the league game – but this match, on 3 March, was a cakewalk. With Hateley back and man of the match Pieter Husitra taking the creative burden from Mikhailichenko, Rangers cruised to a 3-0 win in what McCoist described as one of the best performances of the season. Rangers would return to Perth on 28 March for league business – the week following the defeat to Celtic at Ibrox – and normal service was resumed. There was a win but the 2-1 result was a struggle and once more, injury would strike Hateley, where he took a knock to the back in the very last seconds. Hateley scored both goals that day but would be out for the semi-final with Celtic just three days later. With Rideout not eligible, Smith would have to play McCoist on his own up front and use an extra man in midfield. After six minutes at Hampden, it was just as well.

It was around this time that Stuart McCall was discovering the reality of life as a Rangers player when he took family out for a Chinese meal after the Ibrox Old Firm reverse, 'Everyone was down after the match, but the table was there for 8.30pm so we still went out. To my amazement as we were strolling in this little Chinese guy came up to us and started shouting about how useless bloody Rangers were. He took our coats into the cloakroom but came back with a Rangers scarf and proceeded to stamp on it in disgust, saying Rangers were bloody rubbish today! It was the first time I had been to the restaurant and felt quite embarrassed for my family who thought it was extremely funny. The night went on and so did his verbal tirade and I finally snapped, promising him that in ten days' time we would win and be celebrating. He was carried away too and said that we could bring all the players and their wives next time and get a free meal if we did win the semi. The strangest thing about the way he was ranting and raving was that it was meant, none of it was put on. We had to win that semi or else.'

Celtic were now 14 games undefeated, leading to large parts of the media proclaiming them as the 'best footballing side' in Scotland, despite trailing Rangers on points and goals scored. All of a sudden style was the real measurement of success. The evening of Tuesday, 31 March 1992 however, was not a night for style. The weather was horrendous, with David Livingstone reporting trackside for Sky looking like one of those poor reporters that television news channels send out into the wildest of conditions so that those at home who don't understand isobars on a map can get the picture. Sky Sports, who didn't yet have the English Premier League but did show a lot of Serie A, moved their broadcast of AC Milan v Juventus to 10pm in order to show this. As Glasgow was caught in a tempest, it was never going to be a night for the faint-hearted.

'Joe Miller and I were mates at Aberdeen,' recalled David Robertson when I spoke to him in 2019. 'We were very close and I didn't want a friend to get the better of me in a game. Walter and Archie were winding me up before the game, saying, "You need to sort him out early and do whatever you have to do to stop him." The ball was thrown out to Joe and I was going full steam ahead. He took a little touch past me and I thought "here's my chance" so I took him out. A little more than I planned to! In those days it was an unfortunate red card.' With only six minutes gone, Rangers were down to ten men and the 'curse' showed no signs of lifting. As furious as he looked on the touchline, Walter Smith made the simple changes that gave his team some ballast against the onslaught as Nigel Spackman slotted in at centre-half while John Brown moved over to fill in a left-back. Celtic had much of the ball but opted for crosses too often in conditions such as these and against a tall and imposing defence. And then, right on the stroke of half-time, came the kind of goal that was becoming typical of these encounters. It was Brian O'Neil who was robbed in the middle of the park by the tenacity of the Rangers press, this time by McCall and McCoist. The two combined again to finish another devastating counterattack when McCoist found the only gap he could possibly see without even breaking stride. 'Scenes of extravagant celebration,' shouted Martin Tyler on commentary. 'McCoist is almost in tears of joy and disbelief.'

With a precious lead at the break, Archie Knox did all that he could to ensure that it stayed that way, 'I knew Celtic would throw everything at us in the second half. I went out before the second half kicked off and grabbed one of the ball boys at Hampden. I asked if he was a Rangers fan and he said "yes". So I gave him a fiver and told him to get the message round his pals. If the ball went out for a Celtic throw-in, just leave it until the Celtic fans throw it back. If the ball goes out for a Rangers throw-in, just leave it full stop. I watched him go round all four sides of the Hampden pitch telling his pals not to go for the ball. We needed every advantage we could get and we managed to hang on for the win.'

Knox wasn't wrong and Rangers decided to sit in and defend what they had as Celtic, with the wind now behind them, sought to rescue their season in the remaining 45 minutes. They caused problems but rarely from direct range, with Joe Miller failing to properly connect with the only chance he had in behind Brown. O'Neil hit the post from distance with an effort that deflected off Spackman's hand. Mike Galloway, his replacement later in the half, stung Goram's palms from outside the area. Goram's goal frame was struck twice in quick succession, the first from a Paul McStay shot that left him rooted to the mud bath that constituted a six-yard area, and then he tipped a Crainey header from the resulting corner on to the same crossbar. Almost like a game of rugby, Rangers were conceding both possession and territory as Celtic began to create chances inside the box and the game's second flashpoint was a case in point. With just less than ten minutes remaining, a tiring Rangers defence failed to clear a Celtic move and John Collins appeared to be fouled in the area by John Brown. The replay showed that it was a fatigued and clumsy tackle, and Brown's left foot definitely made contact with the right foot of Collins. However, the Celtic midfielder was already on the way down when the contact took place, his body shape was that of the traditional simulation, and perhaps that created enough doubt in referee Andrew Waddell's mind. If Collins had waited he would have been taken out and Celtic would surely have been presented with an opportunity to force a replay. As it happened, the Edinburgh official spent the final ten minutes much in the same way he did the first, by ensuring that all of Glasgow had something to be incensed about. Galloway had another pot shot from 30 yards, but Goram got behind it and

Rangers saw the remaining time out.

'In the second half I was up in the stand,' said Robertson. 'I was kicking every ball but it shows the fighting spirit that squad had. Even in later years, if you were 2-0 down to Falkirk, you still knew that you were going to come back and win.' Winning in adversity was nothing new to Rangers. Only 15 months previously they had won an Old Firm cup final at the end of a horrid week, but this was something extra. At the end of a season of such transition and challenge, against a Celtic side in genuine form[132] and in such match conditions, this demonstration of unity and spirit arguably surpassed anything that Souness was able to create. 'That's when this Rangers squad had shown exactly what they are made of,' wrote McCoist. 'We reorganised superbly and played as well and as bravely as I can remember any Rangers team in my spell at Ibrox.' The celebrations at the end said it all. The footage of Smith in his suit being held up by the man in whom he had placed so much trust, McCoist, punching and kicking the air with delight, tells a deeper story. Something was born that night that didn't just lead to success in the final two months later, it laid the foundations for the greatest season of all. This was a side coming of age.

For many, McCoist's restoration was crowned by the award of European Golden Boot for his sensational return of 34 league goals in addition to his players' and writers' player of the year awards. The Golden Boot was, along with the same award the following year, technically an unofficial one as L'Équipe and Adidas – the original organisers and sponsors – had both lost interest in the event after some dubious circumstances throughout smaller leagues to try and inflate their players' totals.[133] Adidas made the award for McCoist due to the sponsorship of the club but didn't present it to any of the subsequent winners from Wales, Armenia and Georgia until it was re-instated in 1996, under new weighting rules for coefficients. It could be argued that McCoist's new contact, signed just before Christmas 1991, was the real point whereby the King was returned properly on his throne. Even though he had two years left, the three-year extension ensured that he would be at Ibrox for the peak of his career otherwise, like Trevor Steven, it would take a lot to prise him away. Hateley had signed a three-year extension two days prior and was evidence of a chairman making solid plans for the long term and it was something that David Murray made mention of at the time, remarking about how strange he found it that other clubs would allow their prized assets to run their contracts dangerously close to the end. A dig at Celtic and Paul McStay certainly, but a sound position to take for a chairman who was riding the crest of a popularity wave at that time. Such prudent foresight wouldn't last for ever.

Despite the flood of goals, Hateley was still left with a sense of footballing frustration. The new England manager Graham Taylor, was forced to consider a recall after his visit to the December match at Pittodrie where Hateley was imperious. The niggling injury in January cost him a place in a Wembley friendly against France in February where Alan Shearer made a goalscoring debut but he

---

132   This win arguably halted any momentum that Brady was able to generate. Celtic wouldn't have a run like that again for another four years.

133   The final straw came the season before when the Cypriot league protested Darko Pančev's 1991 award.

was finally given a chance in the friendly against Czechoslovakia in Prague on 25 March. The legendary Guardian football writer David Lacey described Hateley's performance in the 2-2 draw 'intelligent' but this was something of a shift in gear given his reaction to the call-up in the week of the match. Describing Hateley as 'the last of the steam-driven centre-forwards', Lacey felt the selection after a four-year absence was 'just about' warranted, 'If only to show that Bobby Robson was correct in the regarding the powerful but limited striker as a second attacking option once [Gary] Lineker had been joined by Peter Beardsley in the 1986 World Cup.'

The target man was becoming passé even for Taylor although he could have done with that option as he toiled and dithered at the European Championships in the summer. From a position of providing more England players than any other club two years earlier in Italy, there were no Rangers men in that 1992 group, although Trevor Steven would return soon after. Even Gary Stevens – enjoying the most consistent season of his Ibrox career and missing only one game all season – had lost his place to Lee Dixon. He would get it back due to Dixon's late injury but he too would suffer a knock in the final warm-up game against Finland. English football was well and truly back in the fold – in early May UEFA announced that the nation had been chosen to host the next European Championship in 1996, thus marking quite the turnaround – and as such, the brief window of exposure and respect that Scotland could offer was closing. The wind of change was being felt in early February when, according to a report in the Sunday Times, Rangers had frantically called the Football League to ask what on earth this talk was about a new breakaway English league. Rangers had already been having talks with major clubs about a British version. Was this now dead in the water? Yes, it would transpire and with it, another door towards progress would be closed.

All of that, however, was in the future. The present focus was on a double and managing it in style. The week before the league was sealed, Rangers won 2-1 at Tannadice and in doing so broke the Premier Division goals record when Alexei Mikhailichenko and John Brown scored the team's 90th and 91st league goals of the season respectively. The final total would be 101 and is a testament to how positive and aggressive Smith's first season in management was.[134] Appropriately enough, it was McCoist who scored twice against St Mirren at Ibrox as the flag was won with three games to spare, and the ultra-consistent Stevens, who scored the pick of the bunch in a 4-0 win. 'The celebrations went on long into the night, and the next morning,' wrote McCoist. 'If I were to tell you that 5.30am on the Sunday, Andy Goram and I were sharing a bottle of champagne at the bottom of my garden, you'll get a rough idea of the party spirit. Andy and I have booked the garden seats for the same time, same place next year, and, hopefully, for the next few seasons after that.' Being champions was now starting to feel very familiar indeed.

Despite the opposition and being overwhelming favourites, there were still

---

134   It should be noted that this was only the third 44-game season in the Premier Division's history. In terms of average goals per game, it was the fourth-highest by that time. Only 1995/96 and 1996/97 would see a higher Rangers average in the period between 1986 and 1998.

nerves on the eve of the Scottish Cup Final, an occasion that wasn't yet familiar enough. 'Airdrie can't win the cup,' Archie Knox told his players. 'Only you, the Rangers players, can stop yourselves from winning.' This probably didn't ease the tension as Rangers, wearing their brand-new Adidas kit for the first time, toiled a little in the early stages of a final that was clearly never going to be a spectacle. There was breathing space by half an hour and by half-time it was virtually over. Who else but Hateley and McCoist to grab one each to put the champions in the driver's seat? Hateley scored the first from Robertson's low cross, usually making the front-post run that his partner would. McCoist's, right before the interval, came from a left-footed shot driven low across John Martin. Andy Smith grabbed a late consolation but there were no nerves among the Rangers players as they saw the match out. 'Despite the scare, at no time do I think we are going to give up our lead,' said McCoist. 'We are in control. The cup is ours.'

Most of the Rangers team who played that day are low-key in their assessment to the point of apologetic. 'The only let-down was the cup final which was a poor spectacle,' wrote Stuart McCall. 'I felt guilty; we had put on such a poor show for the fans.' McCoist, too, wrote that there was something of a lull just after the final whistle as they players knew that they hadn't played well. Given the run that Rangers had, especially the drama of that semi-final, it was always going to be something of an anti-climax and Smith was quick to remind his team on the field that he had been involved in five Scottish Cup finals where his sides had played well but won nothing, telling them, 'Get celebrating, you've won the cup.'[135] The party atmosphere soon began to build and lasted long into the night with Wet, Wet, Wet on hand to support the singing. There was one moment of poignancy from the season's hero, who now had the full set of medals with his beloved Rangers. Ally McCoist took a moment on that Hampden field – medal in hand and plenty of supporters' scarves around his neck – and looked for the spot on the terracing where he had stood at the 1981 replay win over Dundee United. 'I remembered the hopes and dreams of the teenager who stood there,' he wrote. Even for an optimist like McCoist, dreams were now being surpassed by the magic of reality.

* * *

The story of this season was both one of rich, individual narratives and team cohesion, and one that was quietly orchestrated by Walter Smith. Not as demonstrative that his predecessor but no less authoritative, he was more than happy to allow his players to enjoy the limelight. They were the stars of the show after all; he was simply the director, and it was a production that was a smash hit at the box office.

'I was thrilled for Walter Smith and Archie Knox. Basically, players go out to win matches and championships for themselves and their team-mates. This time I genuinely wanted to do it for Walter and Archie, and I took as much pleasure in

---

135   Ironically, that very same afternoon Graeme Souness ended his own personal FA Cup jinx
         when his Liverpool side defeated Sunderland at Wembley.

their delight as I did in my own,' said McCoist, although this was no post-season platitude, it was a genuine warmth towards the men who had given him a platform from which he was now producing the best football of his career. Smith found it difficult to accept the league title the previous season as his own but this was very much his team both in new personnel and approach. Any fans who feared that the top job would have been too big for a man who had spent so long as someone else's assistant no longer had doubts. Smith didn't fear the history-laden responsibility; he used it as fuel instead. It was his choice to bring the oil paintings of the eight previous managers into his office, 'They were scattered all over the stadium, and I thought it would be nice to have them all hanging together to remind me of the men who had shaped the club's history from the very early days.' Inspiring rather than intimidating.

Smith was now one title in sight of a record belonging to the greatest of those predecessors, Bill Struth. With a fifth championship in succession looking as likely as the fourth which had just been secured, the conversation was increasingly dominated by concerns about how good this was for the Scottish game, especially as this was only coming as a result of Rangers' off-field power. Smith was quick to point out the hypocrisy of the national discourse. When he and Souness arrived, they were told by the footballing literati that they couldn't buy success. 'A couple of years down the line, with the trophy room looking pretty full, the same people were accusing us of buying success,' Smith said. Either way, it wasn't dull for the Rangers fans or players. 'People may say it's boring that Rangers keep winning the league,' said Richard Gough immediately after the title was secured. 'Well if that's boring, long may it continue.' It wasn't all contentment for the captain, however. He felt that the team had let Smith down against Sparta, in a game that they had won and then 'tossed it away'. It was the only thing that the rest of Scottish football had to beat them with – and it had to change.

Fans may have dreamed about a better charge at the European Cup – now to be re-branded at the UEFA Champions League – but recent experience had made them wary. Now that the Scottish Cup jinx had been lifted, it was the prospect of a total domestic sweep that most supporters felt was within comfortable range. No one could know that the trials and tribulations of 1991/92 had shaped a Rangers side who were ready for something special.

The impossible dream was on.

12

THE TWO DAVIDS

'The chairman has always said, "The club belongs to the supporters. Any money that's made, any money that comes in through the turnstiles is going to be reinvested in players."'
Graeme Souness on David Holmes, May 1987

'I've put a £20m team on the park, pay them £10m a year … and I still get pelters.'
David Murray, August 1997

The Rangers that Campbell Ogilvie joined was a world away from the one that he eventually left. In August 1978 he arrived as an assistant secretary dealing with football administration and he became part of an off-field staff that wholly comprised of an accountant, a bookkeeper, a telephonist, one typist and two part-time ticket office employees. 'There was no commercial structure really. I had no commercial background whatsoever but I was still tasked with putting some commercial things together when I wasn't qualified to do so,' he recalled.

Rangers had won a treble the season before Ogilvie's appointment but had started 1978/79 poorly. So poorly in fact that by November's AGM – with the three trophies on display – the board were booed on to the stage. Whatever success and sense of prestige that had been recovered in the 1970s would soon be a distant memory as the club struggled to put a team on the park worthy of the stadium that it had built, with a board who pushed pens more than they pushed limits. Ogilvie continued, 'When I started, there was a board meeting every Tuesday afternoon. It was sometimes difficult to even put an agenda forward for that. But there were these – not quite factions – but very different shareholders sitting around the table. The new stadium had been completed but the average attendance was only about 19,000. All the jokes at the time were about the stands facing the wrong way. Under Willie Waddell, the club had created this new stadium but had hit a barrier. They weren't going anywhere.' From 1986, they soon would be and Ogilvie worked closely with the two men who dominated the boardroom as Graeme Souness and Walter Smith would do in the dressing room.

David Holmes, the former joiner and then chief executive for John Lawrence (Glasgow) Ltd., had originally been involved in the re-building of the stadium throughout the late 1970s and early 1980s, the modern monument to those who perished in 1971. In preparing the work he had been clear about the vision. Speaking in 1987, he recalled, 'We'd pay attention to the fans first. Make sure that they were safe, comfortable and surrounded by something that matched their support of the club. Once that was done then it was time to turn attention to the field. Some say that there should be a plaque for those who were killed that day. The stadium is the plaque.'

By the time Holmes arrived at Rangers in 1985, he wasted very little time in shaking the business out of its slumber so that it was fit and in shape to realise the next and most important part of that plan. His boardroom ruthlessness enabled the club to start moving quickly and his 6am starts to the working day sent a clear message around the growing number of offices. 'The whole place took off,' remembered Ogilvie. 'It was one thing Holmes coming in but he needed the vision to make it happen. David professionalised the club both on and off the field. Freddie Fletcher coming in to look after the business and commercial side is one good example of that. There was now a focus. Previously some directors looked at it like a hobby. There was no specific responsibility for things like commerce or the stadium development. Before David came in, if there was a decision to be made, I had to phone around six or seven directors. It was difficult.'

In order to fuel the revolution on the pitch, Holmes immediately took steps to use Ibrox in new ways. Speaking in the summer of 1986 he said, 'We pay overheads 52 weeks of the year so we must use our facilities to the fullest. We have to take the club forward, and while we hope to do well in the league and Europe, that takes cash. An ambitious club like Rangers cannot exist solely on income from a home game every second Saturday.' The paint was barely dry on the new Thornton Suite, the first hospitality lounge of its kind, for the pre-season friendly with Bayern Munich on 5 August 1986. By late October Holmes was telling shareholders that the new commercial operation was well on its way to raising £1m that year. Ogilvie had sat down with Holmes and Fletcher and sketched out the drawings themselves. Ogilvie said, 'At the time the area was an old storage space and a gents' toilet. The design of the Main Stand probably wasn't built to take suites but there were areas where we could be creative. The Thornton Suite was the first real commercial venture. David brought in Luigi Guisti from the Fountain Restaurant at Charing Cross in Glasgow to oversee the catering. All we had before was the small manager's lounge downstairs, sponsored by Tennent's Lager. Now, after a game, you'd have 140 sponsors in there and the players would come and mix with the sponsors. Betty [Holmes's wife] and David would host it and move around.'

The last part was another important reason why many considered Holmes to be such a success at Ibrox. Ogilvie said, 'David wanted to create a family feel and Betty, his wife, was key to that. It was a big club but it still felt like a family. Through Terry Butcher's wife and Chris Woods's wife, they started a creche where the players could bring in their kids in when they were needed at the stadium. We maybe lost that as years went on.' This was exemplified by the fact that every employee was invited back to Ibrox to celebrate the 1986 League Cup victory and players like Derek Ferguson have spoken about how good Holmes's people skills were, that he would always have time to stop and ask how he was and how his family were getting on. As chief executive, Holmes was at his most comfortable, going about his business in a low-key way on behalf of the owner. His move to the chairmanship in November 1986 – a role with far more profile and an increased remit – was something he took on reluctantly.

'When you're chief executive, you get a lot more done,' Holmes said as the litter floated about Pittodrie, hours after that first title had been secured. 'As chairman, you've got to go to interviews with Jim White.' An intensely personal man, Holmes's discomfort was clear when he spoke about the new role back in the November, 'Power is something I'm just not interested in. Yes, I want to be attached to success and be a top businessman, but that's it. Power can be a destructive thing and I am trying to create something with Rangers. The intrusion into my private life over the past year is something I have been forced to accept but it's something I could've done without.'

Holmes was consistently clear, however, about who he believed he was doing the job for, 'I want Rangers to be a team with a million players. The supporters are as much a part of this club as the employees and that's the way I want it to stay. It's my ambition to stay in touch with the punters and in no way will I be aloof from them.' On the first anniversary of his time in the job he reiterated that belief, 'This is for our fans. They are part of the club because Rangers are part of their life. We still have 2,500 shareholders and I'll never do away with that. Rangers belong to the people.'

The greatest bit of marketing, Holmes said, was a winning team. The fans responded with average crowds rising from 19,000 to 36,000 in that first season alone. Holmes promised, in that 1987 STV review, that the club would continue to reinvest their money, 'Business generates its own cash. Rest assured we are going to make a big sell on season tickets and that money will be used to take the club through the close-season. We started off with the bank's money but we'll give theirs back and will use our own money now. That is what business is all about.' But, as the overdraft grew and grew as Souness demanded more and more, that was something Holmes didn't control. In a manner that was almost unthinkable from him in his construction 'day job', it was emotion that drove his decision-making as the draw of the football consumed him.

Holmes is something of an enigma. The private man who consensually agreed to take on one of the most public roles in Scottish life. The nicest chairman who many players had ever come across and who was committed to creating a family atmosphere at a huge football club but who ruthlessly cut an underperforming board down to size while blindsiding shareholders. The man who publicly made the fans the centre of his purpose but who some – mostly the pre-Souness regulars – complained didn't care about them when it came to prices and access. The card-carrying socialist who appealed to the business class on matchday and who appalled those who shared his political beliefs with the way in which he chose to run the club.

Holmes is said to resent the level of recognition he currently receives for his role in the story of the revolution. He has a point. There should arguably be a bust of him with pride of place at Ibrox for his vision and execution. There should at least be a whole book dedicated to his recollections. However, his reclusiveness makes that something of an impossibility in the 21st-century media world. His successor, however – with whom there is absolutely no love lost – could not have been more willing to use that limelight.

* * *

Both men were to suffer financial anguish – Murray's empire took a hit with the global financial crisis of 2008 and Holmes filed for bankruptcy in 1992, following a nationwide recession – but their reputations as custodians of Rangers are very different. Murray never had a Holmes and was never likely to. Although his predecessor briefly stayed on as chairman until the end of the 1988/89 season – at Murray's request – and despite Murray's initial promise that he would be too busy with his other business to make Rangers a full-time commitment and would therefore need a chief executive who would take care of the day-to-day running of the football club, it didn't pan out that way. Alan Montgomery may well have been the right man at a different time but that particular trio of egos – with Souness also in the mix – was never destined to work out. Neither Holmes or Murray grew up supporting Rangers – the former was a Falkirk fan and the latter purported to be a fan of Ayr United – but the intoxication of being responsible for the biggest club in the country proved too much for both. As Souness had predicted, the club got under his skin quickly and there was very little chance that he could be the absentee owner that Marlborough was and allow a senior executive that kind of free rein. He wouldn't be able to help himself.

By November 1988, when Murray took control, the model of the charismatic and autocratic owner was starting to become en vogue, in particular the likes of Silvio Berlusconi at AC Milan and Bernard Tapie at Marseille. Given the success of both clubs at the time – in their domestic competitions as well as in Europe – this looked to many like the future. Those owners would be almost as famous as the players and managers – certainly more infamous – and the ego-driven approach was perhaps less than custodial. Fears would later intensify about Murray's role in transfer targets and that arguably started with the signing of Duncan Ferguson in 1993, a player Rangers didn't really need and nor did they need to stop rivals having. Murray was comfortable talking about the deal publicly months before it happened. Murray took Berlusconi's example a step further when he attempted to bring media into his portfolio of interests but his newspaper, the Sunday Scot, was an instant flop. In trying too hard to avoid being seen as a Sunday version of the Rangers News – paying £10,000 towards Celtic players' testimonials and running front-page stories with very tenuous links between Rangers players and 'gangsters' – it alienated its most natural audience. He did not, however, follow Tapie's road to politics.

Not national politics anyway. The style that Murray increasingly adopted was described by the football finance expert Kieran Maguire as 'presidential whereby he ruled by decree'. One benefit that Holmes enjoyed, even in the more public role as chairman, was that he worked for Marlborough and only ever felt accountable to him or the board, all but one of whom were Marlborough's men. As an owner-chairman, Murray had less direct accountability but far more indirect. The 'president' had a constituency that was extremely vocal and was hundreds of thousands strong. His political handling of Rangers' support is one of the most defining features of his time in charge, mainly what he communicated to them and how.

There is no vote winner quite like tangible success and Murray was always able to point to the trophy room when waters were choppy. The dynamism of those early years felt as if the pace of the revolution not only failed to skip a beat in transition but that it actually increased. He was bringing a new level of energy and that was underlined by the handling of Souness's exit, the transfer strategy and the increasing corporate sponsorship. His intuition for simple political wins was keener then too. When fans complained about the behaviour of the Celtic support at Ibrox in 1992 and 1993, he banned the entire away support in 1994. Despite having no suitable qualifications for the role, he appointed club legend John Greig as the public relations officer in 1990. 'Fans can't relate to accountants and businessmen,' Murray said at the time. Even the most critical of supporters lapped it up and he ensured that no difficult questions about media strategy would come his way. He seemed very much on the ball.

Despite the early successes there remained a sense of unease in some parts of this constituency. The fact that Murray never had any previous interest in Rangers created concern about just how important to him this venture would be. This only intensified when he was perceived to be benefiting his own business empire rather than the club with decisions such as bringing the newspaper and matchday programme in-house, buying the Albion car park near the stadium or the construction of the Club Deck. Many wondered what the primary motivation for some of these deals were but, as the success continued, one would barely hear any dissension. The fact that Murray wasn't Robert Maxwell – the only serious alternative in 1988 – helped his cause too.

There were early signs of some of the trouble that Murray would experience later in his tenure. On the evening of Tuesday, 20 February 1990, Murray – along with Campbell Ogilvie, Jack Gillespie, John Greig and Alistair Hood – met with around 60 supporters at the stadium. Murray reportedly contradicted himself on the issue of further stadium redevelopment to an all-seater capacity when he rejected a report in the Daily Telegraph from October 1989 that Liverpool were aware of these plans, at a time when the fans didn't know. He later admitted, 'We didn't want the plans to get out.' Football chairmen breaking grandiose promises is very common – Holmes did too with respect to the overdraft – but when there is a hint of smoke and mirrors, it erodes the trust that may be required at a later date. Murray also had to apologise that night for a quote that he had given the Daily Record on 16 February about the future of the remaining standing sections, where he said, 'With the greatest respect, £4 Enclosure tickets don't allow us to buy players like Mo Johnston.' He admitted that he had been dismissive and that many fans made huge contributions relative to their own income to support the club. It wouldn't, however, be the last time this problem arose.

The issue of contribution soon became a constant theme of Murray's messaging and, unlike Holmes, he would too often play down the support's role while building a mythology about his own. Ticket pricing – especially for European games – was a never-ending source of consternation as Murray ridiculed fans for wanting to pay £6 for Champions League quality – no one had ever argued for that – and that you would expect to pay top dollar to go and see Diana Ross, ignoring the fact that not even her biggest fan would go and catch her six to eight times every year. Incredibly, in an interview with Graham Spiers in Scotland on Sunday during October 1997, Murray said, 'They [Rangers fans] basically got the stadium for nothing.' This ignored the Rangers Pools, gate receipts and the Bond scheme for the Club Deck as just three ways in which supporters regularly contributed to the building of the stadium. The Club Deck in particular was something that he was keen to spin as an addition that he had made happen or that Trevor Steven had to be sold so as to afford it. The Bond scheme was thought to generate around £8m, and there was an extra £2m from a government grant not to mention the prospectus of the scheme that said, 'This method of financing will ensure that Rangers can continue to invest its own resources in the best available players.' Huge sacrifices had been made by generations of Rangers fans and it was short-termist to make light of that especially when his initial investment of £6m went straight to Marlborough and not Rangers.

'As a self-made and busy businessman', said Ogilive, 'it was never in his interest to sit around a table of ten people discussing football admin so he was happy for me to take care of that and be kept in the loop if there were problems coming up.' The regularity of board meetings was diminishing. The officiousness that characterised the Rangers that Ogilvie joined was, by the 1990s, approaching the other extreme. The appointment of Walter Smith, for example, was never discussed with other directors. There was no emergency board meeting to discuss how to deal with the sudden succession crisis. Even by November 1994, it was clear that a more relaxed style of corporate governance had taken root. In an interview with The Scotsman that month Murray said, 'We don't have board meetings at Ibrox. To be honest we did have a board meeting for the first time in years about six weeks ago. We are in touch regularly, and if things need to be done then we are in contact by phone or at matches.' But, as Ogilvie told me, in that first ten years of Murray's regime, everyone was happy to go along in that manner. It was a natural extension of the same style that Holmes had adopted, with someone at the top of the club willing to make decisions. When most of those decisions are good, why hamper that dynamic with pesky bureaucracy? What could possibly go wrong?

It's not a coincidence that the forward-looking, energised years of the Rangers revolution – 1986 to 1992 – saw them use the ideal model of corporate leadership for the time. Relative to the boards that came before and would come later, from the second half of Murray's era onwards, this appears to be something of an idyll. Dynamic, ruthless leadership with the power to enact change quickly and the clear vision to see what needed done. No excessive power struggles to slow everything down but, crucially, no untethered fantasies either. More than anything the chairmanship of Holmes and early Murray was still connected to reality, and had ambition that was self-aware enough so that, more often than not, words would match action.

English clubs had majority power blocks too – often families such as the Edwards, Swailes and Moores at Manchester United, Manchester City and Liverpool respectively – but few, if any, entrusted a chief executive with the power that Holmes got. United, Arsenal and Tottenham were restless and keen to enact a lot of the lessons that they were learning from the NFL in terms of stadia and fan experience and safety, but English football was still a pariah until the new decade began. Rangers were indebted, yes, but Holmes was able to convince the bank that the club was good for it as turnover soared. In English football – even at a time of

100 per cent mortgages – no bank was willing to allow the 'slum sport' the chance to gentrify itself. Again, it was this perfect window of opportunity that Rangers were able to exploit well.

In the summer of 1992, Rangers had the second highest wage bill in British football, only behind Manchester United, but this represented only 46 per cent of turnover. According to Kieran Maguire this figure was both healthy and impressive, a perfect example of responsible ambition. The success of this boardroom dynamic, however, was still shaped by circumstance and it would be caught out when that changed. Between 1986 and 1992 the balance of football business was perfectly weighted for a club like Rangers. Gate receipts were still the major source of revenue – Rangers were a big club attracting big crowds – and corporate sponsorship and hospitality were a new and thriving supplementary income, an opportunity which they were the first in Scotland to maximise. However, television revenue would soon dwarf it all, tipping that balance completely upside down. Simply existing in a big footballing market would be enough for some clubs to bring in millions. One man alone wasn't going to do a deal to fix that, no matter how good they were at it.

'You're only limited by your own ambitions and this club has got ambitions. They'll put their own limit on it,' said Holmes on that first title day of the new era. As time went on, it was the lack of understanding of those limits that would prove so costly and, as is almost always the case with history, there were early signs of concern. At that meeting with fans in February 1990, Murray spoke with assurance that a European Super League – a closed shop with no relegation – was on its way. But it was only ever a stalking horse, something with which to frighten UEFA into modernising their existing competition and ultimately Rangers duly assisted in forcing that into being. In the same vein as his panicked call to the Football League the following spring to see what could be done to stop the breakaway Premier League, it was an early signal that Murray's vision was becoming detached from reality. In February 1996 he would tell Scotland on Sunday that Ajax's academy system was the future but by the end of the year, it appeared that asking Kenny Dalglish to scout players from home via his various satellite channels would do. In the summer of 1997, the 'massive structural changes' that he promised amounted to replacing Davie Dodds on the coaching staff with Tommy Møller Neilsen. Eventually what he said and did were too often miles apart. Evidence of a word – 'moonbeams' – that would characterise his legacy more than any other.

It would be tempting to argue that this was both tragic and wasteful, especially when it was a legacy that was originally founded on such strong foundations. As if Murray could have suddenly changed course and started to bulk up board meetings and downsize his rhetoric as the reality of the football world changed around him. But this would be to ignore the likely truth. Not for the first or last time in the story of Rangers in the post-Souness era, the tale of the two Davids is a reminder that circumstances change a lot quicker than people do. In sport and politics, those who remain convinced that their previous success is a cast-iron guarantee for the future so often get trapped by their own narcissism. Those who get out just in time however, leave with their legend untouched.

EPILOGUE

Revolution (noun) : a very important change in the way that people do things.

By the summer of 1992, the Rangers revolution was over. Its aims had either been achieved or exhausted and the pace of change had slowed down to a stroll. The primary goal – to be the best in Scotland – was now firmly cemented. In what historians may have called the 'First Rangers Revolution' – had the drive continued apace into the 1990s and kept in step with the wider trends – Rangers were undisputedly the dominant force in Scottish football. Six years after having to scramble past Dundee on the last day of the season for fifth spot, they had secured their fifth title in six years with bags of style, over 100 goals and plenty of comfort. There were bumps along the way and a huge scare in May 1991, but the tone of the football writers that summer, as they looked ahead to the new season, told its own story. No one could predict anything else and retain a scintilla of credibility. Rangers had gone from laughing stock to lions, court jesters to the kings of all they surveyed.

'The championship is a foregone conclusion,' the Herald's preview of the 1992/93 season sighed. At least in the opinion of the bookies, where Rangers were 3/1 on to lift the title again, with Celtic as far out at 7/2. That summer, Liam Brady was quoted as saying, 'I said before the start of last season that we would win a trophy and although we didn't I am saying the same thing this time.' It was reaching parody, a bad joke. There was no competition to be had and the depressed tones of that season's previews tell that story. There could have been reason for optimism, however, as Scotland – although exiting an international tournament in their traditional manner – at least put up an impressive show at the European Championship in Sweden, in an incredibly hard group. There was even a win, which was more than England could manage. But no, 'Where exactly are we going?' asked the Herald, wearily as another 44-game endurance test awaited everyone.

Other clubs had tried to follow the Souness lead by broadening their horizons – Dunfermline Athletic's £550,000 signing of István Kozma from Bordeaux in 1989 being the highlight – but, without the backing from the stands that Rangers had, it was always risky. When the UK recession started to bite in the early 1990s – along with the reality of the Taylor Report – Scottish clubs became shy of further expansion. A Price Waterhouse report in the summer of 1992 stated that all Scottish clubs other than Aberdeen and Dundee United were living 'well beyond their means' and only Rangers could manage that debt due to their commercial potential. Even within the respectability of that showing in Sweden, there was a message of decline. Only five of the national squad of 20 played outside of

Scotland, a significant drop from what had become the norm.[136] It would pick up again in the two or three tournaments that saw Scotland involved after 1992, but the days of an array of Scots winning European trophies with England's finest sides were numbered. It was a nation looking inward again. The revolution may have been good for Scottish footballers – who were earning far more – but it was arguably less so for Scottish football.

Needless to say, these six years were great for Rangers. The other result of the revolution was that it ensured a two-horse race at the top forever more. In the 36 years before Souness's arrival, there were eight seasons where neither of the Old Firm ended up on top, and six different clubs – Hibs, Hearts, Dundee, Kilmarnock, Aberdeen and Dundee United – had enjoyed their moment. In the 36 years since, only on that final-day drama of 1991 has any other club had a sniff. The economic style of the revolution – that which opened true potential and unleashed real power – meant that the time of varied competition was over. Also, it breathed life into the legend of Rangers' supremacy. The Souness and Smith era and Bill Struth's incredible dominance from the 1920s to the 1950s account for over half of the 55 league titles Rangers have amassed at the time of publication. No other generation has experienced that level of consistent and repetitive success and it makes a piece by Mark Dingwall, written in early 1991, very interesting when he mocked the audacity of Celtic fans to complain after only one season without success (at that time it was just 1989/90). 'Try five or six years, try a decade and see how it feels,' Dingwall expressed. Celtic had finished worse than second only four times in the last 25 seasons at that point, winning 15 of those titles. 'Celtic supporters have very little to complain about,' said Dingwall. It is jarring to see contemporaneous writing that has a certain underdog tone to it but it was justified. Rangers had amassed just two more league titles than Celtic when Souness arrived but so much of that legacy was owed to a bygone age. The notion that Celtic were Scottish football's premier club would have made sense to many in 1986, however uncomfortable, but not by the time Smith had departed.

Alas, the 'Second Rangers Revolution' – that of consistent European success – did not arrive. Not that anyone would know that at the time, but that too was over by 1992. Indeed, if you had said that in the summer of 1993 you would have been laughed out of the room, but the glorious effort of 1992/93 was an aberration and was always destined to be so. The basis of this success story was good decision-making in a window of perfect opportunity and, when it came to Europe, that latter part of the equation was very small. Few decisions, if any, drove Rangers towards their fabled domestic glory more than the one taken by UEFA at the Old Course in May 1988. By the time it came to move onwards in a new direction, when David Murray was arguably still ruthless enough to do so, the rules on foreign players meant it was almost impossible. Repeated humiliation on the continent would follow but by then, despite the lip service being paid to European ambition, the focus was on something else entirely. The benefit of history is that we can see the whole picture from a better vantage point. By 1992,

---

136   Squads had contained nine to 15 players playing outside of their country from the 1974 World Cup to 1990.

there was never any chance of those dreams being realised on a consistent basis. Football was about to leave Scotland behind.

One Rangers fan from Oban shared concerns in Follow, Follow about future success in Europe at the start of the 1991/92 season and he signed off by saying, 'If it's not to be then we always have the heart warming consolation of the league being won to keep us going. Roll on ten in a row.' It is the earliest I found anything on record that mentions the possibility of reaching and breaking Celtic's record. From 1992/93 on, especially in the manner in which that was won, it became the overriding obsession at Ibrox.

That's the thing with modernisation. Others don't stop just because you slow down and very soon everything can feel stale again. There is a sarcastic line, popular with fans of a certain generation, that 'there actually was football before 1992 you know', but it is difficult to think of a year more significant in the history of the game. A wider revolution – one of such scope and wealth – had been brewing throughout the period of the Rangers version and indeed, they had helped bring it into being with the Champions League. It really was something of a footballing year zero and with it, ended the days where a club like Rangers could shape change so dramatically.

The story of the next six years is a very different one in many respects. Despite Rangers talking about new and bigger horizons, they would turn inwards as the obsession with nine grew more intense. Ironically, the support's relationship with home – in particular the national team – would disintegrate and this would be a common theme along with professionalism, celebrity and a rapidly changing sport. What wasn't different, though, was the silverware, which poured in with just as much frequency meaning that Rangers fans ended the era with much more self-assurance than when Souness and Smith arrived in 1986.

Ironic then that, for all the future-looking and dynamic changes that the revolution sought to bring about on and off the pitch and for all the constant excitement that the era produced, perhaps the biggest impact was on our understanding of the past, as a famous old story was given new life and swagger.

A natural order felt restored.

BIBLIOGRAPHY

Books

Alistair Aird, *Rangers FC in the 1980s: The Players' Duties*, (Pitch Publishing, Durrington, 2019).

Terry Butcher & Bob Harris, *Butcher: My Autobiography*, (Highdown, Newbury, 2005).

Neil Drysdale, *Silversmith: The Biography of Walter Smith*, (Birlinn, Edinburgh, 2011).

Ian Durrant & Iain King, *Blue & White Dynamite*, (First Press Publishing, Glasgow, 1998).

Ronnie Esplin & Graham Walker, *The Official Biography of Rangers*, (Headline Publishing, Edinburgh, 2011).

Ronnie Esplin & Graham Walker (Eds), *Rangers: Triumphs, Troubles, Traditions*, (Fort, Ayr, 2010).

Ian Ferguson & Ken Gallacher, *Fergie: The Ian Ferguson Story*, (First Press Publishing, Glasgow, 1999).

Andy Goram & Iain King, *The Goalie: My Story*, (Mainstream Publishing, Edinburgh, 2009).

Richard Gough & Ken Gallacher, *Field of Dreams: My Ibrox Years*, (Mainstream Publishing, Edinburgh, 1993).

Mark Hateley & Alistair Aird, *Hitting The Mark: My Story*, (Reach, Liverpool, 2021)

Mark Hateley & Ken Gallacher, *Top Mark!*, (Mainstream Publishing, Edinburgh, 1993).

Jeff Holmes, *1986: The Rangers Revolution*, Pitch Publishing, Worthing, 2016)

Ian Jack, *Before The Oil Ran Out: Britain In The Brutal Years*, (Vintage, London, 1997).

Sandy Jamieson, *Graeme Souness: The Ibrox Revolution and the Legacy of the Iron Lady's Man*, (Mainstream Publishing, Edinburgh, 1997).

Archie Knox & Roger Hannah, *The School of Hard Knox: The Autobiography of Archie Knox*, (Arena Sport, Edinburgh, 2017).

Archie Macpherson, *A Game Of Two Halves*, (Black & White Publishing, Edinburgh, 2009).

Archie Macpherson, *More Than A Game: Living with the Old Firm*, (Luath Press, Edinburgh, 2020).

Andrew Marr, *A History of Modern Britain*, (Pan, London, 2009).

Stuart McCall & Alan Nixon, *The Real McCall: Stuart McCall's Own Story*, (Ally McCoist & Crawford Brankin, *Ally McCoist: My Story*, (Mainstream Publishing, Edinburgh, 1998).

BIBLIOGRAPHY

Ally McCoist & Crawford Brankin, *Ally McCoist: My Story*, (Mainstream Publishing, Edinburgh, 1992).

Hugh McIlvanney, *McIlvanney on Football*, (Mainstream Publishing, Edinburgh, 1994).

Bill Murray, *Glasgow's Giants*, (Mainstream Publishing, Edinburgh, 1988).

Alan Pattullo, *In Search of Duncan Ferguson: The Life and Crimes of a Footballing Enigma*, (Transworld Publishers, London, 2014).

Dominic Sandbrook, *Who Dares Wins: Britain, 1979 -1982*, (Penguin, London, 2019).

Walter Smith & Ken Gallacher, *Mr Smith: The Fan Who Joined The Ibrox Legends*, (Mainstream Publishing, Edinburgh, 1994).

Graeme Souness & Douglas Alexander, *Football: My Life, My Passion*, (Headline Publishing, London, 2017).

Graeme Souness & Mike Ellis, *Souness: The Management Years*, (André Deutsch, London, 1999).

Graeme Souness & Ken Gallacher, *A Manager's Diary*, (Mainstream Publishing, Edinburgh, 1989).

Graeme Souness & Bob Harris, *No Half Measures*, (Grafton Books, London, 1987).

Adrian Tempany, *And the Sun Shines Now: How Hillsborough and the Premier League Changed Britain*, (Faber & Faber, London, 2016).

Alwyn W. Turner, *A Classless Society: Britain in the 1990s*, (Aurum, London, 2013).

Alwyn W. Turner, *Rejoice! Rejoice!: Britain in the 1980s*, (Aurum, London, 2010)

Mark Walters & Jeff Holmes, *Wingin' It: The Mark Walters Story*, (Pitch Publishing, Durrington, 2018).

Chick Young, *Rebirth of the Blues: The Story of the Rangers Revolution*, Mainstream Publishing, Edinburgh, 1987).

Other Sources

Rangers Season DVDs

Rangers TV archive

Rangers matchday programmes

Various newspapers (titles cited in text)

Follow, Follow fanzine

Glasgow Rangers Revisited audio tape

Scottish Football Today magazine

The Rangers Historian magazine